THE COMPLETE BOOK OF
PORSCHE

BY THE AUTO EDITORS OF CONSUMER GUIDE®

CHRIS POOLE

BEEKMAN HOUSE

Copyright © 1988 by Publications International, Ltd. All rights reserved.
This book may not be reproduced or quoted in whole or in part by mimeograph
or any other printed means or for presentation on radio, television, videotape,
or film without permission from:

Louis Weber, C.E.O.
Publications International, Ltd.
7373 N. Cicero Avenue
Lincolnwood, Illinois 60646

Permission is never granted for commercial purposes.

Manufactured in Yugoslavia, by Zrinski
h g f e d c b a

ISBN 0-517-66188-8

This edition published by
Beekman House
Distributed by Crown Publishers, Inc.
225 Park Avenue South
New York, New York 10003

CREDITS

Principal Author
Chris Poole

Principal Photographer
Nicky Wright

Photography
The editors gratefully acknowledge Porsche Cars North America, Inc.; Dean Batchelor; Roland Flessner; Bud Juneau; Milton Gene Kieft; Douglas Mitchel; Gary Versteege.

Owners:
Without the cars, there could be no book. With this in mind, the editors extend heartfelt appreciation to the owners of all of the featured cars for their cooperation— and particularly for their enthusiasm in wanting to share the delights of their cars with other enthusiasts. Special thanks to C.A. Stoddard, owner of many of the rarest Porsches featured within these pages, and to Patrick I. Garvey, Michael F. Hartmann, Dan and Barb Pankratz, and the Porsche Museum.

CONTENTS

Driving in Its Purest Form

Titles can be misleading, and so it is with this volume. Actually, there can be no such thing as a "complete" book of Porsche because the saga of these superb German sports cars is too dense, too rich in technical detail and historical significance to be contained within a single volume. Entire books have been devoted just to Porsche's competition cars, its road cars, the 911 Series, and the company (as Dr. Ferry Porsche, son of the great Ferdinand, did with *We At Porsche*). Then too, recorded history is only a snapshot of time, and most always outdated the moment it's finished. The moving hand, having writ, moves on.

But if it can't be the absolute in depth, this book is complete in breadth, covering the full spectrum of what has become known as "The Porsche Mystique." That, of course, is a worldwide phenomenon, an enthusiasm—nay, reverence—for the cars from Zuffenhausen that crosses most all lines of age, sex, geography, and social status.

This is the second Porsche book produced by the Auto Editors of Consumer Guide. The first, *Porsche: A Tradition of Greatness,* was completed in early 1983. In preparing this one, we were again struck by the speed at which today's news becomes tomorrow's his-

tory, and the fact that the Porsche story is replete with ironies, each of which has a constant as its "flip side"— traditions that are vital to understanding these singular cars and the company that builds them.

Let's start with the former. Irony: With the possible exception of Henry Ford I, Dr. Ferdinand Porsche had more impact on automotive progress than any other single person on earth, yet never earned a formal engineering degree. He became *Herr Doktor* by dint of two honorary degrees that merely acknowledged his towering native talent and relentless drive. Constant: Ferdinand Porsche's life was a 75-year

pursuit of excellence. And a stunningly successful quest it was. His fierce dedication would be inherited by son Ferry (Ferdinand Porsche II), who then carried it forward into the modern Porsche company and every car it has ever built.

Which brings up another irony: The elder Dr. Porsche barely lived to see the cars bearing his name and only glimpsed the potential of his most monumental creation, the Volkswagen. But though he spent his life working for others—the cream of Europe's prewar automakers, in fact—he gifted the world with concepts so intelligent, so highly advanced that they wouldn't become commonplace for decades: unit construction, torsion-bar suspension, the rotary engine, even front-wheel drive. Is it any wonder, then, that Porsche—the cars and the company—has always been at the forefront of technology?

And typical of Porsche that technology has never been confined to the track, but most always shows up on the road. It's another tradition that stems from the elder Dr. Ferdinand's earliest years, and explains why a Porsche is engineered and built like no other car. Even today's 959, the most formidable roadgoing Porsche ever built, reflects the same philosophy that guided Ferry in shaping the first humble 356: start with the best possible design, test it in the heat of competition, use what you learn to improve it, and then keep on improving it year after year.

Needless to say, change for the sake of change has never been a way of life at Zuffenhausen, and never will be. Porsche has been criticized for maintaining this particular tradition, especially with the 911 Series, which is now nearly a quarter-century old. Yet when "form follows function" is part of your credo—and when you understand automotive functions well enough to devise forms that are consistently and inherently right to begin with—evolution, not revolution, becomes your natural path.

Following that path, as Porsche has, tends to produce cars that defy the ravages of time. In fact, the 911's long, considered evolution bespeaks the engineering artistry that is part and parcel of the great *Herr Doktor*'s legacy. Said Ferry Porsche in 1984: "You must not change every year. If you do, you have the nicest car [only] at the begin-

ning....It has happened many times in the car business. If you change only the necessary things, as we are by putting 4WD or a turbo into the 911, you keep up with the competition and keep the concept good."

Finally, an irony that is also a constant: Though Porsche has become almost synonymous with cars having rear-mounted horizontally opposed air-cooled engines, the elder Dr. Porsche, his son, and their colleagues have, over the years, produced fours, V-8s, flat eights, V-12s, and V-16s; engines with water and air/water cooling; cars of mid- and front-engine configuration. In other words, Porsche has never been mentally bound to a single design concept or technology; rather, it employs those best suited to particular needs.

Those needs, as anyone who has ever driven a Porsche surely knows, always include the highest standards of performance, but not at the expense of durability or practicality. Porsches are built to take it because that's what the race track and Porsche's own engineering ethics demand. And while they may be sports cars designed primarily for the pleasure of "driving in its purest form," as Dr. Ferry Porsche describes it, you can live with them day in and day out, something that can't be said of every British and Italian sports car. For proof, look no further than the high number of 10-, 15- and even 20-year-old 911s still in daily service—and still bringing broad smiles of satisfaction to their owners.

With all this, it may truly be said of Porsche that the more things change, the more they stay the same. Of course, there are many other constants in Porsche history: top-quality craftsmanship, the sure precision with which every Porsche responds to its driver's commands, a skein of victories in most every form of competition Porsche has entered, and a sort of periodic "backtracking" in which new, more affordable Porsches appear once evolutionary improvements begin making an existing model more expensive. Examples of the last include the winsome mid-Fifties 356 Speedster, the mid-engine 914 of the early Seventies and, recently, the rejuvenated 924.

Alas, world economics and today's upward-scaling car business seem certain to make owning a new Porsche an increasingly rare privilege in the years

ahead. Yet exclusivity is also a Porsche tradition. As Dr. Ferry Porsche told Steve Cropley of Britain's *CAR* magazine in the aforementioned 1984 interview: "...For us to do a cheap car? It is not likely. You would have to [build] so many to make it worthwhile, and if there are so many [of them] on the road, the car itself is not attractive. I do not think all that many people would want to drive a Porsche so common...." True enough, but as we know, the price of excellence is never cheap. Porsche has not come this far over nearly four decades to sacrifice excellence on that dubious altar.

Excellence, exclusivity, a great engineering heritage, race-bred performance—all make up the "Porsche Mystique." But there's more to it than that. In his 1964 book, *The Porsche Story,* the late Ken Purdy asked: "Why does this car, of which so few, comparatively, have been made—not the biggest, not the fastest, not the most expensive automobile in the world—still do things that no other car will do? What's the magic answer? There is no magic answer....Just genius, the simple, inexorable application of intelligence over a period of many years, intelligence intent upon bringing into being the very best thing of its kind in the world."

And Porsche, being Porsche, continues to do just that. In the five years since our first Porsche book we've seen the advent of the hot 944 Turbo, multi-valve engines in a new 944S and the posh 928, the otherworldly 200-mph 959, two more all-conquering racers in the 956 and 962, an entry into the rarefied world of Indy-car racing, and the factory's historic takeover of sales and distribution in the U.S., its most important market.

Of course, the Porsche saga is far from finished, another reason why this book can't be complete in the literal sense. But we hope you enjoy the tale related here as far as 1988, the year in which we celebrate the 40th anniversary of the first production Porsche. We also hope that, if not in your past or present, there's a Porsche new or old lying somewhere in your future.

Meantime, let's all raise a glass to Porsche, to driving in its purest form, and to many more years of both.

The Auto Editors of Consumer Guide®
January 1988

Ferdinand Porsche: A Legacy of Greatness

L ike most of the great automotive pioneers, Ferdinand Porsche was special. Like Henry Ford, he dreamed of the day when automobiles would be not toys for the rich, but "universal" cars almost anyone could afford. He was certainly as complex a personality as Ford: "wayward, brilliant, contradictory and utterly single-minded," with "a firm belief in his own ideas," to use David Owen's words—and even more naive about politics. Both were mechanical geniuses possessed of enormous native skill. Both were primarily "engine men." And though not always right, both ultimately succeeded through a relentless drive that inevitably inspired loyal associates who contributed more to each man's legend than was generally appreciated.

But while Ford was a technician, Porsche was an artist, an engineer "having more in common with a painter than a designer of machinery," said Owen. He was, notes Leonard Setright, "one of those creatively fecund individuals whose vision penetrated the obscurantist orthodoxy of more than mere cars." His advanced concepts and lifelong pursuit of mechanical excellence are reflected in today's Porsche company and its cars, neither of which can be fully appreciated without an account of his extraordinary life.

Ferdinand Porsche was born September 3, 1875, (a dozen years after Ford), in the Austrian village of Maffersdorf, located in Bohemia near the town of Reichenberg. It is now known as Liberec, Czechoslovakia, and is located southeast of Dresden and northeast of Prague. The Hapsburg Empire was at its zenith, stretching from the Carpathians to the Alps and embracing scores of nationalities among its 50 million subjects. At least five generations of Porsches had lived and worked around Reichenberg as tailors, weavers, carpenters, and metalsmiths. Among the last was Ferdinand's father, Anton Porsche.

In 1890, Anton Jr., the eldest of Anton's three sons, died in an accident, leaving Ferdinand heir apparent. The 15-year-old soon began an apprenticeship in preparation for one day taking over the business as head of the family. But, to his father's chagrin, Ferdinand was no good at metalsmithing. Worse, he hated it. Ferdinand's mother ultimately intervened, persuading Anton Sr. to let their son attend the Imperial Technical School in Reichenberg.

It was there that young Ferdinand discovered the mysteries of electricity. Soon, he'd secreted an array of wires and batteries in the family attic where, after a 12-hour day, he'd experiment with a form of power that Bohemia had hardly heard of. Anton was furious when he found out about his son's only hobby, considering it a frivolous waste of time. On one occasion, he even stomped on Ferdinand's batteries, ruining a shiny new pair of boots and suffering severe acid burns.

But Ferdinand persisted. By 1893, again with his mother's encouragement, he'd designed, built, and installed a complete electrical system in the family home, including a generator, switchboard, incandescent lighting fixtures, door chimes, even an intercom system. Greeted one evening by the blaze of the new electric light, Anton Porsche realized there might be more to this "frivolousness" than met the eye. Accordingly, he allowed Ferdinand to go to Vienna to find work; the youngest son, Oskar, became the apprentice metalsmith.

Ferdinand Porsche's formal education would be spotty. He'd done poorly at the Imperial School and was too poor for university training. But in Vienna he became a handyman at Bela Egger, an electrical equipment manufacturer that later became the giant Brown Boveri concern. After sweeping floors and oiling machinery, he'd sneak into lecture classes at a nearby university—an enthusiasm which so impressed college authorities that they let him continue even after they found out about it. The only trouble was, Ferdinand wasn't a registered student, and thus couldn't take the formal examinations. But his determination was rewarded at Bela Egger, where by 1897 he was manager of the test department and first assistant in the calculating section.

Then, a turning point. In 1898, Porsche signed on as an engine designer with Jakob Lohner, patron Viennese coachbuilder to the Hapsburgs and assorted rich and famous personages. Two years before, Lohner had begun moving into the business for newfangled horseless carriages. Now, deciding that gasoline engines were too crude for his high-class customers, he wanted someone to design an electric for him. Young Porsche was only too happy to oblige.

The result was the Lohner "Electric Chaise." Built on the *Radnabenmotor* principle, it had an electric motor at each front wheel, eliminating the need for a transmission, gears, and driveshafts—and their weight. It was thus the world's first car with front-wheel drive—Ferdinand's first "first"—and could travel up to 50 miles on one charge. Porsche demonstrated it in 1900 on a run to Versailles from the Universal Exposition in Paris, a feat that earned him a Grand Prize, and the Lohner soon began selling well from England to Prussia. The Rothschilds had one. So did Archduke Franz Ferdinand.

But the Lohner was heavy (2156 pounds, of which 990 pounds were batteries), and thus slow. Porsche duly modified it, then went to the Semmerling hillclimb course on September 23, 1900, where he set a new record time of 14 minutes, 52 seconds, handily beating the previous best of 23:27.

Striving for even better performance, Porsche next reduced battery weight by developing a "mixed-drive" Lohner—what we'd now call a hybrid-power car—with a small gasoline engine to drive a generator feeding the hub motors. Even if the engine failed, the car could still go 38 miles on its battery power. But Jakob Lohner, now earning tidy profits, wasn't interested in improving his cars, and so he sold his patents to Emil Jellinek in 1906. Ferdinand decided it was time to seek new opportunities.

He found them at prestigious Austro-Daimler, the Austrian branch of the German Daimler company. By 1908, Porsche had completely redesigned A-D's four-cylinder "Maja" (honoring one of Emil Jellinek's daughters, the sister of Mercedes, a name with which Porsche would soon be familiar), giving it a few extra horsepower and a four-speed transmission with either shaft or chain drive. A trio of racing versions were entered in the 1909 Prince Henry Trials (after Prinz Heinrich, the

Dr. Ferdinand Porsche (*above*), shown here at the age of 48, wielded great influence over the development of the automobile. In 1898, he joined Viennese coachbuilder Jacob Lohner, who had just launched his own vehicle but felt that gas engines were too crude. Porsche designed him an electric, the world's first front-drive car, shown as a 1900 Lohner (*opposite top*) and as a rear drive 1902 Lohner-Porsche (*bottom*).

German Kaiser's car-enthusiast brother). They were unsuccessful there, but Porsche himself drove one to victory in the Semmerling Hillclimb on September 19. That same day, his wife gave birth in Neustadt, in suburban Vienna, to a son: Ferdinand Anton Ernst Porsche, later most always called Ferry.

Austro-Daimler made an eight-car assault on the 1910 Trials with the Porsche-designed 27/80. Its 5.7-liter (348-cubic-inch) racing four was patterned after one of A-D's aircraft engines, with steel pistons, inclined valves, and a single overhead camshaft. Though small for its day, it produced 95 horsepower. Porsche took great pains to make the cars it powered as light as possible to counter the brute force of the competition's 20-plus-liter (1220-cid) engines. He also took pains with aerodynamics, evident in *tulpenform* (tulip-shape) bodywork: rounded at the front, tapered at the rear, curved upward and outward on the sides. There weren't any wind tunnels then, but these A-D racers must have been quite slippery, for their top speed was near 90 mph, remarkable for 1910. The result was a 1-2-3 finish, with Porsche himself in the winning car.

But 1910 would be the high point for the Austro-Daimler team. Indeed, it was one of the last times that the old Hapsburg Empire of Franz Josef would win any kind of honor. Big-power rivalries—beginning with the Kaiser's decision to match Britain's navy, and France's new alliance with Russia—were about to plunge the world into a cataclysm that would sweep away the old royal houses and redraw the map of Europe. War came in August 1914, though the Great Powers had been preparing long before (Britain and Germany with their naval race; France, Russia, and Austria-Hungary by piling up armaments).

Meantime, Ferdinand Porsche had been designing aero engines at Austro-Daimler. First came a water-cooled inline six, then his first air-cooled horizontally opposed unit, a four-cylinder engine with pushrod-operated overhead valves. He'd later devise several V-type engines, a rotary (though nothing like the late-Fifties Wankel), and even a W-type engine, with three rows of cylinders on a common crankshaft.

Perhaps anticipating the war, Austro-Daimler in 1913 had acquired

Skoda, the great armaments firm that survives today as an automaker in what is now Czechoslovakia, which in those days still belonged to Franz Josef. Skoda was naturally assigned to provide army artillery, and Ferdinand Porsche was assigned to Skoda. His task: find a way to move Skoda's big guns. Drawing on Lohner experience, he developed a four-wheel-drive tractor with gas/electric power for hauling a monster 305-mm mortar. This gun leveled the fortress of Naumaur, helping the Central Powers roll through Belgium in August and September of 1914.

Soon afterwards, Porsche conceived an incredible "land train" comprising a mixed-drive tractor that pulled as many as eight self-steering cars, each with electric front-wheel hub motors receiving power from the tractor via cable. It was ideally suited to the enormous 420-mm Skoda mortar that weighed 26 tons and fired one-ton shells—one of the most devastating weapons of World War I. Thanks to these and other achievements, Porsche was awarded an honorary doctorate from the Technical University of Vienna in 1917; the following year, he became managing director of Austro-Daimler.

But the walls came tumbling down with war's end in 1919, the Treaty of Versailles forever carving up the Austro-Hungarian empire. Porsche found himself the boss of a car company with bleak business prospects—and technically a citizen of another country: His native Bohemia had been taken from Austria and given to the new Czech Republic.

Ferdinand Porsche never cared much about politics, but he didn't ignore the new postwar realities. Indeed, he recognized that no European automaker could survive by returning to the big, extravagant products of prewar days. Small affordable cars were what the struggling new war-formed nations needed most, and he was determined to supply them.

An opportunity came in 1921 when Count Sascha Kolowrat, a wealthy Austrian filmmaker, asked Porsche to design a small 1.0-liter (61-cid) car, all expenses paid. The result, inevitably called "Sascha," was a lightweight, open two-seater with a single-overhead-cam four capable of hitting an astounding 90 miles per hour. In that

year's Targa Florio road race, standard Saschas driven by Kuhn and Poecher finished 1-2 in the 1100-cc class. A third car with a slightly larger engine placed 7th in the hands of Alfred Neubauer. He would soon follow Porsche to Daimler in Germany, where he would become legendary in the Thirties as Daimler-Benz racing manager. Interestingly, Ferry Porsche, then only 12, helped his father break in one of the Saschas.

Still, there was no getting around the dissention and decline then setting in at Austro-Daimler, which was still wedded to *luxus* automobiles and wealthy clients. In 1922, the board decided to withdraw from racing, ostensibly after an A-D driver was killed in an accident. But the real reason was money—or rather, the lack of it. A-D's foreign-exchange earnings were being converted into rapidly devaluing Austrian schillings, and the resulting need to economize prompted the board to

> During his career, Porsche designed a wide variety of vehicles, such as the early 1900s Lohner auto built for Englishman E.W. Hart (*top*) and military vehicles, such as "Big Bertha" (*bottom*), a four-wheel-drive mortar tractor with gas/electric power that saw service in World War I.

cut off development funds for a Porsche-designed 2.0-liter racing Sascha capable of 106 mph. Never one to suffer fools gladly, Porsche hurled a gold cigarette lighter at the directors and stormed out.

Given his small-car dreams—and the board's opposition—he was probably right to do so. Though Karl Rabe, later Porsche's righthand man, replaced him at Austro-Daimler, the firm would be out of business within 10 years. Porsche, meantime, had gone to Germany, where he became technical director and a board member at Daimler in Stuttgart. It was another timely move.

It's unclear how much Porsche ac-

tually contributed to his first assignment at Daimler. Before he arrived, the firm had built a new 2.0-liter supercharged engine with competition in mind. David Owen has written that Porsche spent nine months transforming it from also-ran (at the 1923 Indianapolis 500) to class champion (1-2-3 at the 1924 Targa Florio), but Leonard Setright claims Porsche only inherited it. Regardless, the University of Stuttgart recognized this achievement by awarding Porsche his second honorary doctorate in 1924, which says something.

There's much less argument over the big supercharged sixes that Porsche conceived for the K- and S-Series Mercedes of the late Twenties and early Thirties. They rank among the greatest engineering feats in automotive history.

Michael Frostick has written of these Mercedes that "brute force and bloody ignorance is hardly a fair description," yet there was some of both in their engines. Each was a masterpiece in light alloy, a veritable King Kong among period European powerplants. All stemmed from Porsche's basic 6.0-liter racing six, with which D-B won the 1926 German Grand Prix.

But the blower was their Achilles heel, for driving with it engaged for even a few miles could easily destroy these engines. Connie Bouchard, a distinguished collector who owns a magnificent 540K, still keeps the bits he left on Woodward Avenue in Detroit one afternoon after answering a village hot rodder's challenge. It's been said that the blower was never intended to run on gasoline. If you wanted to use it, you were supposed to fill it with benzol. And in fairness, the owner's manual advised against prolonged use. Yet, even with its assistance, these supercharged Mercs were more sluggish than their spectacular looks suggested because their bodies

and chassis were ponderously weighty.

Setright has written that on the basis of these cars' handling, Ferdinand Porsche was "utterly hopeless on chassis design." But he took pains to note that "occasional errors can be forgiven in anybody; even though a man might be a divine creation, his design has shown the need for some developmental work.... Let us at least give [Porsche] the credit for having been, in an admittedly special sense, an artist."

It would be well here to sort out the various Porsche-designed Mercedes. The first was the Model 24/100/140, a huge touring car of relatively little aesthetic appeal. It quickly evolved into the K (for *kurz* or short, i.e. wheelbase), also known as the 24/110/160. Arriving in 1926, the year Daimler merged with Benz, it packed 160 bhp (DIN) at 3000 rpm and could reach 90 mph.

The Model S followed a year later, with an engine bored out from 6.25 to 6.79 liters for 120/180 bhp (normal/supercharged), good for up to 100 mph. The SS of 1928 saw displacement boosted to 7.0 liters, horsepower to 225, and top speed to nearly 100 mph—impressive considering its great size. The SSK, with a still shorter chassis and somewhat lighter body, was commensurately faster. The final development, in 1931, was the fabulous SSKL (*sehr schnell, kurz, leicht*—very fast, short-wheelbase, light). Offering 300 bhp at 3200 rpm with supercharger, it could reach an unprecedented 140-150 mph.

The Mercedes SSK/SSKL would simply have to be included on any list of, say, the world's 10 greatest cars. No matter that they were a handful to drive, that they delivered only 5 mpg with all the stops out, that their cable brakes were useless against the lofty speeds achieved by that unbelievable engine, or that only a handful of people could afford them. They were otherworldly beasts, part of the razzmatazz

that was the Roaring Twenties. And roar they did, on road and track, to the astonishment and delight of all who appreciated things mechanical. The SS won the 1928 German GP. The SSKL simply won everything in sight.

But great though they were, these mighty Mercedes were a long way from a people's car, the *Volkswagen* that Ferdinand Porsche continued to think about and plan. He'd been waiting for another chance to try one ever since the Sascha's untimely demise, but Daimler-Benz was no better place for realizing his dream than Austro-Daimler. Indeed, some D-B managers (mostly conservative former Benz people) looked on the SSK's creator as

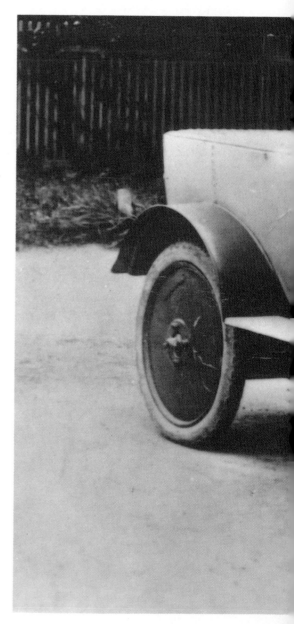

Porsche's first light-car effort was the 1.0-liter (61-cid) "Sascha," designed in 1921 at the behest of Count Sascha Kolowrat, a wealthy Austrian filmmaker. The lightweight open two-seater, running a single-overhead-cam four, was capable of hitting an astounding 90 miles per hour.

something of a dreamer, and thus were strangely cool with him on the subject.

The closest Porsche came to his universal car at D-B was the medium-priced "Stuttgart," forerunner of the production early Thirties 370S Mannheim. In 1929, managers asked him to prove that he'd finally licked cold-starting problems by firing up any of 15 prototypes that had been left outside through a cold night. Porsche failed, flew into a fury, told them to go to the devil, and resigned on the spot. (Ironically, someone else succeeded with a similar test just three weeks later.) Nobody tried to coax him back.

Returning to Vienna in early 1929,

Porsche developed a Stuttgart-like car for Steyr, and it was a big hit at that year's Paris Auto Show. Then the failure of a Vienna bank, one of Steyr's main shareholders, made a merger with Austro-Daimler inevitable, and Porsche was on the move again. The last thing he wanted was another bout with *that* outfit.

But why put up with bosses of any kind? Porsche didn't really need to by now, and decided to set himself up as head of his own engineering and design company back in Stuttgart (at 14 Kronenstrasse). The date was December 1, 1930, which Ferry Porsche would always regard as the start of the modern Porsche company (hence, its

50th anniversary observance in late 1980).

The firm opened under an appropriately imposing name: *Dr. Ing. h.c. Ferdinand Porsche, G.m.b.H., Konstruktionsburo fur Motoren-, Fahrzeug-, Luftfahrzeug- und Wasserfahrzeugbau*—literally "Doctor Engineer (honoris causa) Ferdinand Porsche, Limited, Design Office for Motors, Motor Vehicles, Aircraft and Ships." Porsche's nine-man team was equally impressive. He brought in Karl Rabe from Austro-Daimler and added Adolf Rosenberger, a financier who liked motor racing. Also on hand were Joseph Kales, a specialist in air-cooled engines with experience at Skoda and Tatra (Czechoslovakia's other auto-

15

Dr. Porsche's racing accomplishments during the Thirties are less known than his cars, but no less vital to his story. Having conceived a rear-engine racing car for Wanderer (which became a part of Auto-Union), Porsche demanded—and received—the same racing subsidy as Daimler-Benz. One result was the 16-cylinder R-Type Auto-Union GP car, tricky to handle—but blindingly fast. In 1937, it broke 17 records, including the flying kilometer at 252.47 mph.

merged with Audi, DKW, and Horsch in 1932 to form Auto Union (whose linked-rings emblem survives on today's Audis).

By April 1931, *Porsche Konstruktionsburo* was registered in Stuttgart and Porsche was hard at work laying out his dream car. It would be a *Wagen für das Volk*, a car any German could afford new. The engine would be rear-mounted to avoid a long, heavy drive-shaft and allow plentiful interior and luggage space, air-cooled to obviate the need for a weighty water-cooling system, and made of light alloy to preclude a severe rear weight bias. Porsche also decided it should be a horizontally opposed four, compact and thus ideally suited to the small body size envisioned. It would also hook up easily to Frohlich's proposed aluminum-case transaxle.

Borrowing aircraft techniques used at Austro-Daimler, Porsche planned unit construction, the body welded to a central-backbone platform chassis to avoid the weight of a conventional frame. Suspension would be by simple, low-cost swing axles, springing by the torsion bars that Porsche would invent in 1932, located transversely front and rear. Styling would be aerodynamically efficient, again for best performance and fuel economy.

Though certainly ambitious, this *Volksauto* was long overdue. At the time, America had a car for every six people; Germany had one for every 200. Porsche's car could change all that—if he could find a backer with the same vision.

He found one in Dr. Fritz Neumeyer, head of the Zündapp motorcycle company in Nuremberg. Zündapp had wanted to get into cars since 1925, but hadn't been motivated to do much until the Depression put a big dent in its motorcycle sales. Neumeyer had heard of Porsche, and he paid a visit, offering to foot the bill for the *Volksauto*'s construction and production development, provided Porsche would make a few changes. Porsche complied within four weeks, and Project 12 was underway.

Soon, three prototypes were being built in nighttime secrecy at the Reutter coachworks in Stuttgart. All had rear-mounted engines, but they were water-cooled five-cylinder radials, rather too elaborate for a low-cost "people's car." Porsche himself favored

maker); body designer Erwin Komenda, who would later design the first Porsche car; son Ferry, a skilled technician in his own right (he'd already worked at Bosch and Steyr, too); and gearbox expert Karl Frohlich.

Of course, this was hardly an auspicious time for starting any new business. The Depression was in full swing, and a politician named Adolf Hitler was telling Germans he could alleviate their miseries.

Nevertheless, Porsche had a client

even before he opened his doors. It was Wanderer, the German maker of medium-price cars, for whom he conjured up a smaller, 1.8-liter model with overhead-valve engine and swing-axle suspension. It was the first job for his new firm, but Porsche labelled it Project 7 for fear that "Project 1" conveyed the wrong image. But the little Wanderer was a success, so much so that the company asked Porsche to do an upsized eight-cylinder version. Alas, it was left stillborn when Wanderer

Porsche never lost interest in developing a car for the masses, which meshed with Herr Hitler's plans for a *volkswagen*. With government funding, Porsche refined his previous small-car efforts to come up with the Type 60 prototype of 1935 (*above*), which evolved into the pre-production 1938 Beetle prototype (*right*).

a three- or four-cylinder unit, but was overruled. Not that it mattered. Numerous failures cropped up once prototype testing began in early 1932. With that, and a sudden upturn in motorcycle sales, Zündapp lost interest.

Later in 1932, Porsche visited Russia at the invitation of Joseph Stalin, who wanted to make him the country's "state engineer," effectively the czar of the Russian motor industry. *Carte blanche* authority and an unlimited budget were promised to sweeten the deal, but Porsche soured when he learned that he wouldn't be allowed to leave the country without direct permission from the Kremlin.

Returning to Germany, Porsche was greeted by the head of another motorcycle firm, Dr. Fritz van Falkenhayn of NSU in Neckarsulm. The result was a new small-car project—Porsche Type 32—a slightly larger version of the Zündapp design, but with Ferdinand's favored air-cooled flat four in a 1.5-liter size. There were far fewer prototype problems this time, and tests showed a top speed of over 70 mph. The path to production seemed clear until an agreement with Fiat, under which the Italian company would handle NSU's auto development, put an end to the relationship in 1933. (One Type 32 was discovered in

Germany by an NSU employee in 1945; today, it's owned by Volkswagenwerk.)

Porsche's dream might have ended right there had it not been for the aforementioned Herr Hitler. Rising from obscure mediocrity, he came to power in 1933 on waves of jingoistic sloganeering and grandiose theories for building Germany out of the Depression. Part of the latter involved a network of *Autobahnen*—the world's first superhighways—plus an affordable car for the average German to travel them. Hitler asked his advisors which engineers were best qualified to design such a car. "Somebody foolish got up and mentioned three names," wrote Erik Eckermann: "Joseph Ganz, Edmund Rumpler, and Ferdinand Porsche. There followed an icy silence, because Ganz was Jew and so was Rumpler. That left Porsche."

The apolitical Porsche wasn't concerned about Hitler's racism, only his interest in a people's car. Apparently encouraged by it, Porsche sent a memo outlining his ideas to the Transport Ministry in January 1934. Three months later, he was summoned by Jakob Werlin, one of Hitler's inner circle, to a meeting with *Der Führer* at Berlin's Hotel Kaiserhof.

Hitler laid down his requirements: a roomy, rear-engine car with a 100-km/h (62-mph) cruising speed, 30-40-mpg economy, and low maintenance costs. It must be air-cooled, he said, because most Germans don't have garages and German winters are harsh. It must seat four, he said, because "we can't separate children from their parents." So far, so good. But when Porsche finally asked about price, he was stunned. "Any price," said Hitler. "Any price below 1000 Reichsmarks."

In retrospect, it's easy to dismiss these mandates as lunatic ravings—especially that price: equal to about $240 at the time. That one, as we know, was never met, while the others weren't achieved until Germany lay prostrate after the war she started.

But the fact is that Hitler knew something about automobiles. For instance, he knew about and admired Henry Ford (years before, he'd read a Ford biography while in Landsberg prison, where he wrote *Mein Kampf*). Then too, he personally attended every Berlin Auto Show (it was at the 1933 event that he promised *Autobahnen* and *Volkswagens*, as well as lower car taxes, fewer rules, and *Deutschland über Alles* in racing). He was also the single reason why Mercedes-Benz and Auto Union came to dominate the world's Grand Prix circuits in the Thirties. As a politician, he knew his RM1000 *Volkswagen* would be well received. As a dictator, he knew he could subsidize the price down to that level even if Porsche's design couldn't be built for so little. So, as in most of his industrial recovery programs, there was a degree of reason behind Hitler's airy rhetoric. Indeed, Dan R. Post has recorded that in mid-1934, when Porsche said he couldn't get the price below RM1500, Werlin told him that Hitler would solve that problem in "an administrative way."

Porsche had certain advantages in realizing Hitler's people's car, including the Zündapp experience and the NSU prototypes (on which he retained full rights). He also had some disadvantages, chiefly an impatient *Führer* and a doubtful, if not incredulous, RDA (*Reichsverband der deutschen Automobilindustrie*, German Auto Manufacturers Association). Hitler ordered the RDA to sponsor what all Germans now knew as their *Volkswagen*, but all it offered was a faintly ludicrous $50,000 budget. With that, Porsche could only revise what he'd already developed. But tests of three new Type 60 prototypes, built at Porsche's home in 1934-35, proved the

design well up to claims. By the time testing concluded in late 1936, the RDA grudgingly admitted that this *Volkswagen* deserved further study and development.

Not that anyone in the RDA really wanted to back it. Obviously, a successful small car selling for even RM1500 would be a serious competitor to the economy models on which most German automakers had been working since the Depression. Accordingly, Hitler organized a state-owned corporation, the *Gesellschaft zur Vorbereitung des Volkswagens* (VW Development Company), with Dr. Porsche on its board, and testing went forward from 1937. With unlimited government funding, 60 development VWs were run over a million miles by SS soldiers in secret long-distance tests near the German army barracks at Kornwestheim.

Meantime, Porsche had visited the U.S. in 1936, talking to rear-engine exponents like John Tjaarda, visiting the Fords in Dearborn, and touring the Franklin Automobile Company in Syracuse. He returned with several production experts—of carefully selected Aryan stock—to help set up the *Volkswagen* factory near Castle Wolfsburg in Lower Saxony, a site the Nazis promptly confiscated. Hitler himself attended the dedication ceremonies in May 1938.

In due course, Porsche Project 60 became the VW Series 30 and, finally, the Series 38. The latter was the final pro-

While Dr. Porsche languished in an unheated Dijon dungeon, son Ferry kept the company alive and acquired the million-franc bail requested by the French by designing this '49 Cisitalia Grand Prix car.

duction prototype, marked by the now-famous beetle-shape body with its high beltline and tiny divided rear window. Hitler had wanted to call it KdF for *Kraft durch Freude*—strength through joy—but even Josef Goebbels couldn't sell that one. *Volkswagen* the people called it; Volkswagen it became.

To sell it, the *Deutsche Arbeitsfront* (government labor organization) issued booklets in which would-be owners pasted stamps, creditable toward the purchase price, buying them for a minimum of RM5 weekly. Of course, this money promptly went into the Third Reich's war effort from mid-1939, and nothing but pilot VWs were produced through 1945. But Volkswagenwerk did honor the stamps through 1961 to the tune of 600 Deutsche Marks credit or DM100 cash.

Ironically, it was the British, then the dominant car exporting people, who got Wolfsburg back into serious production postwar. Heinz Nordhoff, formerly of Opel, was picked to run the place, and put VW firmly on its feet. It would take 10 years, but the lowly Beetle would overwhelm the likes of Austin and Morris in world markets, notably the U.S. Germany thus accomplished in the auto field what she failed to do on the battlefield: achieve industrial supremacy over the hated plutocrats of France and Britain.

Even as the VW drama unfolded, Ferdinand Porsche was accomplishing great things on the sporting side of

The 1949 Cisitalia Grand Prix car designed by Ferry Porsche was highly advanced, with four-wheel-drive, fully synchronized gearbox, and a mid-mounted 1.5-liter supercharged flat 12 producing no less than 385 horsepower. Ironically, the Cisitalia never raced.

motoring—less well known, perhaps, but a vital part of his story. As we've seen, he was hardly a stranger to competition cars by the early Thirties, and it was in 1932 that he began work on his most awe-inspiring creation: the Auto Union P-Wagen.

Its design was prompted by the new 750-kg Grand Prix formula for 1934. Typical of Porsche, it emerged as an incredibly sleek single-seater with light-alloy monocoque construction, mid-mounted supercharged V-16, five-speed transmission, and VW-style all-independent torsion-bar suspension with front trailing links and rear swing axles. Initial DIN horsepower was an incredible 295 on 7.0:1 compression. To ensure it all got to the ground, Ferry Porsche later conceived the world's first limited-slip differential. Nearly 50 years later, he modestly recalled that his father "became very enthusiastic about it."

Originally conceived for Wanderer, the P-Wagen ended up an Auto Union, thanks to that 1932 merger. The following year, Porsche met with Hitler to request the same $250,000 in racing support that the new Chancellor had just granted Daimler-Benz. Hitler told Porsche that only D-B could produce a champion for Germany. At that, Porsche turned five shades of red and, wrote David Owen, "launched into a typical flood of technical argument, explaining just what his new racing car was, what it could do, and why no other car could do it. Hitler tried to interrupt, but for once in his life, he was forced to listen.... At first astonished, finally he was impressed. He changed his mind completely and signed an order awarding Auto Union the same government subsidy."

The first P-Wagen, called Type A, was completed by late 1933. Hans Stück drove it to win the Grands Prix of Germany and Switzerland in 1934 as the Auto Unions generally demolished the factory Alfas, and even the GP Mercedes. A Mercedes onslaught gave D-B the Manufacturers Cup in 1935, though the squirrely but blindingly fast Type B Auto Union, with 375 bhp, won the Italian and Tunisian events, with Stück and new team member Bernd Rosemeyer starring.

Rosemeyer was particularly adept at using the car's awesome oversteer to advantage. Indeed, he seemed about the only one who could really control the beasts (except for Ferry Porsche, who drove them during much of the development testing). Rosemeyer won the 1936 Italian, Swiss, and German GPs with the 6.0-liter 520-bhp Type C. In 1937 he drove the ultimate 6.3-liter 545-bhp version to win Germany's *Eifelrennen* against Mercedes' best. Before Hitler rang down the curtain on peace, Auto Union won the GPs of Romania (Stück), France (Müller), and Yugoslavia (the great Tazio Nuvolari). The last would be the final Grand Prix for the duration, and was actually run while the Germans were beating down the Poles on September 3, 1939.

The P-Wagens were also impressive high-speed record breakers. Rosemeyer set 17 new marks in October 1937, including the flying kilometer at 252.47 mph on the Frankfurt-Darmstadt autobahn. He alternated between the R-Type, a special speed-record version that made the 252-mph run, and a smaller-engine car for the 3000-5000-cc class. The following January, he took out after the new 270-mph record of Rudi Caracciola's Mercedes; tragically, a crosswind sent the devilishly tricky AU out of control, and Rosemeyer was killed.

Unquestionably, the Thirties was a golden age for motor racing in general and German GP cars in particular. Driven by the likes of Rosemeyer, Caracciola, Nuvolari, Hermann Lang, Dick Seaman, and Werner von Brauchitsch, Germany's silver missiles ruled the circuits for a decade: wildly beautiful and truly unforgettable for anyone lucky enough to have seen them. Yet all these immortals—the Auto Unions directly and the Mercedes at least tangentially—owed their concept to the same gifted man.

Alas, the winds of a new war ended Ferdinand Porsche's brief years at the pinnacle. Wolfsburg was soon given over to military production (one of its first tasks making stoves to warm the *Wehracht* for the frigid invasion of Russia) and the Volkswagen was shunted aside.

But Ferdinand Porsche was too talented to be left idle. His first wartime project was the Type 82 *Kübelwagen* ("bucket car"), the German Army Jeep, a go-anywhere VW that carried Rommel's *Afrika Korps* across the Sahara. He then rendered the *Schwimmwagen*, an amphibious derivative with four-wheel drive and detachable propeller.

Porsche also designed the Tiger tank, which spearheaded the 1940 invasion of France and the Low Countries, staved off the advancing Russians for months, and fought the Americans to a standstill at the Bulge until the Germans ran out of gasoline in late 1944. He also had a hand in

some of Hitler's "secret" weapons. Among them was the 20-foot-high *Maus*, conceived as a sort of impregnable, far-ranging mobile fort but, in practice, almost *im*mobile on soft ground. Only three were built before the Third Reich collapsed in 1945.

Shortly before this, at the end of 1944, the Porsche design business was evacuated to Gmünd in Austria when Allied bombs began devastating Stuttgart. Nevertheless, *Herr Doktor* Porsche was arrested by the British, though saved from immediate imprisonment by Albrecht Speer, the architect who'd interpreted Hitler's grandiose plans for a new Berlin. Speer told them that this plain-bolts engineer cared nothing about politics and wasn't a Nazi. Porsche was released.

But in November 1945, Porsche was invited to visit French headquarters in Baden-Baden, ostensibly to discuss an idea from Industry Minister Marcel Paul for a French people's car, a VW with a different body. Porsche said he would help, only to be arrested a few days later as a Nazi "collaborator," along with Ferry and son-in-law Anton Piëch (who'd married Ferdinand's only daughter, Louise). The idea was to divert French public attention from the arrest of Louis Renault on the same charge. Porsche was soon marched in chains through Dijon by the all-conquering French, who nevertheless had the presence of mind to tap his brain at the Renault factory, obtaining suggestions that ultimately produced the postwar Renault 4CV. They then locked the 72-year-old Porsche in an unheated Dijon dungeon and demanded a million francs bail.

Ferry Porsche, released in mid-1946, raised the money by signing a contract with Italian Piero Dusio to develop a new Grand Prix Cisitalia. The result was highly advanced, with four-wheel drive, a fully synchronized gearbox, and a mid-mounted 1.5-liter supercharged flat 12 producing no less than 385 bhp. Ironically, it would never race, but it helped bring the elder Porsche home. He was later tried in absentia by a French court and acquitted of all charges, but the million-francs ransom was never returned.

Ferdinand Porsche would continue working in the few years remaining to him, but war, politics, and betrayals had broken the once-indomitable spirit that had survived countless setbacks

and had even stood up to Adolf Hitler. He approved Ferry's Cisitalia design, though Leonard Setright opined that it "set at nought the experience garnered with the 1938-39 Grand Prix Auto Unions... [reverting] to a form of independent rear suspension that once again imposed camber variations and toe-in aberrations without any means for controlling them."

In November 1950, barely two months after his 75th birthday, Ferdinand Porsche suffered a stroke from which he would not recover. When he died on January 30, 1951, the first sports cars bearing his name were just beginning to excite the motoring world. Their basic design reflected engineering tenets he'd espoused for decades, though their direct predecessor dated only from 1939. This was the Type 114 F-Wagen, conceived with Ferry as a sporting evolution of the VW. Though Ferry would be left to realize the first Porsche cars, his father truly founded the marque, and the great *Herr Doktor*'s spirit lives on in every rear-engine Porsche built since.

As a man, Ferdinand Porsche was mercurial, subject to violent temper. He couldn't abide slipshod engineering—or engineers—and he expressed his dislikes in the bluntest of terms. Yet as David Owen notes, "he was a child" politically. He saw Hitler only as a sponsor, and a useful one at that. He was never a Nazi, and the evidence is that Nazi practices abhorred him. Ironically, he prevented the Gestapo from arresting and probably killing Jean-Pierre Peugeot (after the French Resistance bombed the occupied Peugeot factory), only to be branded a "collaborator" by Peugeot after the war, resulting in his needless imprisonment.

Fortunately, Ferdinand Porsche lived to see his two greatest dreams fulfilled: an efficient small car for the masses and an unbeatable competition car. Owen relates that Ferry drove his father to Wolfsburg for a 75th birthday celebration in September 1950. "On the way [they] passed shoals of VWs crowding the autobahns. For [the elder] Porsche, coming at the end of his captivity and illness, it was too much. He broke down and wept. Yet if Porsche was an artist—and he was— he was unusually fortunate. Not many artists are lucky enough to see their work valued at its true worth before they die."

Dr. Ferdinand Porsche was finally released from prison in the late Forties, shortly before this photo was taken. He died on January 30, 1951.

356/1 & 356/2: Birth of a Legend

With its Nazi-ordered departure from Zuffenhausen as too tempting a target for Allied bombs, *Porsche Konstruktionsburo* had all but disappeared by May 1945. The Berghof, Hitler's getaway nest at Berchtesgaden near Salzburg, was blown up by an American detachment. British forces combed the countryside to the south, finding little of significance—until they entered the sleepy little Austrian village of Gmünd, where they were startled to discover a makeshift Porsche operation, including most of the firm's top engineers.

Gmünd was a useful, out-of-the-way place for the Stuttgart refugees. Ferry Porsche had thought it better than Berlin's suggestion of Czechoslovakia, mainly because that country was becoming increasingly restless as the Germans fell back. Some machine tools were shipped to Gmünd, but not all. The Porsche family had decided they could no longer chance a single repository for their valuable equipment. Thus, some tools and files remained in storage at Zuffenhausen; other materials were secreted at the family estate at Zell am See, Austria.

Naturally, the first order of business was to get the business going again, and Ferry Porsche threw himself into the task as soon as the French released him from prison in mid-1946. In a 1979 interview with veteran journalist Jan P. Norbye, he recalled that "matters became quite serious for me after the war, since it all came down to my own initiative. My father was [still] interned at Dijon. When he was finally released...his health was failing and

he never recovered completely." Meanwhile, Ferry's sister, Louise Piëch, held things together, assisted by the loyal Karl Rabe.

The war years had been filled with bitterness and disappointment for all the Porsches. Ferry, in his interview with Norbye, recalled the wrenching turn from *Volkswagen* work: "That was one of our most important and most difficult tasks....[But] once the war began, we worked exclusively on military projects. At first we were largely unsuspecting and torn away from our preparations in Wolfsburg in the middle of the job. We had to leave all peacetime projects behind—such as an exhaust-gas turbocharger for the VW engine, using the same principles we apply today....We had to set aside all such plans and drawings. In 1948, we worked in very primitive conditions in Gmünd, and were happy just to have some VW equipment on hand."

Even so, early progress was brisk despite the circumstances. Notes author Karl Ludvigsen: "By December of 1946 the works employed 222 people, 64 more than it had a year earlier.... Their total 1946 business volume was 1,319,000 Reichsmarks, only 17 percent less than it had been in 1938." One of the first and most important contracts was the four-wheel-drive Cisitalia GP car, the proceeds from which Ferry used to pay off his father's French jailers, securing his release on August 1, 1947.

As noted, that Cisitalia never raced, this despite strong interest from Tazio Nuvolari, by then aching to race again, especially in something designed by

Dr. Ferdinand Porsche and son Ferry pose next to the 356/1 (*opposite page*). Below it, a 1949 356/2 coupe, whose spartan instrument panel (*top*) lacked even a gas gauge. A modified VW flat four provided power (*above*). *Previous page*: Owner C. A. Stoddard says this 1948 356/2 is "the oldest known Porsche in the world...the sixth car to be completely built by Porsche."

the father of the great prewar Auto Unions. The reason it didn't was that Cisitalia founder Piero Dusio saw more profit in roadgoing sports cars, in his case based on off-the-shelf Fiat components. It was hardly a new idea: Ferdinand Porsche had wanted to do something similar way back in the Twenties.

Trouble was, he didn't have the money then, and his decision to join Mercedes in 1923 reflected that. But by 1937, when he *did* have funds (courtesy of the VW project), Dr. Porsche was again thinking about a sports car with his name on it.

"In the last two years before the war, in 1938 and 1939, [my father and I] had wanted to develop a small sports car based on the Volkswagen," Ferry Porsche recalled. Their first effort was the Type 64, built around stock VW components, with a special body and a hotter engine. Unfortunately, it was done in by its very concept. When the Porsches applied to the *Deutsche Arbeitsfront* for the necessary hardware, "we were told then that a state-owned firm [VW] couldn't deliver parts for private business use." The Porsches didn't accept this for long, and in 1938 produced the direct forerunner of the first production Porsche, the Type 114 F-Wagen.

An astounding technical achievement, the Type 114 was largely finalized by transmission specialist Karl Frohlich, with chassis design completed by early 1939. Like the great Auto Union P-Wagens, its engine was placed ahead of the rear-axle centerline, with a Frohlich-designed five-speed gearbox dangling out behind, but the engine was a complex water-cooled V-10 displacing 1493 cc on a bore and stroke of 58.0×56.5 mm. Typical of Porsche, it employed aluminum block and cylinder heads, six main bearings, domed pistons, hemispherical combustion chambers, and a single overhead camshaft per cylinder bank. Magneto ignition was provided for each bank, driven off the intake camshaft. Carburetion was via three one-barrel downdraft instruments squeezed within the 72-degree valley between the banks. Radiator and cooling tubes were initially mounted up front, later transferred to the rear. Again, suspension was VW-like—swing axles, trailing arms, and torsion bars at the rear; parallel trailing arms and

transverse torsion bars up front—carried on a tubular chassis.

In plan view, the Type 114 looked like one of the streamliners penned by pioneer aerodynamicist Paul Jaray, with a smooth, rounded nose and flowing, two-passenger cockpit tapering to a ground-hugging tail. Wheelbase was initially 106.3 inches, later 108.3; tracks measured 53.2 inches.

Three Type 114s with special coupe bodies were built for racing. Designated Type 60K10, they were blessed by *Korpsführer* Huhnlein of the Nazi Motoring Corps (NSKK) after *Herr Doktor* Porsche sold him on the idea of a special Berlin-Rome road race to show off their mettle. But the contest, scheduled for September 1939, was cancelled by Hitler's invasion of Poland. Ferdinand Porsche used one of these cars, modified for the road, for daily driving in the early war years, and Ludvigsen records that Porsche's capable chauffeur, Josef Goldinger, once averaged 85 mph on a trip from the VW factory to Berlin.

The Porsches were obviously quite adept at building remarkable sports cars from ordinary components, but it would be left to Ferry to realize the first production Porsche. By the late Forties, he had shared that dream with his father for a long time. "Cars like that had been a hobby of mine before the war," he told *CAR* magazine's

Early production Porsches were built in Austria, and in small numbers—only 51 had been produced by the spring of 1951. This 1948 model 356/2 was made of aluminum, hand formed over a wood buck (full-scale model form). Like all Porsches of the era, it featured a four-speed crash box. Despite the engine's modest 40-horsepower output, a low 1300-pound curb weight and an aerodynamically slippery body allowed it to approach 90 mph flat out, while averaging about 30 miles per gallon at a 70-miles-per-hour cruise.

Steve Cropley in 1984. "I liked a machine that was speedy, had good acceleration and roadholding compared with ordinary cars. During the war I had an opportunity to drive a supercharged VW convertible with about 50 horsepower, which was a lot of power then. I decided that if you could make a machine which was lighter than that, and still had 50 horsepower, then it would be very sporty indeed."

Ferry and Karl Rabe again began thinking about a VW-based sports car in 1947. By the time Ferdinand rejoined them in August, they had the specifics firmly on paper. Ferry recalls his father being "very interested...of course. He took an interest in everything but didn't have the energy anymore, nor that once-inexhaustible vitality he previously possessed. I had to assume the risk myself."

What ultimately emerged was Porsche Project 356, a smooth, aerodynamic open two-seater with an 85-inch-wheelbase tubular chassis, air-cooled VW engine, and a dry weight of about 1300 pounds. The chassis was a sturdy affair, anchored by bulkheads in the cowl and behind the seats; they turned inward front and rear and were connected by hefty transverse tubes at each end.

The Type 114 and Frohlich's Auto Union concepts, rather than those of the production VW, influenced the chassis. The flat four was located amidships, behind the cockpit and ahead of the rear-axle centerline, and VW swing-axle rear suspension was reversed so that the transverse torsion bars mounted at the rear and the trailing arms became leading arms. This would theoretically result in considerable oversteer, but the tendency was reduced by careful attention to fore/aft weight distribution, which ended up nearly even, and an ultra-low center of gravity. Front suspension was stock VW, as were the steering and cable-actuated nine-inch-diameter drum brakes. Special Porsche-modified cylinder heads with larger intake valves and ports, plus higher compression (7.0 versus 5.8:1) boosted brake horsepower from the stock Beetle's 25 (DIN) to near 40 (at 4000 rpm). Displacement remained at 1131 cc on a 75 × 64-mm bore and stroke.

"We built that car only for experience," said Ferry Porsche in 1984. "It was to see how light we could go

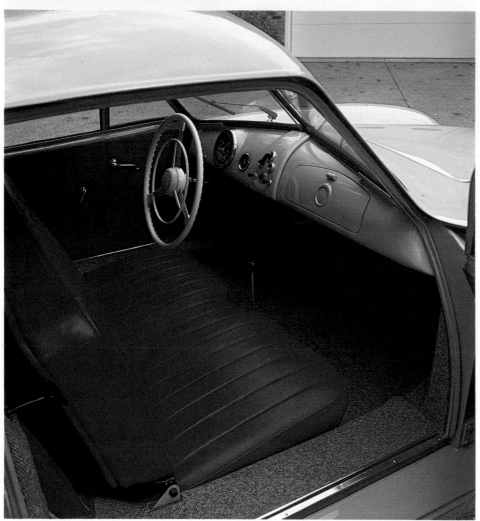

The '48 Porsche 356/2 lacks a tachometer (*above*), an item that didn't become standard until 1952. Most early models, however, were equipped with a clock. The "cat's whiskers" seen on the front of the 356/2 (*right*) disappeared when production was moved to Germany.

and how many VW parts we would need." Ferry and Robert Eberan von Eberhorst, a bright young engineer, first tested the running chassis in March 1948 on a natural proving ground not 20 miles from Gmünd: the daunting, 32-percent grade of the Katshberg Pass. It easily passed every test, confirming that the VW components would hold up under the most demanding conditions.

That mountain test site should come as no surprise given the Germans' historic fondness for hillclimbs and the Porsches' long experience with them. Mountain testing still figures heavily

in the way Porsches are engineered, and helps explain why they not only perform so well, but last so long. "I remember how, after the war, American visitors used to try and keep up on our Volkswagen test runs," Ferry Porsche related in 1984. "The result was usually a boiling radiator at the second turn of the Grossglockner, the highest mountain in Austria, while we could drive our Beetles from bottom to the summit flat out."

Retrospectively known as 356/1, the first prototype Porsche was finished in May 1948 after receiving its aluminum roadster body, designed by long-time

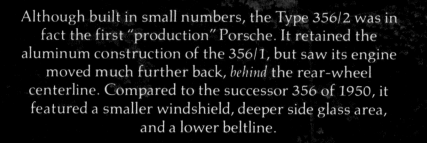

Although built in small numbers, the Type 356/2 was in fact the first "production" Porsche. It retained the aluminum construction of the 356/1, but saw its engine moved much further back, *behind* the rear-wheel centerline. Compared to the successor 356 of 1950, it featured a smaller windshield, deeper side glass area, and a lower beltline.

Porsche hand Erwin Komenda the previous month. Smooth and low, with a two-piece unframed windshield, it set the pattern for the production 356s to come, though it had many unique touches. For example, there were no air grilles in back, and engine access was via a long front-hinged lid that lifted as a unit, not like a hatch as on the production design. Behind the en- gine was room for the spare wheel, a six-volt battery, and a small amount of luggage. Inside was a rudimentary semi-contoured seat. A speedometer was the only instrument, though a clock was built into the glovebox at the far right. Up front, the Porsche name was proudly spelled out in letters not unlike those used today. In all, the 356/1 was sporty and good-looking, constructed with obvious attention to aerodynamic detail, and different from anything else on the road.

On a shakedown run from Gmünd to Zell am See, Ferry and one of his en- gineers encountered only one problem with the 356/1: a terrific pounding on the rugged pavement of Grossglock- ner Pass bent one of the rear frame tubes. Limping into Grossglockner,

they fashioned a two-piece metal sleeve to cover the weakened nub, a reinforcement later applied to production 356s. A July showing at Berne, Switzerland, earned good reviews from the British and European press. That same month, the prototype won a 1000-1200-cc-class road race in Innsbruck, Austria, the first of the 356 Series' competition victories.

The next development was 356/2, which Ludvigsen determined "was developed in parallel with the space-frame roadster and not as a successor to it, as has often been maintained. Planned in both coupe and cabriolet models, the Type 356/2 Porsches differed sharply in design...[with] new frame construction, body style, and engine position." They were, in fact,

the first production Porsches.

And once they appeared, little was heard of 356/1. Komenda modified the roadster's lines, moving even closer to the inimitable 356 style while retaining aluminum construction for both body types. The engine now sat much further back, behind the rear-wheel centerline, which encouraged severe oversteer that was only partly countered by reverting to normal positioning for the VW rear suspension.

But there was, of course, a reason for these changes. "We felt the mid-mounted engine had little interest for the customer," Ferry Porsche explained later. There was also his conviction that even a sports car should have good passenger and luggage space. A more "out of the way" engine provided it within the same overall package size. Besides, "Our goal has always been to build cars for normal purposes, that can go on all kinds of roads and in all weathers"—hence the advent of the definitive beetle-like fastback.

Backed by good-faith orders from two Swiss enthusiast-businessmen, R. von Senger and Bernhard Blank, *Porsche Konstruktionen GmbH* planned to build 50 Type 356/2 chassis, of which 10 would have coupe bodies. Initial publicity brochures pegged the coupe at $3750 and the cabriolet at $4250, prices that were hardly small change at the time. Americans could buy two 1947 Chevys for such sums, while VWs were selling in Germany for about half as much.

But it didn't matter, for Gmünd simply couldn't turn out many cars very quickly. Only four 356/2s were built by the end of 1948—by hand—followed by 25 the next year and 18 in 1950. By spring 1951, just 51 had been sold. But as Ferry Porsche recalled: "Today it seems almost a miracle to me that we managed to build...cars in Gmünd and then sell them." The coupe/cabriolet breakdown has been variously quoted as 45/5 and 42/8; the latter seems more likely, as six cabrios bodied by Beutler of Switzerland are known.

Bernhard Blank, a successful Zurich car dealer, sold most of these first Porsches. A few had engines with a 73.5-mm bore instead of 75 mm to keep displacement below 1100 cc for class racing purposes. Historians doubt the published 7.0:1 compression ratio; 6.5:1 was more like it. But it's interesting to note that the Porsche was at least as economical as the Volkswagen, maybe more so. Despite its piddling 40 horsepower, the 1300-pound curb weight and slippery body allowed the car to approach 90 mph while returning (according to contemporary road tests) no less than 27 mpg—and usually closer to 35. Testers commonly reported 30 mpg at a 70-mph cruise.

This unusual frugality would characterize later roadgoing Porsches capable of far higher speeds.

As noted, most 356/2 cabriolets were built at the Beutler works in Thun, Switzerland, near Berne, with bare chassis shipped from Gmünd. They were slightly more elongated than the coupes, undoubtedly the coachbuilder's doing. The last one was delivered in August 1949. Between five and eight were completed—probably six—but the accepted total may be low. Serial number 57 is known, though some lower numbers could have been skipped.

A minor sales demand developed as the months passed and word spread about the Porsche. Karl Rabe had enthusiastically promised 150 units by the end of 1948 but, as noted, things moved slowly in Gmünd. The aluminum bodies, for instance, had to be hammered out over wooden forms by

The contours of the rear of the '48 Porsche 356/2 were more bulbous than those of the 356 that was to follow. Likewise, wheel arch shapes were more rounded. Note also that the 356/2 sported vent windows, which would be dropped on the Zuffenhausen-built models. Erwin Komenda was responsible for the design evolution from the 356/1 to the 356/2. He also penned the lines of the first German-built cars, the now-familiar shape known to generations of Porsche enthusiasts.

hand. Engines varied from car to car, not because of engineering problems but because everything was in such short supply. Still, the ledgers were being written in black, even if the numbers weren't impressive.

In September 1948, Ferry Porsche, seeking even firmer footing for his company, concluded a multi-faceted deal with VW's Heinz Nordhoff, whom the British had installed at Wolfsburg. "We agreed on a new license for the VW [design], a consulting contract [thus reestablishing the prewar Porsche/VW relationship, Porsche's becoming] the import agency for Austria, favored status on delivery of VW parts for building our own sports cars, and joint use of the worldwide VW sales organizations. That was the basis for our fresh start." The Marshall Plan and a reviving German economy would do the rest.

Gmünd posed a thornier problem: too small, too remote, and completely removed from the car-building heart of industrial Germany. Designing and building cars there made about as much sense as General Motors setting up its Saturn plant in rural Tennessee.

Porsche clearly needed to return to Zuffenhausen, but the Americans had been using its old premises for military motor pools and weren't eager to give them up.

But the GIs agreed to leave in mid-1950, and Porsche duly made plans to close up at Gmünd and move back home. The decision was not made lightly, however. VW work was Porsche's most profitable at the time; sports cars were but a hobby by com-

The 40-horsepower rating for the 356/2's engine may sound woefully inadequate today, but the contemporary VW engine—on which it was based—could muster only 25 horses. The increase was accomplished via special Porsche-modified VW heads with larger inlet valves and ports and a boost in compression ratio from 5.8:1 to an alleged 7.0:1.

parison. Conceivably, Porsche viewed returning to Zuffenhausen as a tax write-off against the payments starting to come in from VW, as Nordhoff and company began their drive to success among economy cars. But sports cars were more fun than people's cars, and there was no question of building tanks or any other military hardware. The one fly in this ointment was a big one: the costs of starting production in Stuttgart were relatively astronomical, considerably higher than Porsche's income from Wolfsburg.

The problem was solved when Alfred Prinzing, Ferry's wily business manager, took a Porsche coupe on a tour of Germany's main VW distributers. It was a literal door-to-door sales job, but Prinzing was a born salesman and returned with orders totalling DM200,000. Adding that to its VW receipts gave Porsche at least a fighting chance. Plans were made for chassis assembly in part of the Reutter works, and Porsche began moving out of Gmünd in early 1950. In April, the first of a long and distinguished line rolled out the Zuffenhausen door: the first German-made Porsches.

CHAPTER THREE

1950-55 Type 356: Porsches for the World

Despite great strides at Gmünd, *Porsche Konstruckstionen GmbH* was still struggling to establish itself in 1950. It wouldn't have to struggle much longer. With components and consultancy fees from Volkswagenwerk assured, Porsche had the "fresh start" it needed to begin producing sports cars in earnest. With the return to Stuttgart-Zuffenhausen that year, it got down to business.

"We signed a contract with Reutter to build bodies for the 500 cars we planned to start with," Ferry Porsche recalled 29 years later. "Since Reutter had no experience with welding light alloy, we had to change to steel for the coupe. We had only perhaps $50,000 on hand to start production and never dreamed we would eventually reach... 78,000 of the 356-model cars."

As luck would have it, Reutter Karosserie was located right next door—a good thing, as Porsche had to rent 5000 square feet of the coachbuilder's plant for final assembly since it wasn't able to use its own factory at first. A bit later, Porsche purchased a nearby 1100-square-foot building for administrative offices and design space. The company soon changed its name again, to *Dr. Ing.-h.c. F. Porsche KG* (the KG denoting the German term for limited partnership).

"Having Reutter nearby was a great advantage for us," Ferry said later. "In those days, chassis and body construction were far more separated than they are today. Later we took over the

Reutter firm so that we could build the bodies, which are the most expensive part of an automobile, ourselves."

In preparation for the ambitious 10-fold production boost, Erwin Komenda cleaned up the lines of the 1948-50 Gmünd-built 356/2 coupe and cabriolet, creating the now-familiar shape of what was simply called the 356. The windshield (still divided) was enlarged, side-window area reduced (via a higher beltline), and vent wings eliminated. Inside, an oil temperature gauge was added and the clock moved from the glovebox to beside the speedometer. There was still no gas gauge, though, Porsche relying for now on VW's reserve-tank system and a thoroughly un-Porsche measuring device, a wooden dipstick.

The engine remained the 40-horsepower (DIN) Porsche Type 369 air-cooled flat four, still VW-based with special Porsche heads, but now boasting twin carburetors (Solex 32 PBI). Chassis changes followed those of VW, which in 1950 adopted hydraulic shock absorbers, mounted in steel towers, and hydraulic drum brakes. The latter proved inadequate in the Porsche, and were replaced by 1951 with twin-leading-shoe Lockheed front drums supplied by the German Alfred Teves company (Ate). At the same time, the previous lever-arm rear shocks were ousted for modern tubular units.

Porsche completed its first Stuttgart car on Good Friday 1950—and never

looked back. Deliveries were underway by April, with the coupe priced at DM9950 (about $2030). By midyear, sales were running at 33 cars a month, versus the 8-9 projected in the original Reutter contract. Sales totalled 298 at year's end. Sadly, the great Dr. Ferdinand barely lived to see the swift progress of the cars and company bearing his name. By the time of his death in late January 1951, the factory was claiming output of 60 units a month.

Meantime, Porsches were gradually getting into the hands of non-German testers, who would presumably render the harshest judgments. But the folks in Zuffenhausen needn't have worried. Typical of the reviews was that of Britain's weekly *The Autocar*, which evaluated a 356 in April 1951: "Even a short run serves to give the characteristic impression of a really well streamlined car. The acceleration above 50 mph is quite beyond what would be expected from the engine size, and is achieved in extraordinary quietness. About 60 mph is available in third gear.... It is a rare car these days in which the designer has gone all out for certain qualities with the limited means at hand and has accepted certain disadvantages instead of trying to achieve a well-balanced mediocrity.... It is not a car for everyone's taste, but it offers a unique combination of comfort, performance and economy, for which some people will pay a very good price."

At the Frankfurt Automobile Show

that same month, Porsche introduced the Types 356/1 and 356/3, its first 1300-cc models. Their new engine—precisely 1286 cc (78.5 cubic inches) on a bore and stroke of 80.0 x 64 mm (3.14 × 2.52 inches)—was a bored-out Type 369 with aluminum instead of cast-iron cylinders, chrome plated on their working surfaces for greater durability. The 369's compression may be disputed, but this Type 506 derivative definitely had a 6.5:1 ratio, and this, plus the greater displacement, boosted output to a claimed 44 bhp (DIN) at the same 4200 rpm. Reflecting Porsche's traditional concern for craftsmanship, each engine was assembled by a single worker, a job that took 25 hours.

The modest compression made Europe's lower-grade fuel more palatable to the 1300 than the 1100 engine had found it, but there was a slight performance gain nevertheless. Factory records show the 1300's top speed as 92 mph, about 2-3 mph faster than the 1100.

Also introduced at Frankfurt as across-the-board changes were: improved defrosting provisions, optional tachometer, the new VW-based suspension, tube shocks, and Lockheed-Ate brakes. In all, the 1300 was a definite step forward that earned more good marks from the press.

Volume began taking off in 1951. Porsche completed its 1000th Stuttgart car on August 28, and output for the year totaled 1103 units for a profit of $3 million. Not widely appreciated is the fact that Porsches were still built in Gmünd through March of this year. From then on, production was centered solely in Zuffenhausen.

Part of that 1951 revenue, though admittedly a small part, came from the U.S., then the home of hard currency, bigger-is-better, and numerous well-heeled buyers. Most was owed to Max Hoffman, the veritable godfather of postwar America's import-car business, who in 1950 had added Porsche to the select nameplates sold at his New York City dealership on Park Avenue. Hoffman initially had his doubts, perhaps because some of his customers thought the 356 curious: shaped like a well-worn bar of soap and as costly as a Lincoln. But he had a weakness for Porsches, being Austrian-born and a great admirer of Ferry and his father. Hoffman had also introduced the Volkswagen to America, selling two in 1949 but eventually giving up the franchise (one of his greatest mistakes, he later admitted). But he did sell Porsches, slowly at first

Perhaps the most important of the early Porsche 1500 Supers was the America, a rakish roadster with aluminum bodywork by Gläser. Only four were sold in the U.S. in 1952, the year model shown, and total production reached only 15-50 (estimates vary widely).

but rising to 10 a week by 1954. Hoffman later allowed that sales—and his own approval rating—picked up considerably once Porsche dumped the VW-based "crashbox" for its own four-speed synchromesh transmission in 1953.

That gearbox was developed from a design conceived for the GP Cisitalia and patented in 1947. Gear synchronization was its most unique feature, accomplished by intermediate servo rings instead of conventional cones. Each pinion had a servo ring revolving

with it at equal speed; as a shift was made, the appropriate servo ring matched the clutch ring's rate of rotation to that of the rear output shaft. The result was quicker shifts than the cone system allowed, owing to shorter gear braking/acceleration time. The arrangement was also more compact, and Porsche claimed the new transmission was no larger than the previous one. Synchromesh was eventually extended to all Porsches, though the factory regretted that fitting it to earlier models wasn't possible. Predic-

tably, other carmakers were quick to adopt this superior system, including Alfa Romeo, BMW, Ferrari, even Daimler-Benz (beginning with the racing 300SLR of the mid-Fifties).

There's no substitute for cubic centimeters. If the 1100/1300 could perform so well while sipping tiny amounts of fuel, why not a 1500? Porsche began working on such an engine in mid-1950, mainly because 1500 cc had become the upper displacement limit for several racing classes; moreover, the size seemed ideal for a small,

The Porsche America was planned with racing in mind, and so weight was kept to a bare minimum. More importantly, perhaps, it was the forerunner of the legendary Speedster.

light sports car like the 356.

Since the 1100 flat four was bored to get 1300 cc, it was only logical to lengthen stroke to get 1500. The Hirth company of Stuttgart devised a connecting rod compact enough to allow a 10-mm increase, to 74 mm, giving 1488 cc. Hirth also supplied a new crankshaft with roller bearings, which reduced friction but soon had people like Max Hoffman complaining about durability. Prolonged low-rpm running and/or inattention to regular oil changes most always led to early crank

failure. Avoiding it was as easy as reading the owner's manual but, of course, not everyone did (collectors, take note). Interestingly, this engine began the practice of "keeping the revs up" that many Porschephiles—especially 911 owners—still follow even though it's long been unnecessary.

Initially, the 1500 retained the small twin carbs and developed 55 bhp (DIN) at 4500 rpm, but only 66 of these Type 502 engines were built before Porsche switched to a new Type 547 derivative with Solex 40BPI instruments and 60

bhp (the smaller carbs could be fitted if desired). The original Solex 32s reflected caution on Porsche's part rather than engineering error. The company felt the gearbox might not be up to the extra power, but the new all-synchro transmission ended that worry.

A squad of 356s—1100s and 1500s—went to Monthlèry, France's huge banked oval track, for some speed-record attempts in September 1951. All performed brilliantly. The 1100s set three new marks, averaging better

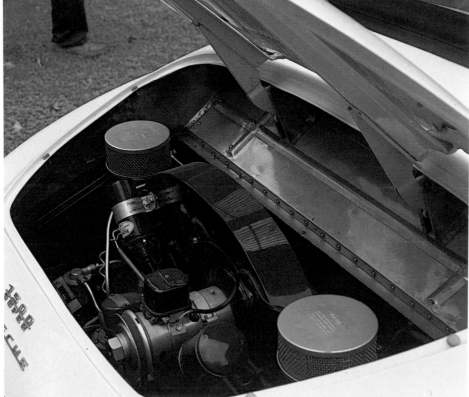

than 100 mph for 500 miles, 1000 kilometers, and six hours. The 1500s, including a mildly modified car from Volkswagen dealer Walter Glöckler, broke no fewer than 14 records. The factory car raised official averages to over 97 mph for 3000, 4000, and 5000 kilometers; 2000, 3000, and 4000 miles; and 24 and 48 hours. It also averaged 95.75 mph for 10,000 km and 94.6 mph for 72 hours. The Glöckler, a streamlined roadster, ran 500 and 1000 km and the six hours at 114-116 mph, breaking three more records. The 72-hour mark came despite a disabled top gear that forced drivers to run in third at 90 mph with the engine whirling at a busy 4500 rpm. It was a tremendous performance that conclusively proved the 356's mettle.

Ferdinand Porsche once said that it makes no difference where a car's engine is located, so long as it's light. The 1500 unit weighed a mere 160 pounds, while early 356s rarely exceeded 1750 pounds at the curb. Fore/aft weight distribution was approximately 780/970 pounds, but this wasn't as big a difference as it might seem. In unofficial tests conducted by an unnamed Southern California aircraft company,

This page: In order to reduce weight, the America's interior (*top*) included aluminum-frame seats and a hole in the dash instead of a glovebox. Wind-up windows gave way to Plexiglas side curtains, the padded soft top to a thin snap-on canvas roof. Its Type 528 engine (*bottom*), good for 70 DIN bhp and 80 lbs-ft torque at 3600 rpm, was strong enough to propel the 1600-pound car to 110 mph and from 0-60 in 9.3 seconds. *Opposite page*: The 356 assembly line stood in sharp contrast to the mass production methods of Detroit.

it was learned that the 356 body generated 175 pounds of front aerodynamic downforce that effectively equalized weight distribution.

Balance of another kind impressed editor Dick von Osten of the U.S. magazine *Auto* when he tested a 356/1500: "The top-speed runs were made with two different drivers on a level, measured quarter-mile at sea level. I expected to clock slightly over 100 mph, so it was quite a shock when [I] reached that figure with no apparent effort and kept on going. [We] both managed to hit the maximum speed of 111.1 mph on both an east and west run. Five mph were probably added to the top speed by the perfect wheel balance, a typical detail of this car: all Porsches come from the factory with the wheels and tires in a perfect state of dynamic and static balance. Dr. Porsche once said that...wheel balance can add or subtract 500 engine rpm at top speed." (Incidentally, his reported maximum was 15 mph *higher* than the factory claimed, a conservatism that still marks Porsche's official performance figures.)

Despite the more powerful engine, fuel economy was hardly affected. Von

Osten covered 329 miles (75 in city traffic) on one tankful, including top speed, acceleration, and braking tests, and a highway run at an average 70-75 mph. This required 11 gallons of gas for an overall average of close to 33 mpg. Somehow, results like these make you wonder if we've learned that much in the last 35 years.

Significantly, Von Osten mentioned that others remarked most often about his test Porsche's "unmistakable quality. From the gentle 'click' of the door to its smooth paint, from the handling ease to the engine's performance, the Porsche reflects genius in design and pride in craftsmanship.... Although it is not a low-priced car (approximately $4284 for the coupe and $4560 for the convertible), it is a car to which every owner can point with pride, one of the rare sports cars that makes the owner feel that he has cheated the factory by paying so low a price." A lot of folks would still agree with that even though new Porsches now run something like 10 times as many dollars.

Even in these early days, the 356 Series reflected the Porsches' belief in the perfectibility of a given design—

provided it was good to begin with—and detail refinements have been the standing order most every year since. By mid-summer 1952, all 356s had acquired a one-piece windshield (albeit with a vertical bend in the center), perforated disc wheels, and bodywork wrapped down more beneath the bumpers. A large 6000-rpm tachometer became standard, replacing the clock, and both it and the speedo were newly hooded to prevent unwanted windshield reflections at night.

The ultimate developments of the original 356 were the 1300S and 1500S, the "S" denoting Super. The latter came first, in October 1952. Its heart was a new Type 528 powerplant with the same displacement as the 502/507 but running 8.2:1 compression, good for a rated 70 DIN horsepower and 80 pounds-feet torque at 3600 rpm. That highish peak torque speed was a clue to Porsche's intentions—production-class racing—and the Super was predictably less sudsy below 3500 rpm than the normal 1500. Both 1500S and 1300S (announced in November '53; same CR, 60 bhp) benefitted from a revised camshaft designed by future Porsche chairman

Ernst Fuhrmann, a Gmünd engineer who'd been involved with the GP Cisitalia. The factory assigned the 1300S an official top speed of 100 mph, the 1500S 105 mph. But again, the evidence is that these were conservative claims, especially for cars given careful tuneups.

Perhaps the most important of the early 1500 Supers was the America, a rakish roadster with aluminum body-work by Gläser, marked by an ultra-low beltline. Almost unknown in Europe, it was hardly familiar in the U.S. either, priced at a lofty $4600. But it was a start toward what would be one of the most beloved Porsches of all: the immortal Speedster.

Like many of the Fifties' more interesting European imports, the America sprang from the fertile mind of Max Hoffman, who wanted a lighter open Porsche without the heavy top and side windows of the standard 356 cabrio. Of course, he had racing in mind, and there were many touches designed to save pounds, which didn't exceed 1600. Included were light aluminum-frame seats, Plexiglas side curtains, thin snap-on canvas roof, a hole in the dash instead of a glovebox, and a divided windshield that could be replaced by a racing windscreen. With

By 1954, the 356 was nearing the end of its production run. Shown here in Adriatic Blue, this coupe sports chrome wheels and is powered by the 1500N engine. Although a production run of only 500 units was planned initially, car number 5000 was built in March, 1954.

all this, the America was even more exciting than the regular 1500S. *Auto Age* magazine's test showed a 110-mph top speed, 0-60 mph in 9.3 seconds, and the standing quarter-mile in 17.9 seconds.

Alas, not many Americas were built, largely because of the way they were built. Reutter sent rolling chassis from Stuttgart to Gläser in Ullersricht, north of Munich, where artisans hand-hammered the aluminum body-work and welded it to the chassis. Semi-finished, the cars were then trucked back to Zuffenhausen for final assembly. Only four were sold in the U.S. in all of 1952, and production ended the following year. One Porsche expert puts the total number at 20, another at 50. Regardless, the America remains a rare and thus highly collectible Porsche. A seemingly limited market and high production costs (aggravated by transportation expense) condemned it to an early grave, though it would not be forgotten.

A change symbolic of Porsche's progress marked the 1953 models: the now-famous Porsche crest. This, too, was prompted by Max Hoffman, who thought all cars should have emblems. He suggested this while lunching in New York one day with Ferry Porsche,

who quickly sketched out a bit of heraldry on a napkin. As finalized by freelance graphic designer Eric Strenger (who at the same time developed the Porsche logotype still used today), it bore the Stuttgart coat of arms, a rampant black horse on a yellow shield representing an old part of the city where a stud farm had once been (Stuotgarten); surrounding this were the colors and six staghorns from the crest of the state of Baden-Württemburg. Ferrari, of course, also uses the prancing stallion. It's said that Enzo Ferrari took his design from the emblem of the World War I air squad-

The instrument panel (*top*) looked less spartan in 1954 than it had in 1948. The badging above the license plate light (*above*) indicates the "Normal" 1500-cc engine. Note the twin taillights. Styling had changed little since 1950 (*right*).

ron commanded by Italian pilot Francesco Baracca, an insignia connected with Stuttgart's in Ferry Porsche's view.

Other 1953 changes were more tangible. Parking lamps moved inboard to beneath the headlamps, taillamps were now circular pairs on each side instead of circle/oblong duos, and a separate trip odometer joined the total mileage recorder as standard equipment. Engines stayed the same: 1100/1300/1500 "Normal" and 1300/1500 Super. The Type 528 gave up its Hirth crank for one of forged steel, as Karl Rabe was able to shorten the original rod design by making a diagonal cut across the big end, thus leaving adequate clearance for the longer stroke. The 1500 Normal had 6.5:1 compression and only 55 bhp at 4400 rpm, but the factory claimed that sufficient for a 96-mph top speed. It was an ideal foil for the 1500S, more tractable at lower speeds and thus better for everyday driving. All engines, each available in coupe or cabriolet, would persist through 1955 except for the 1100s, which vanished after '54.

Only the 1500s came to the U.S. in '53, where the Normal was called America and impressively priced at $3445 for the coupe and $3695 for the cabrio—the most affordable Porsches yet. (The equivalent upmarket Supers listed at $4284/$4584.) Max Hoffman had struck again (as he would a dozen years later by bringing in the first BMW 1600 2-doors for under $2500). But what he gave with one hand he took away with the other, having Porsche delete the reclining seatbacks, wheel trims, the fold-down provision for the vestigial back seat, the radio, passenger-side sunvisor, and the tachometer; all were standard on European 1500s.

Porsche passed a production mile-

stone on March 15, 1954, by completing Zuffenhausen car number 5000, followed a few weeks later with another batch of running changes. Parking lamps were now flanked by tiny grilles that, despite their size, efficiently channeled cooling air to the brakes and opened up hooting space for new twin Bosch horns. Inside were a semicircular horn ring (real Detroit, that), passenger grab handle, and instrument-lighting rheostat. Windshield washer and oil filter were also newly standard.

Porsche's big event of 1954 arrived in September: the charming, sporty Speedster. It was yet another bit of marketing magic from Max Hoffman who, despite his experience with the 1952 America, didn't think U.S. demand for roadsters was quite *that*

limited, and that an inexpensive model should be a permanent part of the Porsche line.

His arguments were sound. As he told Ferry, the U.S. market had become crucial for Porsche. The firm was then producing an average of nine cars a day. The U.S. was taking four, and Hoffman was selling nearly half of those: 22 percent of Porsche's total volume. Moreover, Americans had been flocking to sports cars with enthusiasm since the war. MG and Jaguar had started the trend, but Triumph and Austin-Healey were getting into the act, and by 1953 even Detroit was muscling in with production two-seaters like the Chevrolet Corvette and the Anglo-American Nash-Healey.

Hoffman was a firm believer in the

salability of open sports models, and his suggestions to Daimler-Benz at about this time resulted in the 190SL of 1955, another car he'd move in good numbers. But while the Mercedes had to sell for upwards of $4000, Hoffman wanted a Porsche priced under $3000. Maxie knew his market, and Porsche listened.

The result was the Speedster, an evolution of the first America, bearing the same Type number (540) but designed by Reutter for the lowest possible production costs. It started with the ordinary cabriolet bodyshell, but had none of its ordinary accoutrements. Like the America, the Speedster came only with a simple canvas top and side curtains instead of a built-in padded top and roll-up door windows, and its windshield was cut about

At the behest of Max Hoffman, the American importer of
Porsche automobiles, U.S. models were called the
Continental (*both pages*) in 1955. This was not to last,
however, as Ford "owned" the name, and was about to bring
out its own Continental for 1956—the Mark II. All
Porsches received thoroughly revamped engines for 1955.

Porsche celebrated its silver anniversary as a company in 1955. Production came to a satisfying 2952 units and the marque had by now established a fine reputation. Enthused *The Autocar*: "There is a feeling of rushing through space with the road disappearing rapidly...."

3½ inches shorter than the cabrio's for an extra dash of raffishness. The cockpit was as spartan as a Triumph TR2's, with minimal instrumentation (just speedo, tach, and temperature gauge), a painted dash, and simple bucket seats with fixed backrests. Exterior appearance was standard Porsche from the waist down, save the near full-length

bodyside chrome strips running neatly through the door handles, which greatly helped aesthetics. Nevertheless, the Speedster was typically likened to an inverted bathtub (recalling some late-Forties Detroiters), and it looked a bit bizarre buttoned up. Technically, the tachometer and heater were extras, but as it was hard to find a

car without them, they were effectively "mandatory options" that pushed the typical delivered price over $3000. But Hoffman realized his target base: $2995 POE New York, plus delivery and options.

Not surprisingly, the 1500 Normal engine was standard for the Speedster, but the Super spec was available for

about $500 additional. Speedsters weren't immediately sold in Europe, but were well received in the U.S. After an exploratory 200-unit run for 1954, the factory upped output. By the time the last one was delivered in 1958, the total exceeded 4900.

Visually, the 1954 and '55 Speedsters were quite similar, the differences confined mainly to gauges, bonnet handle, and emblems. Like all 356s since the first, they rolled on 16-inch-diameter wheels and tires.

The Speedster seemed born to race, and was certainly quick enough for it. The base model weighed nearly 200 pounds less than the 1500N coupe and was thus about a second faster in the 0-60-mph sprint, though superior aerodynamics let the coupe pull away from about 80 mph. The 1500S was commensurately faster, though again deficient at the top end next to its coupe counterpart. Comparing Super and Normal Speedsters, respective 0-60-mph times were 10 and 14 seconds; figures for the standing quarter-mile

were 17.5 and 19 seconds; top speeds 95 and 100 mph.

Of course, being Porsches, the Speedsters did race, and with considerable distinction. John von Neumann, Porsche's west-coast counterpart to Max Hoffman, started running them in SCCA events in November 1954, when his 1500S finished 8th overall in a six-hour enduro at Torrey Pines, California, and won its class the following day. Bengt Sonderstrom drove one to win the national SCCA F-Production championship in 1955.

And Speedsters have continued racing ever since. Nowadays you see them mainly in vintage events, although a few still show up—and win—in production classes against cars many years newer. Never has there been a better expression of the race-and-ride sports car.

Walt Woron waxed enthusiastic after testing a Speedster for the July 1955 issue of *Motor Trend* magazine: "Its size, power, easy shift and steering make it fun to drive.... The brakes are extremely good. They have a servo action [and] are very positive; they get you out of situations where you may have delayed too long.... For a sports car, and especially such a small one, the Porsche Speedster has a very smooth ride. It recovers quickly after a dip or bump, which seems to be inherent in torsion-sprung cars. There's absolutely no wallowing when it comes out of a dip; you've always got it under control."

Like most drivers, Woron felt slightly claustrophobic within the Speedster. "With the top up... you have to jackknife in; the top is extremely low [overall height was a mere 48 inches] and if you're over six feet, your head is going to touch. It doesn't leave much room between the top and doors for seeing out; and with the side curtains on, you may as well be content with just looking forward."

Though rudimentary next to the cabrio roof, the Speedster top was high-tech stuff compared to the erector-set affairs of British contemporaries. "Putting up the soft top is absurdly easy," said Woron. "You reach behind you, grab the top's forward bow, pull forward so that it reaches the windshield and snap the two locks in place." He also noted that Reutter had managed to sneak in a little padding between the top's inner and outer

Opposite page: Porsche's immortal Speedster (*top*) sported side curtains and an unlined top. Bowing in September 1954, it had evolved from the America; its cockpit (*bottom*) was spartan because Reutter (*this page, below*) designed the car for the lowest possible production costs. At $2995 POE, it came with the 1500 Normal engine; $500 more bought the Super (*above*).

layers, an advance unknown in darkest Coventry.

Summing up the Speedster's appeal, Woron rhetorically asked, "Where else are you going to get a sports car that has the performance, the ride and the workmanship of this one? There are few cars in its price class or above that can compete with it in an across-the-board comparison. Sure, it lacks certain features like roll-up windows, but if you want an open-air car you'd have no complaints on this score. If you drive for the fun of driving, you'll *love* this one."

As indeed, people do today. In fact, the recent rash of Speedster replicas—some good, others less so—is proof that, as with so many well-liked cars, demand for the original still far outruns available supply.

Shortly after the Speedster's debut, Porsche completed a wholesale revision of its engine lineup for 1955. The 1100 was abandoned, as noted, while the four remaining powerplants became "/2" types (e.g., 546/2 and 528/2 for the 1500 Normal and Super). Among other things, they benefitted from improved valvegear, strengthened castings, virtually square cylinder dimensions on 1300s (74.5 × 74.0 mm), and three-piece, 4.5-liter aluminum crankcases instead of the previous two-piece, 3.5-liter magnesium affairs.

These "/2" engines put further distance between Porsche and VW engineering, being designed for easier servicing and quicker camshaft swapping under race conditions. This meant that fewer parts now interchanged with VW's, which was okay with Ferry Porsche. His cars were rapidly becoming more specialized and thus increasingly removed from their humble origins, marking his firm's emergence as a manufacturer in its own right and, just as important, reducing its reliance on VW components. Porsche didn't make much of these changes (indeed, they're listed mainly in factory documents), but they reflected the continual quest for perfection that remains a fact of life at Zuffenhausen.

There was one other change for '55. Again at Hoffman's behest, U.S. models were called Continental that year—and that year only, because Lincoln "owned" the name and was about to bring out its new Continental Mark II for '56.

The Autocar captured much of the early Porsche essence in its November 1953 test of a 1500: "By virtue of its very low build and fine aerodynamic lines it attracts immediate attention and interest from young and old. It is so obviously a car designed by [those] who knew what they wanted and were able to carry out their ideas. Its very appearance suggests speed, and as soon as one is seated...any desire to loiter is quickly [forgotten]. The Porsche [holds the road] in no uncertain manner, the soft torsion-bar springing allowing it to hurry round main road corners without roll, while the rather direct steering gives the driver exact control over the front wheels."

Uncharacteristically, the editors allowed that they extended their test time simply because the 1500 was so much fun: "The high top gear makes cruising effortless, with an indicated

75-80 [mph] on the speedometer. One can imagine the car being thoroughly at home storming Alpine passes, where the admirable third gear and also second could be used to advantage. At night there is the impression of being in an aircraft cockpit, with the close curved windscreen and discreet lighting from the fascia, the suspension ironing out any sudden undulations in the road surface and no squeal being evident from the tyres when cornering fast. There is a feeling of rushing through space with the road disappearing rapidly immediately in front and the subdued beat of the engine from the rear." That was about as lyrical as the conservative British weekly ever got, but then the 356 experience was, as Ford would later say of the Thunderbird, "unique in all the world."

As the last of the original 356s—the first Porsches *for* the world—came off the line, Porsche could look back on 25 successful years. The company had certainly come a long way since the great *Herr Doktor* opened the doors on Kronenstrasse back in 1930. Calendar 1955 production was a satisfying 2952 units. Even more important, Porsche at last got back into its original premises, restored by the West German government on December 1 of that year. But though few believed it then, even greater things lay ahead.

Even with the top down, the Speedster looked racy with its cut-down windshield. Almost 5000 Speedsters were built during its lifetime.

1956-65
Type 356A/B/C:
Pursuit
of Excellence

At first glance, the 1956 Porsches seemed little different from earlier ones, but closer inspection revealed a new approach sufficient to warrant an "A" suffix for the type designation. As was now customary for Porsche, the new 356A Series was launched at the Frankfurt Auto Show, in September 1955, then went into production a few weeks later. It would see the end of the 1300/1300S models and, alas, the winsome Speedster. But it would bring a slew of running changes and the first of the fabulous Carreras—the fastest "street" Porsches yet, capable of 120-125 mph in normal trim (and worthy of separate coverage in the following chapter).

The 356A Series initially comprised coupe, cabriolet, and Speedster body styles still supplied exclusively by Reutter in Stuttgart. Styling was subtly altered. Most obvious were a one-piece curved windshield without the previous vertical crease, and slim rocker rub rails. On Speedsters, windshield height and the top-frame bows were raised about 2½ inches' to improve headroom (a running change actually made in mid-1955). Less noticeable, but a key chassis improvement, was the switch from 16- to 15-inch-diameter wheels in a new "super-wide" 4.5-inch size. These carried correspondingly fatter tires, 5.60-15s versus the previous 5.00-16s.

Inside, the all-metal center-bulge dash of yore gave way to a new flat-face panel with padded top and, Speed-

sters excepted, a radio mounting slot. Ahead of and readily visible through the steering wheel were three large gauges: a centrally placed tachometer flanked by an equal-size speedometer on the left and a combination fuel level/oil temperature gauge on the right. Headlight flashers were now standard, except on Speedsters, and handbrakes were more conveniently located. Entry/exit and front legroom improved via a floor lowered 1½ inches, and the ignition switch now incorporated a starter detent. Car for car, more thorough sound insulation in strategic places made 356As quieter than 356s.

Besides the chunkier wheel/tire combination, the A boasted a heavily revised version of the now-familiar 356 chassis, based on a prototype (nicknamed "Ferdinand" after the elder Dr. Porsche) that had been used for testing since 1954. Suspension was modified for increased travel and a softer ride. For the latter, leaves were removed from the laminated front torsion bars and the rear bars were both lengthened (from 21.8 to 24.7 inches) and reduced in diameter (by 1 mm, to 24). This, together with the lower-profile rolling stock, had been found to improve roadholding. Shock absorbers got suitably higher rates all-round and were repositioned, with the rears mounting vertically instead of at an angle. Up front, suspension mounts were beefed up and a stiffer, larger-diameter anti-roll bar fitted. Outer

suspension-arm bearings were now of the needle-roller type. Steering geometry was altered, and a small hydraulic damper was added to absorb road shock and reduce kickback through the wheel. While the chassis tuning definitely aided ride, roadability was unaffected, so a 356A feels considerably more "modern" by today's standards than a 356.

Avid Porschephile John Bentley opined that the updated chassis gave the 356 "a brand-new personality. If the steering had lost its feather-lightness, it also shed that alarming front-end tendency to 'float' and wander at high speed. Then too, the traditional oversteer gave way to neutral steering; and although the car offered a slightly 'softer' ride than before, it became as tractable as a front-engined machine and could be driven in much the same way."

Road & Track magazine put it a little differently: "[The car's] suspension system...gives an impressive combination of control and true riding comfort. The inbuilt oversteer, an old story to those who know Porsches well, can still make the novice a little jumpy until he is sure just what the car is going to do. Then he will find himself hunting up sharp curves for the sheer pleasure of being in control of so exceptionally maneuverable a car."

Inevitably, Porsche also improved its flat-four engines, which now numbered five: 1300, 1300 Super, 1600, 1600S, and 1500GS. Only the last

Although there was technically no such thing as
a '59 356A *Speedster* Carrera GT, a few were
built from left over parts in early '59. GT
pieces included aluminum doors, hood, and engine
lid; heavy-duty brakes; four-cam, twin-ignition
engine; larger gas tank; and roll bar.

three were sold in America. All engines were available in all body styles save for a non-existent 1300N/Speedster combination. All were still air cooled, of course, and all but the 1500GS retained overhead valves actuated by pushrods and rocker arms.

The big news was that brace of 1.6-liter engines. Prompted by the FIA's new 1600-cc competition limit, they were created by simply fitting larger cylinder barrels to the previous 1500 block, enlarging bore by 2.5 mm. The results were bore/stroke dimensions of 82.5 × 74 mm and total displacement of precisely 1582 cc. Higher compression yielded 60 DIN horsepower (70 SAE) at 4500 rpm for the Type 616/1 Normal unit; the Type 616/2 Super delivered 76 bhp (DIN) at 5000 rpm (88 bhp SAE). With their extra cc's, both offered more low-end torque and were thus more tractable at low and midrange speeds. Incidentally, transaxles received longer-lasting mounts, and the clutch was also redesigned.

Though covered in the next chapter, the 1500GS engine, we should note here, was nothing less than a detuned version of the twincam 550 Spyder unit introduced in Porsche's 1954 sports-racing cars. It was dubbed "Carrera" in honor of the famed Mexican Road Race (*Carrera Panamericana*) where Porsche had competed with distinction in 1953-54. Featured were a built-up Hirth crankshaft with one-piece connecting rods, roller bearings for both mains and rods, 8.7:1 compression, and dry-sump lubrication. Output was an impressive 100 DIN horsepower (115 SAE gross).

Magazine reviewers generally judged the new 1600 better behaved than previous Porsches. It responded, said Britain's *The Autocar*, "more like an orthodox high-performance sports car, although a certain skittishness at the rear, partly attributable to the swing-axle rear suspension, can still be felt....Stability remains very good indeed, and the design as a whole gives a liveliness to the controls of which the skilled driver can take advantage."

The editors noted than even Germany's *Autobahnen* had curves and rough sections, yet a 1600N pegging 4500 rpm could take such tricky stretches without slowing: "Off these main highways the car is more enjoyable, for its modestly sized engine does

The 356A was launched at the Frankfurt Auto Show in September 1956. Among the three body styles was the Speedster (*opposite page*), which in "1959" guise shows the padded instrument panel with three large gauges (*this page, top*) and the Speedster's side curtains (*below*).

so much without fuss, provided that the driver expends on the gearbox energy equivalent to a housewife cutting soft butter.... As the car will so willingly cruise at 90 mph, it is made to do so by most drivers when traffic conditions permit, making the mpg range of 29-36 [Imperial; 23-29 mpg U.S.] all the more creditable.... At under 1500 rpm the characteristics of the flat-four engine and the transmission result in a reduction in response and a slight feeling of snatching." Then again, who would routinely drive a Porsche at such low revs?

Although Porsche had increased its workforce, it had also increased its output per worker. Yet there had been no compromise in the by-now-famous Porsche workmanship. The Germans' painstaking attention to detail must have been as mind-boggling to the British as it was to Americans, perhaps more so. For example, all steering mechanisms were run-in "on the bench," lock to lock, for the equivalent of 5000 kilometers, and the quality of trim, upholstery, and paint was a cut above the norm, even for Porsche's price class.

Concluded *The Autocar:* "The superbly controllable Porsche brings back to motoring some of the joy that those privileged to drive sports cars in the earlier spacious days must have experienced. At the wheel one feels to be one up on the other fellow in all the things that matter in driving for its own sake. The imposition of duty and purchase tax make the total price formidable for British buyers [£1891 or $5300 U.S. for the 1600 coupe] but the car remains, nonetheless, highly desirable."

Having made such a long leap for '56, Porsche was content to let the 356A carry into '57 unchanged, then made some detail refinements in the spring of that year. The speedometer exchanged places with the combination gauge, horizontal teardrop taillights substituted for the previous four round units, the license

plate/backup-lamp bar moved from above to below the plate, and padded sunvisors became standard.

Evolution was again the watchword on the '58 models, designated T-2. Vent wings appeared in cabriolet doors, and coupes could sprout extra-cost windwings on the outside of their window frames. Exhaust tips on all models now poked through the lower part of the vertical rear bumper guards, and a double-bow front bumper overrider replaced the former single-bow item. Larger rear windows improved top-up vision in Speedster and cabriolet, and both open models were offered from late '57 with a lift-off fiberglass top as a factory option (made by Brendel in Germany for Europe, Glasspar in California for America). Though controversial, that Cadillac-style exhaust routing was practical in that it better protected the tips and raised exhaust-system ground clearance.

On the mechanical front, the 1300 engines were dropped, the 1600 engines reverted to plain bearings, and cast-iron cylinders returned on the 1600 Normal to reduce both cost and noise for what was basically a touring Porsche. Carburetors were now Zenith NDIX instruments, a Hausserman diaphragm clutch replaced the coil-spring Fitchel & Sachs unit, the shift linkage was reworked for shorter throws, the old worm-and-peg VW steering gave way to a Ross type mechanism by ZF and, from late '58, progressively wound single valve springs replaced dual springs in all pushrod engines.

Along the way, Porsche also instituted improved door locks, a one-piece aluminum transaxle (replacing the previous cast-magnesium unit), redesigned oil coolers and, for the 1600N engine, offset-wristpin pistons (to eliminate cold-engine piston slap) and fiber camshaft gears. Later came FIA-homologated gear ratios and a 5.17:1 final drive. Convenience and appearance were served by repositioned heat-

The 356B debuted at the Frankfurt Auto Show in September 1959. The most noticeable change, as shown on this 1962 model, was the bumpers, which had been raised about four inches.

er controls, new outside door handles and inside window winders, revised rear package shelf, optional gasoline heater, slim-back bucket seats, larger-diameter steering wheel, and new hubcaps bearing the Porsche crest.

A change in sales tactics was evident in August 1958, when Porsche got a head start on model year '59 by replacing the Speedster with the Speedster D, retitled Convertible D shortly before its public debut. The D denoted Drauz of Heilbronn (about 20 miles from Stuttgart), which built the bodies. Still a two-seater but priced $500 higher, the Convertible D had a taller, chrome-framed windshield and a top somewhere between the original Speedster's low, simple design and the cabrio's deluxe padded top. Also featured were roll-up windows (no more side curtains) and reclining front seats as on other Porsches. Retained was the unique Speedster dash design with no glovebox (kick-panel map pockets substituted) and a hooded bulge over the instruments. The Speedster's body-side chrome strips were also retained, giving the D some of its visual character.

The Convertible D's rationale was simple: Ferry Porsche had never liked the Speedster. He felt a "stripper" didn't really fit the Porsche image, and cited low sales while making a case against it on cost grounds as well. As usual, Ferry was right. Though more like the regular cabrio and thus, perhaps, less charming than the Speedster, the Convertible D earned plenty of press praise, *Road & Track* calling it "the best buy in a highly desirable line [offering probably] more driving pleasure per dollar than almost any car you can buy." Which was saying something, considering that it cost only some $200 less than a 1959 Corvette.

Apparently noting that narrow price spread, *Motor Trend* conducted an unorthodox comparison test between the Convertible D and a fuel-injected example of America's sports car. While concluding that both were great buys for the money, writer Wayne Thoms admitted throughout that the Porsche was superior on most counts: fit and finish, handling, braking, low-speed tractability, passenger comfort, fuel economy. The Vette only won points for acceleration (7.8 seconds 0-60 mph versus 15.2) and more readily available service.

Road & Track was amazed at "how a company can continue to improve a car so much over a period of years with only detail refinements." This was simply Porsche's way, though planning for the 356's successor had already begun—back in 1956, in fact, just as the first A-models were reaching customers.

Still, the 356 had a lot of life left in it. As if to prove it, Porsche trotted out the new 356B in time for the Frankfurt Show in late 1959. It was as close as Zuffenhausen would ever get to a GM-style facelift. Indeed, General Motors itself could have come up with the cowl-forward makeover that seemed pretty frightening to old Porsche hands. Erwin Komenda, still an active company designer, conjured up a more massive front bumper with jumbo guards, the ensemble riding about four inches higher for better body protection than on the A. Rear bumpers were larger too, and higher by the same amount. Headlamps sat more upright, prompting near straight front fenders (versus the 356A's curvier panels) and blowzier lower front sheetmetal. A more garish chrome handle adorned the hood, phallic parking lamps sprouted from the outboard ends of the horn grilles, and a pair of brake-cooling slots was cut in below the front bumper. Among reviewers, the more fervid carped that Porsche had "done a Detroit." But like most of the factory's changes, these were soon accepted as typically Porsche. As Karl Ludvigsen later wrote, many people by this time were inclined to think that if Porsche did something, it must be right no matter how it looked.

Regular engines now encompassed a trio of 1600-cc Type 616s: the Normal with 60 bhp (DIN) at 4500 rpm and a claimed top speed of 100 mph; the 110-mph Super with 75 bhp (DIN) at 5000 rpm, and thus sometimes called Super 75; and the new Super 90, with 90 bhp (DIN) at 5500 rpm and an official 116-mph maximum. The last, though announced at Frankfurt, didn't actually reach production until March 1960. Body styles (designated T-5) carried over from the final 356As: coupe, cabriolet, and Convertible D, the last renamed Roadster in 1960. As before, all were available with any engine, giving a total of nine separate models (save Carreras).

The 356B featured raised headlights and a straighter fender line. New on the '62 was an outside gas filler cap on the right front fender. This car was bodied by D'Ieteren of Belgium, a Porsche supplier beginning in 1961.

Aside from the more blatant changes already mentioned, the B arrived with a stubbier gearlever and a rear seat lowered to increase headroom. The latter's fold-down backrest, a feature since the earliest 356s, was newly split so that three persons and some luggage could be carried inside. All models acquired door vent windows, and defroster vents appeared inside below the backlight.

Alterations to chassis and running gear were subtle but noteworthy. The new Porsche synchromesh, with an easier-to-engage first gear, was carried over from late 356As. Though their days were numbered, drum brakes returned as new cast-aluminum units with 72 radial fins (instead of circumferential ones) and cast-iron liners secured by the Al-Fin process. They were not only stronger but better sealed against moisture. After the first 3000 cars, transaxles reverted from single to dual mounts.

In his March 1960 test for *R&T*, Hansjoerg Bendel observed that the Super 90 was "developed because Porsche wanted to [provide] performance similar to that of the original Carrera, using the simpler, less expensive pushrod [engine], which is also less exacting in maintenance than the sophisticated 4 ohc engine." Its power was accordingly produced through conventional means: higher-lift camshaft, improved carburetion (two twin-choke Carrera-style Solex 40 P-II-4s with larger throats and high-performance jets) and tighter compression (9.1:1, versus 8.5 for the Super and 7.5:1 for the Normal).

This was basically minor but precision tuning, nothing exotic or beyond the car's limits—which was also Porsche's way—and nothing was lost in flexibility. *Sports Car Graphic* magazine said the Super 90 was "tamer in traffic and [the] lower speed ranges than the 1600 Super. Getting off the mark fast from a standing start takes some practice, as the big carburetors can't be dumped open too fast. Once the biggest chunk of inertia is overcome, you can [floor the accelerator] and start moving out very fast indeed. In fact, one of the most impressive

The 356B was in its last year in 1963. This T-6 series cabriolet (*below*) came equipped as a 1600S, with 75 DIN/88 SAE horsepower (*top left*). The interior (*top right*) retained its traditional Porsche look.

things about this engine is the feeling of torque—the sheer push in the shoulders—that one gets on booting the throttle....There isn't the feeling of wild acceleration from a standing start but, once under way, it comes on with increasing force [and] builds up faster than one would believe possible."

Objectively, the Super 90 *was* quick: under 10 seconds 0-60 mph in *SCG*'s test. Bendel, however, could only manage 12.5 seconds with his Roadster. Still, he found "the level of performance...remarkably close to that of the Carrera, though...the acceleration times are not quite as good as those of [our 1958] Super Speedster... because the new body is heavier and because 4th gear is now 3.78 instead of 3.91."

Testers generally praised 356B handling, especially in 1961, when Koni shock absorbers became standard for both Supers, accompanied by suitably lower spring rates. More significant was a reduction in rear roll stiffness via 1-mm-smaller torsion bars (23-mm diameter) and the addition of a transverse leaf spring, called a "camber compensator," as standard for S-90s (optional elsewhere). "Normal procedure," said *SCG*, "letting the front end plow to compensate for the rear coming out...will net you a trip through the tules [sic]. It must be set into a high drift attitude before the corner and varying amounts of power applied." This was on German Dunlop Sports tires; with harder racing tires, handling was more like what Porsche drivers were used to.

Nevertheless, *R&T*'s Bendel stated that "the present chassis remains practically neutral up to very high cornering speeds. This means the driver is in control of a most responsive car, which goes around corners with deceptive ease and stays on its course even when the road surface is decidedly bumpy and/or cambered. The springing is a good compromise between firmness and comfort, damping is good and [the suspension] never bottoms. As far as we are concerned, the standard chassis without the transverse spring is already very good. Our test [Roadster] appeared particularly surefooted and could not be caught on the wrong foot even in very quickly succeeding bends. The steering is wonderful, highly accurate and yet light....It gives superb contact with the road without unde-

Opposite page: Among the changes on the 356B were the protruding parking lights (*top*) and, for 1962, the twin air-intake grilles for the engine lid (*bottom*). The 356C (*below*) looked little different, but it sported a new wheel and hubcap design and four-wheel disc brakes.

CHAPTER FOUR

sirable feedback...."

Super 90s could be revved about 800 rpm higher than other 356B 1600s thanks to a special cooling layout that gathered in more air, plus nitrided crank and cam-bearing surfaces, lighter flywheel, stiffer valve springs, light-alloy rockers, larger-diameter (by 5 mm) main bearings, and cylinders lined with Ferral, a coating of steel over molybdenum. S-90s also had a unique oil pickup system that allowed the engine to draw oil from the sump's full side in hard cornering, thus ensuring proper lubrication at all times. It was an important advance that

Porsche racers had wanted for several years, and was especially welcome in the high-performance 90.

Meantime, models and coachbuilders had been proliferating. Bodies for the Drauz-built Roadster, which continued into the early part of model year '62, were also supplied by D'Ieteren Freres, and Karmann in Osnabrück began production of a new fixed-roof notchback coupe looking much like the cabriolet with optional lift-off top.

Subtle body changes marked the '62-model 356Bs (designated T-6). Coupe windows were enlarged, there were twin grilles on a deeper-cut

engine lid, the front lid acquired a flatter lower edge, an external gas filler appeared (under a flap in the right front fender), and a cowl vent was added ahead of the windshield. The series then continued in this form through July 1963 when the 356Cs appeared, the last—and arguably the best—of the early pushrod Porsches, available in steadily diminishing numbers through 1965.

Apart from new flat-face hubcaps and a still-larger coupe backlight, the 356Cs were visual twins to the Bs. Even so, constant improvement was still clearly in evidence at Zuffenhau-

This 1965 356C (*left*), sports a body by Karmann. The SC badge (*bottom*) meant it had the highest horsepower—95 DIN/107 SAE at 5800 rpm—of any 356, except for the four-cammers. The dash (*below*) saw the light switch moved out from under the steering wheel to nearer the clock in 1964.

sen. For instance, a lever replaced the clumsy, VW-derived heater knob (VW itself made this change a few years later), and seats were more "buckety."

More significant were the 356C's mechanical updates—starting with standard four-wheel disc brakes (adoptd the previous year for the Carrera 2). Though a departure from past practice, this development was not only in keeping with Porsche engineering philosophy but, in the end, inevitable. Porsches were getting faster, and they needed to stop with equal authority.

Porsche had been experimenting

The 1965 Porsche 356C (*above and right*) was the last of the line. A total of 16,668 356Cs had been built during its two-year tenure, while production of all 356 models reached an amazing 76,303 units over 15 years. The 356C was the most developed of the line, and is regarded by most 356 enthusiasts today as offering the best combination of comfort and performance.

with two disc systems since 1958: its own (ultimately used on the Carrera 2) and a Dunlop design made under license by the Alfred Teves company (Ate). The choice came down to economics and logic. Using its own system would make Porsche unique among the world's automakers; Dunlop's alternative offered lower cost and easier parts availability, so it was the one selected.

Carrera aside, engines were down to two, as the 60-bhp Normal disappeared. The 75 returned as the 1600C, while the Super 90 was renamed 1600SC and given higher compression (9.5:1), good for 95 DIN horsepower. Positive crankcase ventilation was adopted for the U.S. versions of both, along with reshaped ports that im-

proved airflow. Additionally, the 1600C benefitted from a higher-lift cam and the SC gained small-diameter intake valves and larger exhausts. For 1964, the SC's Ferral cylinder coating gave way to a new Biral treatment. Similar to the Al-Fin brake process, it comprised a finned aluminum shell cast around a cast-iron sleeve and provided better heat dissipation at less cost than Ferral.

Once more, Porsche offered all engines in all body styles, but the Roadster's demise reduced the latter to the long-running coupe and cabrio and the newer Karmann notchback coupe. A corporate move with lasting implications for car enthusiasts generally—and Zuffenhausen in particular—occurred in 1963, as Porsche absorbed

Reutter and spun off a seatmaking division that has since become world famous as Recaro (from Reutter Carozzerie).

Enthusiasts interested in investing in a 356 ("buying" seems inappropriate somehow) should know that the C offers reliable transport, steady (if not escalating) capital worth, and inestimable driving pleasure. As the most refined of a long line, it was—and is—as close to perfect as cars get. For example, Ludvigsen records that in the C's last season, warranty repair costs averaged only $8.38 per car, "the lowest in history for Porsche and incredibly low for any car." The other side of the coin is that 356s of all kinds have long been collectible and thus cost a good many pretty pennies.

After more than 15 years and precisely 76,303 units, the 356 Series was honorably retired in September 1965. Production by type was as follows:

Type	Production	Yearly average
356	7,627	1,090
356A	21,045	5,261
356B	30,963	7,741
356C	16,668	8,334

Those figures wouldn't occasion toasts at General Motors, but for Porsche, which had started from ground zero with this basic design, they told a remarkable story: one of constant evolution and steady, satisfying growth within the original 1947 concept laid down by Ferry Porsche and Erwin Ko-menda. Moreover, the ever-improving 356 had brought Porsche international respect as a builder of fast, durable, superbly engineered performance machines at home on road and track alike.

Prosperity naturally accompanied Porsche's growth and growing renown. The firm had needed four years to build its first 5000 cars (April 1950 to March 1954), yet by the time of the 356B, sales were running far above that in every calendar year:

Year	Unit Sales
1960	7,598
1961	7,664
1962	8,205
1963	9,692*

* incl. 356C

Of course, the cars themselves had come a long way from the Gmünd days and even the early Zuffenhausen 356s. Noted *Road & Track*: "Gradually, and part by part, Porsche adopted bits, pieces, and complete assemblies of its own. Today nothing remains in the way of VW parts, though there are many similarities in arrangement and construction. The modern Porsche is unique, it has had a tremendous success, and it deserves it."

But even better days lay ahead. With the new six-cylinder 911, Porsche would succeed in ways its founding father could never have imagined.

The First Carrera: The Ultimate 356

No car deserves the term "giant-killer" more than the Porsche 356 Carrera. Introduced with the revised A-Series models in late 1955, it combined the 356's uniquely capable basic design with an advanced engine developed expressly for racing. The result, on road and track alike, was a mighty mite that achieved through elegant, efficient engineering what rivals could do only through sheer bulk. As the ultimate 356, the Carrera remains one of the most coveted Porsches ever built. "If the dream of a million VW owners is someday to own a Porsche," said *Road & Track* in 1956, "then the dream of 10,000 Porsche owners must be someday to own a Carrera." Still true, except that the number is more like 100,000.

Dean Batchelor, Porsche historian and former *R&T* editor, records that the engine was born in 1952: "Ferry Porsche and his team of engineers had wondered what the potential of the air-cooled four-cylinder boxer engine might be, and Dr. (later Prof.) Ernst Fuhrmann was told to find out. A figure of 70 horsepower per liter had been [mentioned] and Fuhrmann's calculations indicated [it] was possible—with four camshafts instead of the single camshaft and pushrod/rocker-arm valve actuation.

"The Fuhrmann design followed the basic configuration of the standard Porsche engine but differed in almost every detail. It had four camshafts (two per side, called double overhead

or dohc), twin ignition, dual twin-choke Solex carburetors, dry-sump lubrication, and roller bearings on both mains and rods.

"Fuhrmann's new design was tested on Maundy Thursday, 1953. It was a happy day for several reasons: It was three years to the day after the first Stuttgart-built Porsche...and the new [1498-cc] engine produced 112 hp at 6400 rpm on the first test...74 hp per liter."

Designated Type 547, the four-cam was developed mainly for the racing Type 550 Spyder (see Chapter 15), but in March 1954, as Batchelor records, a developmental unit "was installed in [Ferry] Porsche's personal car, *Ferdinand,* to evaluate the engine/chassis combination...Porsche was still experimenting...in the summer of 1955 [when a 547 was installed in another of Ferry's cars, a] gray cabriolet. The enthusiasm was universal from Porsche personnel, only Fuhrmann having had expectations of this possibility right from the start."

It wasn't long before outsiders got a look. One of the first was writer John Bentley. Among the more diffident critics of early 356s, he'd owned five of them in the early Fifties. After spinning a sixth in an airport race at 90 mph, he vowed never to buy another: "They are front-end happy; they oversteer like mad; they are temperamental beasts—absolutely unbeatable when conditions are perfect, but morose and stubborn when tempera-

ture, barometric pressure, humidity or a combination of these is not exactly to their liking."

But, on a 1955 visit to Zuffenhausen for *Foreign Cars Illustrated* magazine, Bentley casually asked Fuhrmann why Porsche hadn't put the Spyder engine in a 356. Fuhrmann invited him to try the gray cabrio. Bentley did, and returned a believer. The quadcam and the 356 platform were a natural match—so much so that it seemed as if they'd been designed for each other. In a sense, they had.

The model name came from the *Carrera Panamericana,* the famed Mexican Road Race where Type 550s had distinguished themselves in 1953-54. Factory nomenclature for the first roadgoing Carrera was 1500GS, the letters signifying "Grand Sport." Normal 356s already provided plenty of that; the Carrera simply delivered more.

Differences were few between the production four-cam engine (officially 547/1) and its competition counterpart. Compression was initially lowered from the Spyders' 9.5:1 to 8.7:1, but was soon restored to 9.0:1. Also, the twin distributor drives were placed at the opposite ends of the intake camshafts for easier accessibility in the 356 body. As introduced at Frankfurt '55, the Carrera packed a rated 100 DIN horsepower (115 SAE gross) at 6200 rpm (versus 110 bhp for the racing version). The engine was such an easy-revver, though, that it could be rou-

The 356 Carrera, here a '63, is considered
by Porsche enthusiasts to be the ultimate
356. It was named after the *Carrera
Panamericana*, the famed Mexican Road Race.

tinely taken to 7000-7500 rpm without harm.

The 356 package was good enough to handle this extra power without major change but, reflecting its typical thoroughness, Porsche made a few other modifications for the Carrera, notably wider tires (5.90s), 8000-rpm tachometer, and 180-mph/250-kph speedometer. External distinctions were limited to discreet gold name script on front fenders and engine lid, making this a "Q-car" par excellence. Because their engine was heavier, Carreras weighed about 100 pounds more than pushrod 356As.

Per Porsche practice, the quadcam was available in all three body styles, Speedster included. Fuhrmann accurately described the Carrera as "a detuned version [of the Spyder] providing extra performance for high speed, Gran Turismo competition, with more power than the pushrod engine could produce."

Journalist Bentley timed the gray prototype at under nine seconds 0-60 mph and less than 20 seconds 0-100 mph. Still, he was disappointed that the extra weight—most of it out back—had made handling even more squirrely than on his 356 slalom coupe. But the production Carrera appeared as part of the 356A Series, and thus benefitted from all its suspension improvements (see Chapter 4).

In its first Carrera test, *Road & Track* noted that these "do not appear important in detail [but] have made a considerable improvement in the handling. In addition, the Carreras appear to be coming through with about 1° of negative camber at the rear wheels, with no load. This and the larger 5.90-section road-racing tires give as close to neutral steering as is conceivable. With the tremendous power available, a burst of throttle in a corner (in the correct gear) will give

oversteer, just as it does with any machine of comparable power-to-weight ratio [18.5 lbs/bhp for the test coupe]. High-speed stability at over 100 mph in a cross wind still leaves something to be desired in our opinion, but this applies to almost any well-streamlined coupe with [a] preponderance of weight on the rear wheels. In any event, the steering is accurate and quick and requires only common sense and alert attention at over the magic century mark."

Jesse Alexander largely concurred after driving a Carrera Speedster for *Sports Cars Illustrated*: "The car neutral-steers [sic] as long as the driver gives the right amount of throttle [and] can be thrown happily through a series of Alpine hairpins with wild abandon, the steering being quick and precise.... The use of factory-recommended tire pressures seems to be the answer for making a Porsche handle satisfactorily; altering pressures and/or make of tire can change a Porsche's personality completely (especially in the wet)...."

Interestingly, both magazines used almost the same words to sum up the Carrera. "Without a doubt, this was one of the most interesting cars we have ever tested," said *R&T*. "It completed the vigorous performance tests as if it were out for a Sunday drive...." Some Sunday drive: 0-60 mph in 11.5 seconds, the standing quarter-mile in 17.7, a top speed of just over 120 mph. *SCI*'s Alexander called his Speedster "one of the most exciting cars we have ever had the privilege of testing. As always, Porsche is moving forward in design trends. It's intriguing to consider what will come next from Ferry Porsche's team of engineers. Whatever it is, it will certainly represent... advanced thinking in automotive design."

The Carrera itself didn't come cheaply: a minimum $5995 in the U.S.

Contrasting sharply with a group of derelict Porsches around it, the '63 Carrera 2000GS cuts a striking figure. Better known as the Carrera 2, its big attraction was its Type 587 engine, an expansion of Type 547. Displacement came to 1966 cc, and it developed 130 DIN horsepower (150 SAE) at 6200 rpm, close to 1.3 bhp per cubic inch.

Of course, you always could take delivery in Stuttgart, drive the car in Europe and then ship it home as a "used car," which in those days would have saved you about $1700, more than enough to cover the trip. Still, *R&T* held that "the price doesn't seem quite so steep" considering the Carrera's performance, its "fool-proof, if not ultra-rapid" gearbox, and "tremendously powerful" brakes. Cheap at twice the price? Carreras go for that and more today, and there still aren't enough to go around.

May 1957 saw a new Carrera Deluxe replace the "standard" offering. This mainly meant a heater that really heated instead of blowing tepid air at your feet. Announced at the same time was a no-cost GT option for coupe and Speedster, with an extra 10 bhp (and a higher, 6500-rpm power peak), 21- instead of 14-gallon fuel tank, Spyder front brakes with 128 square inches of lining area (versus 115), and Spyder worm-gear steering. Again the intent was competition, so GTs were literal strippers, shorn of heater and undercoating and fitted with plastic windows and lighter bumpers. By 1958, they'd acquired aluminum doors, hood and engine lid, and lightweight bucket seats, all of which pared 150 pounds from the stock Carrera coupe, 100 pounds from the Carrera Speedster.

Journalist Bentley bought and tested a Carrera Speedster GT in 1958, ordering it in silver-gray metallic like the

Although the badging was about the only clue to the Carrera 2 engine under the hood, Porsche fans knew what it meant: an impressive 131 lbs-ft torque at 4600 rpm. Better yet, the torque curve was broad and flat. With longer-striding gear ratios for American conditions, the Carrera 2 had the extra power that made the difference between lugging and pulling away smartly. For this reason, plus its innate civility, it was the most popular Carrera yet.

prototype that had changed his mind about Porsches. His car naturally carried the latest running changes: new crankshaft distributor drive, ram-type air intake (via engine-lid louvers), built-in rollbar posts, and Fren-do competition brake linings. He was too early for the Koni adjustable shock absorbers that later became standard, but he installed a set post-purchase.

Bentley's report is still enough to stir your blood: "Low gear [with the standard 5.17:1 U.S. final-drive ratio] is a shade too low; but in second gear the GT leaps forward with a wild, exhilarating surge.... The muffler is noisy, but that noise is music of a delightful kind. As the tach needle leaps to 5200 rpm and peak torque, the car seems to grab hold and a terrific surge of power becomes available. The savage bark of the exhaust levels off to a high-pitched snarl, and before you know it the tach is indicating 7500 rpm."

The Carrera Speedster tested by *SCI*'s Jesse Alexander was a GT too, and it registered similar impressions: "The engine smooths out at about 4200 [rpm], right where a pushrod Porsche would be getting rather wound up. At 5000 rpm...things start to happen, and from there on you've got that feeling of being pushed in the small of the back. The acceleration is accompanied by the most unholy snarl of power you ever heard...a shattering blast of sound that sends chills up the spine of the uninitiated. The range of speeds in the gears is amazing: 40 mph in first, 70 in second, and 100 in third."

It seemed that everything hung onto the ever-evolving 356 worked that much better on the Carrera. Both the brakes and all-synchro gearbox were not only smooth and precise but light to the touch; the bucket seats (more rudimentary on the GT) provided plenty of support. Handling, in Bentley's opinion, was now beyond criticism: "With 26 lbs [air pressure] in the front [tires] and 27 in the rear you can break the tail loose in the secure knowledge that the machine will respond to correction in the normal manner. There is no danger that the slide will become an uncontrollable spin, as in former years."

Plug fouling was the Carrera's one serious flaw. A week of around-town driving was usually sufficient to gum up the plugs completely. Changing them, Bentley said, "required the dex-

terity of an octopus and the tenacity of a leech."

Still, most everyone agreed that the Carrera was one helluva car. "What an enthusiast's dream," Bentley concluded. "It is in a class by itself." (And now what did you make of a fuelie Corvette, *Motor Trend*?)

Odd though it may seem, Carreras were as reliable as any 356A when carefully run-in. Dean Batchelor notes that all Carrera engines were bench-tested at 4000 rpm for several hours, then given full throttle for several minutes before installation. Bentley didn't follow the owner's manual and paid the price with improperly seated rings, but his engine was rebuilt under warranty. "Now go out and beat the hell out of it," a factory hand told him. "Take it to 7000 rpm if you like—just for short bursts. But don't baby the engine. This is a Carrera GT!"

But any Carrera was rather a fish out of water in American conditions. A car that didn't begin to come alive below 4000 rpm and fouled its plugs on the way to the market was really at home only on Germany's unlimited-speed *Autobahnen*—or race tracks.

Still, the Carrera was meant to sell as well as race, hence the changes undertaken for 1958, developed under technical manager Klaus von Rucker. Included were the new distributor drive already mentioned, a plain-bearing Alfing crankshaft to replace the roller-bearing Hirth unit, and twin oil radiators (mounted behind the tiny horn grilles) to compensate for the higher oil temperatures produced by the plain bearings. This revised 1500GS engine was designated Type 692/1; a roller-bearing version, Type 692/0, was developed for competition. Nominally rated at 110 bhp (DIN) at

6400 rpm, they weren't common: just 14 and 20 were built, respectively.

Von Rucker had designed in room for a bore increase, and it duly arrived during 1958 with the new Type 692/2 engine. An 87.5-mm bore and the existing 66-mm stroke combined for a total of 1588 cc but "only" 105 DIN horsepower (121 SAE) at 6500 rpm—still more than sufficient, though. The GT version, designated 692/3, featured 9.8:1 compression (versus 9.5 on the Deluxe), Weber 40DCM2 carburetors, 12-volt electrical system, free-flow muffler, and sodium-cooled exhaust valves, the last a real competition touch. Output was a smashing 115 bhp (132 SAE), over 1.4 bhp per cubic inch. A year before, Chevrolet hailed the "1 hp per cu. in." of its fuel-injected 283 V-8 as a new engineering benchmark, and with far more fanfare.

Carerras were available in the usual Porsche body styles, shown here in coupe (*opposite page*) and Speedster (*above*) form. The latter was, of course, the lightest model, and therefore best suited for track work. This example, shorn of its bumpers and sporting a roll bar, undoubtedly saw plenty of action.

Still, the Carrera wasn't nearly as potent in the showroom as it was on the road. Sales totalled only 700 units between introduction and January 1960—far less than Zuffenhausen had hoped—this despite the 1959 addition of a plusher, 2100-pound 1600GS. And that wasn't the half of it. As Dean Batchelor notes, 692/2 engine production was a mere 45 units in 1958, 47 in '59, and just two in 1960.

One big problem was that the "cook-ing" 356A was pretty high-strung; making it more so only limited its appeal that much further. Then too, the Carrera cost a bundle, yet those most able to afford one weren't usually cut out for it. They'd typically lug the engine, avoid using the gears, and fail to exercise the car when the (rare) opportunity presented itself. No wonder that many owners complained to dealers, as unhappy with their cars as the Carreras might have been with them.

No, it made more sense to own a pushrod Porsche if you lived in America and didn't race. "There was really not much point in preferring the more sophisticated engine and its exacting demands on maintenance unless the superior performance in the upper speed range could be exploited," wrote Hansjoerg Bendel. "The pushrod units were cheaper to buy and to run, less noisy and, in daily use, just as fast."

To stay ahead of the competition, Porsche commissioned 20 special lightweight bodies; thus was born the Abarth-Carrera GTL. Approved as a production GT by the FIA, it went on to score numerous track victories between 1960 and 1963 (shown here as a '60).

Acknowledging this state of affairs, Porsche offered only detrimmed Carrera GT coupes for 1960-61. Carrying lightweight Reutter bodywork, they were identified by simplified bumpers sans guards, plus aluminum hubcaps and a more spartan interior. The 1960 models retained the 692/3 power unit. An evolution, the 692/3A, arrived for 1961 with larger main-bearing journals, stronger con rods, and redesigned camshafts with a total of six small flywheels for quelling harmonic vibration in the valvetrain. The company also busied itself with new sports-racing cars like the GTL Abarth-Carrera (see Chapter 14).

Despite disappointing sales, Porsche would issue a final series of roadgoing 356 Carreras. Based on the revised B Series of 1960, it bowed at the Frankfurt Show in late 1961 for the '62 model year. Included were a steel-bodied 1600 with a 1582-cc engine packing 90 bhp at 5500 rpm; a lighter 1600GS with 115 bhp at 6500 rpm from 1588 cc; and a new 2000GS, better known as Carrera 2. The last featured the new four-wheel Dunlop disc brakes previously described (Chapter 4). All three had the latest body mods save the Detroit-style bumper-guard exhaust outlets (the tips exited below the bumper as before, but were now surrounded by a protective apron).

Naturally, the Carrera 2's big attraction was its engine, designated Type 587. An expansion of the Type 547, it was decidedly oversquare at 92 × 74 mm—1966 cc in all. Output was 130 DIN horsepower at 6200 rpm (150 SAE), close to 1.3 bhp per cubic inch. Peak torque was an impressive 131 pounds-feet at 4600 rpm; the torque curve was broad and flat. Reflecting lessons learned in the marketplace, the Carrera 2 used plain rather than roller bearings, and its top two gears had longer-striding ratios for lazy Americans:

Gear Ratios

	European	American
1st	3.090:1	3.090:1
2nd	1.765	1.765
3rd	1.130	1.227
4th	0.852	0.885

This wasn't a major adjustment—relatively few Porsche modifications seem more than incremental—but it had the desired effect. The American Carrera 2 had that fraction of extra power that made the difference between lugging and pulling away at proper rpm. For this reason, not to mention its innate civility, it proved the most popular Carrera yet.

Civility was the key. Hansjoerg Bendel commented on the "notable innovation" of a combination fresh-air intake and heater fan (via the optional gasoline heater), the comfortable Reutter seats, the quick gearchange and, above all, the unmistakable feel of a quality car built for the connoisseur. He also noted some beneficial chassis changes: "The steering gave improved response with reduced vibration, the car seemed to stick better to the road and stay stuck during hard acceleration, and the disc brakes, added late to the Carrera 2 specification, were more than adequate."

"The car's acceleration is exhilarating," said Bendel. "The clutch takes quite a bit of throttle without protest,

and when one finds that it is time for 2nd gear, down comes the stick in a flick, more acceleration, and other cars pass by as if in reverse. High up in the speed range, this is it—the effortless superiority of the true high-performance machine."

Bendel had few criticisms. The Carrera was still too noisy he thought—and for a $7595 luxury GT, it probably was—and the engine had a "certain roughness well remembered from older Carreras." Also, and more telling perhaps in the context of 1962, was the almost 20-year-old basic design: "Even the accustomed eye begins to notice some signs of age. The instrument panel, for example, is higher up than is usual nowadays, and visibility could only benefit from a lower waistline." Bendel should have been more patient. The 911 was on its way.

But not before a short run of 356C-based Carrera 2s in 1963. Like the '62s,

they were available with Porsche's usual vast assortment of competition equipment: larger fuel tank, limited-slip differential, special weight-saving body and chassis items—virtually anything a racing customer wanted.

Bendel accurately summed up the Carrera 2 as "certainly one of the most desirable GT cars" of its day, one to "delight the owner looking for a car of high quality and exceptional roadworthiness." Alas, like most good things, it was short-lived, built mainly to homologate the Type 587 engine for competition, initially in production-based cars, later in the factory's more specialized racers such as the 2000GS/GT and the beautiful 904.

But the ultimate 356s had left their mark, the first of the grand roadgoing Carreras that would persist through namesake 911-Series models to this very day. And well into the future, we reckon.

The Abarth-Carrera GTL was as aerodynamic as it was beautiful, and with a light aluminum body, curb weight came to just 1800 pounds. Competition-wise, it debuted in the '60 Targa Florio, and won its class outright.

1963-66 Type 911/912: The Once and Future Classic

To at least three generations of enthusiasts—and most non-enthusiasts these days—"Porsche" means one and only one car: the 911. For those old enough to remember the 356 firsthand, it remains the only "real" Porsche. Ferry Porsche thought his first six-cylinder production model would have a good long life when introduced back in 1963, but even he couldn't have guessed that it would still be around 25 years later, maintaining a grand tradition while overshadowing newer Porsches in the hearts and minds of many marque partisans.

And Porsche's far from finished with it. All indications are that the 911 will run at least another 10 years—maybe longer—albeit with a redesign so thorough as almost to qualify as "all-new." But the familiar looks and layout will continue because there's something timeless about the 911, a quality that sensible Porsche is understandably reluctant to let slip away.

Not that it hasn't wanted to. By the early Eighties, the 911 had been consigned to a coffin more times than Bela Lugosi's Dracula—mainly by the press, though certain forces in Zuffenhausen have also wanted to drop it at various times. Yet, like the Beetle once was for Volkswagen, the 911 had become such a strong symbol of everything Porsche that it ended up outselling erstwhile replacements. VW finally made its great model leap (from rear-engine Bug to front-engine, front-drive Golf/Rabbit), but Porsche

hasn't. The 911 remains too profitable, too vital to corporate survival to be abandoned, the main reason you can still buy a new one today—and marvel at its super cousin, the 959.

AutoWeek magazine once called the 911 "the world's most authentic replicar." Some critics have termed it a "classic" in the pejorative sense: a car that's been allowed to hang on well past the point of being contemporary. Yet, this very durability surely testifies to the inherent "rightness" of the original 911 design, not to mention Porsche's skill at keeping it up to date in the face of economic forces and government regulations its creators couldn't have possibly foreseen.

The result is a living legend, a bridge between Porsche's past and present that's also still very much a part of its future. You may call it a "classic" or old-fashioned, you may think it grossly overpriced today (which it is), but in no way has the 911 ever been dull, ordinary, or unamenable to change. It's proved nothing if not a survivor. And thanks to a quarter-century of Porsche-style honing, it's even more exciting now than it was in the beginning.

Of course, the 911 was good—very good—to begin with. Why? We think the answer lies in the way it preserved the essence of earlier Porsches while setting a new and entirely higher standard of engineering and design. Its shape was recognizably Porsche, yet sleek and modern, as it still is. William

L. Mitchell, former design chief at General Motors, once said the 356 resembled a loaf of bread. While not putting it so bluntly, a good many critics have allowed that, loveable though it was, the 356 wasn't exactly beautiful. But the 911 was.

Moreover, even as people were getting their first look at it, the 911 somehow came across as a car destined for immortality. Consider these rather prophetic words from *Car and Driver* magazine in April 1965: "This is the Porsche to end all Porsches—or rather, to start a whole new generation of Porsches....It's one of the best *Gran Turismo* cars in the world, certainly among the top three or four....Only yesterday, the 356 seemed ahead of its time. Today you realize its time has passed....The 911 is a superior car in every respect, the stuff of which legends are made."

Mechanically, much of that stuff broke sharply with Porsche tradition. The 911 was the first production Porsche without front trailing arms and rear swing axles, though it retained 356-style torsion bars. As mentioned, it was Porsche's first six-cylinder road car, but the engine remained a horizontally opposed air-cooled type riding behind the rear-wheel centerline. Also unlike the 356, the 911 engine was supported at both ends: by the transaxle in front and a transverse mount in back. An all-synchromesh gearbox with overdrive top gear was another link with the past, but instead of four ratios you could now have five, providing greater low-speed flexibility and higher top-end potential.

The 911 originated as Project 695, which also produced Porsche's disc brakes. Planning began in 1956, a mere six years after production began in Zuffenhausen. At first, the new model was seen not as a direct replacement for the 356 but as a larger, four-seat car with performance comparable to that of the charismatic, complex Carrera. Other 356s would carry on even after the "big Porsche" was launched,

as indeed some did. Ferry Porsche later changed his mind about the size, fearing a full four-seater would put his firm in the unaccustomed—and thus uncomfortable—position of competing directly with much larger, high-volume producers, notably Daimler-Benz.

By 1959, work was underway on what would emerge as the T-7 prototype (T-6 was the last 356 body, appearing in 1961). Styling was entrusted to one of Ferry's four sons, Ferdinand Porsche III, known as

"Butzi." Although not a body designer, Ferry knew what he wanted. A family resemblance to the 356 was all-important, but there must also be "more space inside" and a "luggage space that could take an owner's golf clubs," as he later described.

High performance was a given too, but Ferry put new emphasis on smooth, quiet running: "We decided on a 2.0-liter six-cylinder engine because sixes are more comfortable and refined," he said in 1984. "We studied the concept of a mid-mounted engine...

but we could not give it enough interior room for the outside size we wanted." What they *did* want, in short, was a roomier, smoother, quieter, more practical, and somewhat more luxurious Carrera. In this regard, it's interesting to note author Dean

Batchelor's statement that "the four-cam Carrera engine was considered briefly as an across-the-board replacement for the pushrod-and-rocker-arm engine, but was too costly and too complicated to be considered seriously for general use."

Without greatly extending wheelbase, Butzi did a remarkable job of enlarging the 356 interior to full four-seat size. Outside, the T-7 showed a low beltline, lots of glass, and a sharply sloped "hood." The front fenderline remained high and prominent, some-

Despite the sales success of the Porsche 911/ 912, the pace of production didn't seemingly change much from earlier days. Each car still required a lot of painstaking hand assembly.

The biggest problem with the 911 was adequate supply, but workers in the assembly hall (*above and opposite*) did their best to fill orders.
The 911 had its origins in Type 695, the project that produced Porsche's disc brakes, and whose body was given the code T7 (*below*).

thing he considered essential to Porsche identity.

With a huge wrapped backlight and stubby semi-notchback tail, T-7 looked a bit unorthodox, but the interesting thing is that its styling from the B-pillars forward would be retained almost intact for the production 911. When Ferry decided on a more evolutionary car with Porsche's traditional 2+2 seating, Butzi revised T-7 from the doors back, creating the now-familiar fastback roofline with ovoid rear side windows and back-slanting B-posts. Batchelor records that Ferry decreed a wheelbase of no more than 2200 mm, 100 mm longer than the 356's, and that's about how it worked out: 2211 mm (87.0 inches) versus 2100 (82.7) for the 356.

Designated Type 901, the new Porsche made its world debut at the Frankfurt Automobile Show in September 1963. Porsche allowed that it was being shown early; production wouldn't begin sooner than the summer of '64. *Road & Track* magazine's John R. Bond reported that "there were so many rumors circulating that they were forced to show it." In its November issue, *Car and Driver* advised: "Wipe that drool off your chin; it's not going to be ready for almost a year, and it won't be cheap when it gets here." As it turned out, the 911 wouldn't reach U.S. shores until model year '66.

It's widely believed that the new model and the 901 designation arrived together, but they didn't. Porsche has never been absolutely sequential in ladling out project numbers, and it's skipped quite a few. (Remember that the great *Herr Doktor*'s first effort as an independent designer, the 1.8-liter Wanderer, was Type 7; he didn't want anyone to think he was just starting out.) While 901 was chosen to suggest a new direction, that's all there was to it.

The name, of course, was changed to 911 before sales began. The reason was protests from Peugeot, which claimed to have a patent of sorts on three-digit model numbers with middle zeros and threatened to prevent a "901" from being sold in France. (Peugeot seems to have given Porsche and the Porsche family more than its share of grief over the years). But Zuffenhausen got the last laugh by giving middle-zero numbers to a half-dozen of its competition cars, such as the beautiful 904 GTS (see Chapter 16).

Per Ferry's instructions, the 911 boasted a split fold-down rear seatback for greater cargo/passenger-carrying versatility. And despite having a more streamlined tail than T-7, it still offered enough rear room for one adult or two small children.

Yet for all its newness, Bond reported that the chrome-yellow Frankfurt show car was "not as much different from the 356 as it appears in the photos; seen side by side, the actual contours are almost the same. The big difference is the elimination of the broad-beam hip effect that results in a trimmer, narrower look and a roofline that, in plan [overhead] view, no longer tucks in at the rear. The net result of these appearance changes is a car 2.7-in. narrower overall, and more head, shoulder and leg room for rear seat passengers."

As mentioned, the 911 suspension was another departure for Porsche, though still all-independent, of course. At the front were MacPherson struts, something new at the time, and single lower transverse A-arms connected to longitudinal torsion bars. Rear suspension comprised transverse torsion bars and semi-trailing arms, a logical progression from swing axles.

"On all swing-axle Porsches," as R&T said later, "in spite of a very high degree of taming, the 'animal oversteer' could still be sensed. On the 911, the beast is out, and the car is neutral in its behavior and perfectly controllable throughout the whole speed range and even on atrocious road surfaces. True, the suspension is on the firm (not to say harsh) side, but for a high-performance car like this, it appears a small price to pay for the ability to drive the car with an abandon and enjoyment that many other top-class cars would not accept from any but the most wary, experienced pilots."

The steering also parted company, now ZF rack-and-pinion instead of the old VW-based worm-gear mechanism, one of the last remnants of the original Porsche/VW kinship. The new setup was not only more direct—with virtually no free play at the wheel—but light, full of feel, and shock-free (thanks, as usual, to a hydraulic damper).

Porsche also took pains to provide effective heating, typically difficult in air-cooled cars. In the 911 system, air was drawn from the cooling fan to a heat box, then rammed into the cock-pit via under-dash and dash-top (defroster) vents. Still optional was a gasoline heater, with an electric fan that forced more air into the heater boxes, though it was rarely needed once the car was warmed up and moving. Interior ventilation improved with the addition of extractor outlets above the backlight.

But the big news was the 911's heart: its new 1991-cc flat six (which, incidentally, retained the 901 designation, officially 901/01). Developed by Ferdinand Piëch, Ferry's nephew, and Hans Tomala, it featured decidedly oversquare dimensions (bore and stroke: 80 × 66 mm/3.15 × 2.60 inches) and a pair of triple-choke Solex 40 PI carburetors. On 9:1 compression, output was a rated 130 DIN horsepower (148 SAE gross) at 6100 rpm and 140 pounds-feet peak torque at 4200 rpm.

Unlike previous Porsche fours, the 901 six employed a single overhead camshaft per cylinder bank. Each operated two valves per cylinder (arranged in V-formation) via rocker arms and was driven by a pair of roller chains instead of the complex train of bevel gears used on the Carrera engines.

John Bond explained the reasons for the last: "In an air-cooled engine it is very difficult to maintain constant valve-tappet clearances (cold to hot) with pushrods. Hydraulic valve lifters offer a solution, but they are expensive, often troublesome, and they 'pump up' or cease to function at high speed. In addition, the sohc and its en-

By the mid-Sixties, when this photo was snapped, Porsche's annual production was up to around 13,000 units, about two thirds of them four-cylinder 912s. Production 911/912s had a more streamlined tail than T7, but in profile they looked very much like the 356s they replaced. A big difference, however, was the elimination of the broad-beam hip effect. Overall, the new models were 2.7 inches narrower, on a 4.4-inch longer wheelbase, and provided more rear seat room.

The Type 901-series bodyshell was immensely strong. Butzi Porsche designed it for 2+2 proportions, and gave it a low beltline and lots of glass area. The severely sloped front "hood" and high fenderline could by now be considered Porsche trademarks.

closure give the designer more latitude in providing for air flow and cooling fins in the most critical area. The camshaft enclosure also forms a natural barrier for directing cooling air without the need for awkward sheet metal baffles to do it."

Enhancing the greater inherent · smoothness of the 901 boxer six was a six-throw forged-steel crankshaft with no fewer than eight main bearings. A countershaft mounted beneath the crank carried impulses to twin chain sprockets at its rear end, each sprocket driving a camshaft. Ahead of the countershaft were two oil pumps: a large scavenger for circulating oil between the dry sump and a separate, remote reservoir, plus a smaller pump for maintaining oil pressure. An oil cooler was also fitted, reflecting Porsche's passion for proper lubrication and also contributing to overall engine cooling. The factory stated that oil temperature should never rise above 130 degrees. No tester ever recalled that it did, which was only to be expected from a system developed by the literal heat of competition.

Bond compared the 901/911 engine to one of his domestic favorites, the Chevrolet Corvair flat six, which in its moderately tuned 110-bhp version looked anemic next to the Porsche unit. More comparable was the turbocharged 180-bhp Corsa unit:

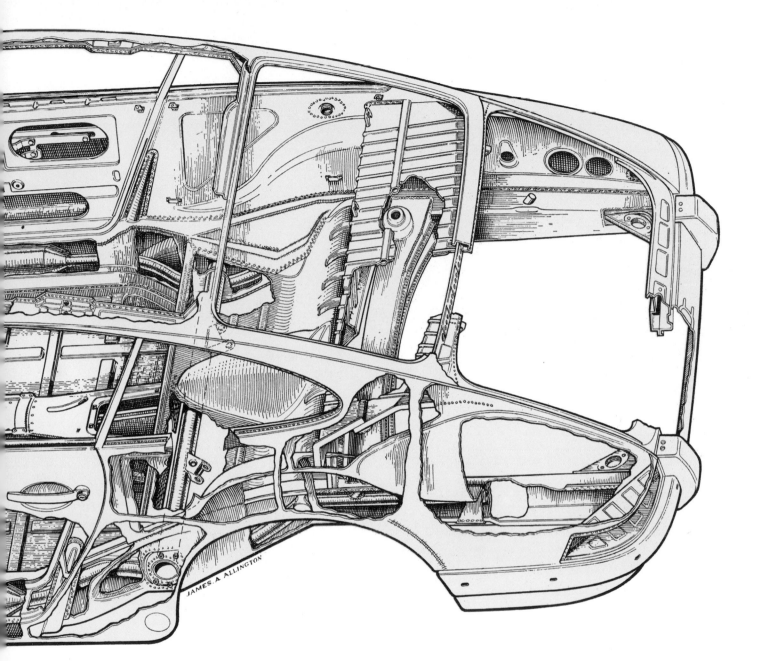

JAMES.A.ALLINGTON

	Corsa	911			
			lbs-ft torque @	232 @	119 @
			rpm	3200	4600
displacement			bhp/cu. in.	1.098	1.235
(cu. in.)	164.0	121.5	lbs-ft torque/		
			cu. in.	0.976	0.983
compression					
ratio	8.0:1	9.0:1	frontal area		
			(sq. ft.)	19.6	18.2
horsepower @	180 @	150 @	approx. top		
rpm (SAE)	4000	6200	speed (mph)	115	125

These figures reveal that the 911 maintained Porsche—certainly Carrera—tradition by being designed for peak performance at relatively high rpm. By contrast, the lower-revving Corsa engine showed excellent torque peaking some 1400 rpm below the 911's maximum crank speed, "an obvious difference of opinion," wrote Bond, "if not basic design philosophy."

Again per Porsche practice, the 911 engine retained a cast-aluminum

crankcase and separate cylinders with hemispherical combustion chambers of crossflow design. Cylinder construction was quite exotic for a 1963 production car, comprising aluminum-silicon alloy with a thin aluminum layer chemically etched away in the bores to leave silicon crystals as the pistons' working surface. This had the advantage of providing microscopic "valleys" that ensured constant surface oiling. For strength, the pistons were made of forged aluminum, the con rods of forged steel.

The rest of the drivetrain was fairly familiar. Power was taken through a Fichtel & Sachs single dry-plate clutch to a fully synchronized Porsche trans-axle, initially with five forward ratios arranged racing style, with first gear to the left and down, below reverse, out of the main H-pattern. The five-speed later became optional and a four-speed made standard to help hold down retail price. Initial rolling stock comprised 4.5-inch-wide, 15-inch-diameter steel disc wheels shod with surprisingly modest 165-15 radials.

As with every 356 evolution, the 911 initially generated mixed reactions from confirmed Porschephiles, though most soon grew to accept it and, inevitably, respect it. Of course, it has since become the most popular production Porsche of all, this despite the later mid-engine 914 and today's front-engine/water-cooled 928 and 924/944 Series.

Press response was enthusiastic. Said *Car and Driver:* "What Porsche has wrought in the 911 is a worthy replacement for all the models that pre-

ceded it. Race breeding and engineering development ooze from the 911's every pore. The whole package, especially the powertrain, is designed to be more reliable and less difficult to service, thus all the better suited to the factory's concept of the Porsche as a sealed machine for ground transportation. Although the 911 costs a lot less than the Carrera [about $6500 in 1965]—and a lot less than the current [356] C and SC—it's worth the price of all the old Porsches put together. More importantly, the 911's appeal should be

considerably wider than the earlier models—which, in truth, you had to be something of a nut to own. Withal, anybody who ever felt a flicker of desire for a Porsche before will be passionately stirred about the 911."

Denis Jenkinson, long-time contributor to Britain's *Motor Sport* magazine and veteran of a quarter-million Porsche miles, was never one to mince words (even at the expense of advertising revenue), yet his glowing assessment of the 911 likely surprised him as much as his readers. As he declared in

The Porsche 912 was developed because the 911's high price eliminated many potential customers. Introduced in Germany in April 1965, it made it to the U.S. two months later. Its flat-four was the 1600SC, slightly detuned to 102 bhp, enough to propel the 2200-pound car to 116 mph.

Acceleration and top speed aside, the 912
performed much like the six-cylinder 911. Both
had strong, virtually fade-free brakes; light,
accurate steering; and German Dunlop SP radials
that worked perfectly with the suspension to
provide strong cornering power and a good ride.

February 1966: "...It is the best car Porsche have yet built for normal road use [and] one of the best cars I have ever driven."

Yet "Jenks" termed his first meeting with the 911 "a little disappointing."

The driver faced a dashboard that seemed a little bland next to the almost classic 356 panel. An elliptical binnacle housed five circular gauges, the largest of which was the tachometer (*not* the speedometer) mounted dead center.

To its left were a pair of combination dials, one for fuel and oil levels, the other for oil pressure and oil temperature; the speedo was on the right, along with an electric clock. Below the cluster was a strip trimmed in genuine teakwood containing various knobs and switches. A molded crash pad stretched full width across the dash top, and there were the usual shapely bucket seats with Reutter's "stepless" backrest recliner adjustment.

Still, the cockpit left Jenkinson unmoved: "Driving quietly away, this lack of character was even more noticeable, so that seasoned Porsche owners commented that it was all right, but hardly a Porsche, and in fact it could have been almost any sort of reasonable GT car."

But Jenks was moved after flogging the 911: "Out into the open country, the whole car immediately became alive and was unmistakably a Porsche in all the true traditions of the Stuttgart firm. The more I drove it and the harder I made it work, the more Porsche-like it became, so that by the end of the week I had no doubts at all that this was a car from the brains of Dr. Porsche and his men, and could not possibly have come from anywhere else."

One attribute that literally helped solidify his impression was Porsche's usual "all-of-a-piece" feeling regardless of surface or speed. "The whole car [seems] indestructible," Jenkinson wrote, "coupled with suspension, ride, roadholding, steering, braking and general good manners that are truly modern, and the nearest to perfection that production cars have yet reached.... Why don't all manufacturers make cars like this? It can't be so difficult."

Porsche's biggest problem with the 911 was supply, as demand was strong from the outset. Buying Reutter in mid-1963 assured better quality control but did nothing to increase production. Accordingly, Porsche contracted with the Wilhelm Karmann works for additional bodies, a move that effectively ended production of the 356C (in September 1965, by which time it was for the U.S. only).

To fill the gap, Porsche conjured up a four-cylinder 911, the 912 (again, the project was 10 digits below the type number in actual order). Both 911 and 912 were "officially" introduced in late 1964, at which time a Porsche repre-

sentative said he feared that new-model announcements were becoming a habit at Zuffenhausen: "We just had one 15 years ago." U.S. 911 deliveries began in early 1965, for model year '66; the first 912s arrived in June, two months behind initial European deliveries.

Inevitably, the 912 was powered by the 1600SC engine from the last of the 356s, slightly detuned to 102 bhp (SAE) at 5800 rpm and 91 lbs-ft peak torque at 3500 rpm. On paper, the 912 should have been slower than the SC because the 911 bodyshell made it about 100 pounds heavier at the curb. But the five-speed gearbox was offered as a $75 option and aerodynamics were superior, so the 912 actually beat the old Super 90 in top speed. Porsche's quoted figure was a conservative 116 mph. *C/D* missed that mark by 1 mph but *R&T* managed 119, both cars with five-speed. Typical 0-60-mph acceleration was 11.5 to 12 seconds, the standing quarter-mile an 18-second affair at 77-78 mph. Predictably, the 912 was much thriftier than the 911: an average 25 miles per gallon versus 16-20 mpg.

"This isn't a car in which one can amble around town in high gear with abandon," said *Road & Track* of the 912. "It's necessary to make full use of the five speeds, and there seem to always be more wrong gears than right ones,"

Opposite page: The basic shape of the 1967 Porsche 912 was still around 20 years later.
This page: As per Ferry Porsche's orders, the 911/912 boasted a split fold-down rear seatback (*top*) for greater cargo/passenger-versatility; there was room for one adult or two children. The cockpit of the 912 (*left*) was more austere than the 911, but the former replaced its three-dial instrument cluster for the five-gauge unit of the 911 in 1967. The 912 received most of the improvements of the 911 as they were phased in.

a reference to the racing-style shift pattern. *The Autocar* in Britain said it was possible to go from first to fourth, instead of the desired second gear, but found that shifting became "subconscious" with practice.

Conversely, said *R&T*, the 912 engine "runs without fuss at low speeds and idles smoothly at 1000 rpm, [though] it's anything but quiet. It never sounds overworked, mind you, but it seems that all the clatter comes right through the bulkhead." The 911 also wasn't particularly quiet inside, so Porsche still had some fine-tuning to do in that area.

Acceleration and top speed aside, the 912 performed much like its six-cylinder sister. Both had strong, virtually fade-free brakes; light, accurate, and well damped steering; and German Dunlop SP radials that worked perfectly with the suspension to provide strong cornering power and a good ride. "Oversteer is a thing of the past," *R&T* concluded, "and one no longer need be an expert to keep from losing it—even in the wet. The 912 is a car that is very responsive to small steering inputs . . . but not at all likely to wag its tail in vigorous cornering. Fact is, it's well-nigh impossible to trip up the 912 on a winding mountain road." *R&T* judged the ride as firm "but most definitely not a harsh one. There's very little tendency to pitch or roll and, true to Porsche tradition, the body itself adds to the impression of a good ride by being absolutely rigid and rattle-

While the 912 (*both pages*) was slower than the 911, it was more thrifty and less expensive. The motoring press took to both models, praising in particular the handling, which was consistently rated superior to that of the 356 series. The ride came in for compliments, too, because it was judged firm, but not harsh.

squeak-free—as if it had been carved from a solid chunk of material....We suspect that a ride [this] firm...just might seem harsh (subjectively) if the bumps produced rattles."

In keeping with its lower price ($4700 POE), the 912 was somewhat "decontented" (to use a current term) from standard 911 equipment. For instance, plastic replaced the teakwood lower-dash appliqué and the clock and oil-pressure/temp dial were eliminated. You also couldn't order the optional gas heater at first. But *R&T* noted "many nice touches," saying "nothing is left out that is really necessary. If you want to order a Porsche with no extras, be assured it will be a 'fully equipped' car." In both 911 and 912, that meant three-speed wipers, windshield washers, rear-window defroster, backup lamps, and a headlamp dip/flash switch incorporated in the turn-signal lever.

The 901 Series saw relatively few changes through 1966. July 1965 brought revised gears ratios for both models and the aforementioned standard four-speed for the 911. Complaints of carburetion flat spots and fouled plugs in low-speed driving were answered in February 1966 by switching from Solex to Weber 40 IDA 3C carburetors. Gripes from early 911 buyers about front-end float and the rather abrupt transition from understeer to oversteer in hard cornering brought a very un-Porsche-like solution: an 11-kilogram (24.2-pound) cast-iron weight bolted and glued to each inner outboard end of the front bumper.

A more sophisticated development appeared at the 1965 Frankfurt Show: an open-air 901 with a clever yet practical new roof design featuring a lift-off section above the front seats and a fixed rear "hoop" for rollover protection. Porsche called it Targa in honor of one of the make's most successful competition venues, the gruelling Targa Florio road race in Sicily. Available in both 911 and 912 versions, the Targa went to export markets beginning in 1967.

Butzi Porsche had objected to retaining the coupe's rear sheetmetal here, saying a conventional "trunked" configuration (as on the original T-7) was the only proper one for a cabriolet, but lower projected sales made the shared bodywork a necessity. The plus side was that it prompted Butzi to design in the strong, functional rollbar. Initially, the Targa had a zip-out plastic rear window and a folding roof panel of rubberized fabric. The rollbar was finished in brushed stainless steel, harking back to the GM exercises of Harley Earl in the Fifties. Butzi said he chose the material to emphasize the hoop's functionality.

As it turned out, the public wanted Targas in far greater numbers than Porsche planned, and the body style's initial 12.7-percent production share proved inadequate. Porsche also found that the 912 sold much better than the 911, though that was hardly surprising given the big price difference. Of the nearly 13,000 Porsches built in 1966, over 9000 had four cylinder engines.

But these were problems of success that everyone in Zuffenhausen was happy to put up with. The new-generation Porsche was a solid hit. All that was left was for Porsche to begin applying the same sort of carefully considered year-by-year improvements it had lavished on the 356 Series, which it would do (you'll find the details in subsequent chapters). A once and future classic was on its way.

The 911 and 912 (*as pictured*) Targa debuted in September 1965 at the Frankfurt Auto Show. It featured a built-in rollbar, folding roof panel, and zip-out plastic rear window (later glass).

1967-73 Type 911: The Classic Evolves

Project 901—the production 911/912—emerged as a great car from the very first. Nonetheless, it allowed ample room for future development, though perhaps only Porsche, being Porsche, could see this. As related in the previous chapter, improvements weren't long in coming, and late 1966 brought even more excitement in the first 911 derivative: the hot 911S—the letter, of course, denoting Super. With this model, Porsche effectively returned to its traditional three-tier lineup of Normal, Super, and Carrera, respectively represented by the four-cylinder 912, base 911, and 911S.

From then on, series developments and model designations would be increasingly difficult to follow, if not for Porschephiles, then surely for others. Actually, year-to-year revisions through 1973 weren't all that complicated and, coming from Porsche, were made in perfectly logical fashion.

The S embodied modifications expected in a high-performance car: re-profiled camshaft, larger valves and better porting, plus higher compression (9.8:1 versus the standard model's 9.0:1) and larger jets for the Weber carbs (which were otherwise little different from those given the base 911 in early 1966). The predictable result was more horsepower: 160 DIN (180 SAE) compared to 130 bhp (148 SAE) on the normal 911. Torque improved but fractionally, from 125 to 127 pounds-feet, but peaked fully 1000 rpm higher. Unlike other models, the S lacked a choke, but pumping the accelerator was usually sufficient for starting—and contributing to the chronic plug-fouling that remained an early-911 problem.

There were, of course, the requisite chassis upgrades to match the extra power: rear anti-roll bar (complementing the one in front), Koni shock absorbers, ventilated instead of solid-rotor disc brakes all-round and—soon to be a 911 trademark—distinctive five-spoke Fuchs alloy wheels that cut five pounds from unsprung weight at each hub. Curiously, the S arrived on the skinny 165-15 tires of the base 911, though it would soon change to heftier rubber.

With this more potent, freer-revving 911, merely blipping the throttle was enough to send the tacho needle scurrying up to its 7300-rpm redline. Recognizing that, Porsche wisely fitted an ignition cutout that momentarily interrupted spark to the plugs near maximum revs, thus protecting the valvetrain from the overly enthusiastic.

Two definite steps in the torque curve were apparent. "The catalogue peak comes at 5200 rpm," noted Britain's *The Autocar* magazine, "but before that, at about 3000, the engine takes a deep breath and literally surges up to the next step, where the extra punch feels like an additional pair of cylinders being switched in. This kick in the back leaves passengers unaccustomed to it slightly winded, and it is sudden enough to cause momentary wheelspin on wet surfaces, even in third."

Gear ratios were evenly spaced except for the five-speed transmission's overdrive top, which was purposely very high. It gave you 100 mph for only 4200 rpm, hardly a strain for the highly tuned flat six. Pulling max revs in the lower gears netted 0-60 mph in eight seconds or less and the standing quarter-mile in under 16 seconds at 90-plus mph—real drag-race stuff.

In *Fahrdynamik* (road manners), the 911S earned mixed reviews. "Oversteer is back—and Porsche's got it!" screamed *Car and Driver*. "At low lateral accelerations it understeers mildly.... By 0.70g, it's in a full-blooded four-wheel drift....Beyond the limit of... adhesion, the 911S reacts like any car with a rearward weight bias, and spins, or, if you're quick enough to catch it, power-slides like an old dirt-track roadster." *Road & Track* reported that the S "has less of the [low-speed] understeer that so surprised us in the 911...but at road speeds above 40 mph we were hard-pressed to detect any difference....Certainly it's easier to hang out the tail if you're in the right gear, simply because of the increased power. But the simple application of steering to the 911S at highway speeds gets the same results as in the 911, which means stick-stick-stick-oversteer! And you'd better know what you're doing in that last phase."

Nevertheless, *C/D* concluded that

"Porsche's admonition, 'not for the novice,' is a bit gratuitous. Within normal driving limits and with reasonable caution, the 911S handles predictably, controllably, and head and shoulders above anything else on the road." As proof, the magazine measured lateral acceleration around a road course, riding with an experienced race driver. The results: peaks of 0.93g in right-hand turns, 0.89g in lefts, and a calculated 0.81 g overall, this despite the modest rubber—well above what many of today's so-called "performance cars" can achieve.

Interestingly, both *C/D* and *R&T* were disappointed in 911S braking, blaming the skinny tires for unimproved stopping distances despite the vented rotors. *C/D* also criticized certain minor lapses in workmanship (though its test car was admittedly "right off the boat," sans dealer prepping). The engines in both magazines' test cars apparently weren't up to scratch either. Even so, *C/D* cut a full second off Porsche's claimed 7.5-second 0-60-mph time, though *R&T* managed only 8.1.

There was no disagreement about the S engine: beautifully smooth, fantastically willing. But *The Autocar* also applauded "the superb lightness of all the controls which, together with excellent seating, immediately put the driver at one with the car and enabled him to go out and enjoy its character to the full. The Porsche 911S is a car one never likes to leave parked when one could be driving it somewhere." *Car and Driver* concurred: "The 911S is a great way for getting from Point A to Point B, even when Point B represents only an excuse for driving somewhere."

As ever, *Road & Track* was a bit more critical, opining that, in American conditions, the 911S "offers no real gain over the 911 and perhaps even a slight loss. It is a bit less flexible at ordinary speeds; deceleration below about 1800 rpm brings on bucking and considerable clatter from the drivetrain, demanding an immediate downshift." But even the hard-nosed Newport Beachers weren't immune from that intoxicating powerplant. "For the driver who really wants to get on with it," *R&T* concluded, "the 911S is bound to be more fun than the 911."

Alas, the fun stopped for 1968 when the 911S suddenly vanished from the U.S. market (though it continued in Europe). While the ostensible reason was that year's new emission standards and the need for engine retuning to meet them, some say it was the persistent plug-fouling, which had proven a tremendous service problem. But the S would return for 1969.

Meantime, three new variations appeared: two for Europe, one for the U.S., both part of what was called the 911 A-Series. America's model was the 911L, replacing the standard issue just after the start of the model year. The L stood for Luxus (luxury) and denoted what was basically an S with the normal-tune engine. An upmarket move, it sold for $600 more than the previous year's base 911, some of the increase reflecting modifications for federally required safety and emission standards.

Europe also got an L-model (from August 1967) as well as a low-priced 911T (Touring). The latter, trimmed to 912 standards, was powered by a detuned 110-bhp (DIN) six with lower compression (8.6:1), cast-iron rocker

Although the 911S disappeared from the Porsche lineup for 1968, it was partially replaced by the 911L (*top left*). The L stood for *Luxus* (luxury) and denoted what was basically an S with the normal tune engine. The L sold for $600 more than the base model from 1967, which was also gone for '68. The Targa (*opposite page*) was now in its third year. Patrolling the German Autobahns, where there were no speed limits, required a fast car, so it's hardly surprising that Porsche was the one chosen by the *Polizei* (*left center and below*). More surprising might be that they drove the more expensive Targa model.

arms and cylinders, milder camshaft, and no crankshaft counterweights. Plain steel wheels and a lighter front anti-roll bar were also specified.

Make no mistake: Early U.S. 911s weren't perfect. Plug-fouling afflicted even the base model (though not as severely as the S) and switching to Weber carbs didn't completely cure the jetting and adjustment problems of the original Solexes. Bosch's WG 265 T2SP sparkplug helped driveability somewhat, but the '68 L met emission limits with an air-injection pump at the exhaust manifold that produced backfiring on deceleration and rough running. This was a makeshift solution, coming from Porsche, and it wouldn't last. In fact, the factory later made amends with a retrofit kit comprising revised jets and readjusted accelerator rods.

It's also true that initial fit and finish wasn't up to previous standards, though a long production run had made the 356 a tough act to follow in that regard. Still, even early 911s ranked high for workmanship next to rank-and-file sports cars, and Porsche would tackle what few lapses remained with its usual thoroughness and creativity.

Outside, all '68 U.S. Porsches were distinguished—if that's the word—by add-on side marker lights, again per Washington edict. Why Porsche didn't simply incorporate them within the wrapped taillight and parking-lamp clusters isn't known, though this would be done later.

Announced in Europe during 1967 was a surprising new 911 option that came to America for '68: Sportomatic, Zuffenhausen's first automatic transmission. Devised by Fichtel & Sachs expressly for the U.S. market, it was, said *Car and Driver*, a throwback to "Detroit's bizarre efforts at clutchless

shifting that died a merciful death in the middle Fifties." That made it in reality a semi-automatic box, here comprising a three-element hydraulic torque converter, single dry-plate clutch, and manually shifted four-speed gearbox, the last Porsche's own creation.

Road & Track described Sportomatic this way: "The converter is a 'loose' one, with a stall speed of 2600 rpm and stall torque ratio of 2.15:1; its oil supply is common with the engine's, adding 2.5 qt. to that reservoir. The clutch is disengaged by a vacuum servo unit that gets its signal from a microswitch on the shift linkage; thus, a touch on the shift lever disengages the clutch. The gearbox is the usual all-synchro 4-speed unit but with a parking pawl added."

Gear ratios differed considerably between Sportomatic and the normal four-speed:

	Manual	Sportomatic
1st	3.09	2.40
2nd	1.68	1.63
3rd	1.12	1.22
4th	0.86	0.96
final drive	4.43	3.86

With this, a Sportomatic 911L was slower off the line than its manual counterpart but almost as fast all out, maximum converter efficiency being a very high 96.5 percent.

Driving with Sportomatic took a little practice. "For all normal acceleration from rest, D (2nd gear) is used," *R&T* explained. "The converter lets the engine run up to 2600 rpm immediately and…gets the car moving briskly, but noisily, if need be. A direct shift to 4th at some casual speed will be the usual upshift. For…vigorous driving, the Sportomatic is just like the manual 4-speed except that one shifts without the clutch….We found that the best technique was to engage 1st gear, let the clutch in (by taking the hand off the stick), 'jack up' the engine against the converter while holding the brakes, and release the brakes to start." A little rough on the transmission, perhaps, but this method netted 0-60 mph in 10.3 seconds and a very good quarter-mile run of 17.3 seconds at 80 mph.

Car and Driver did even better: 9.3 seconds to 60 and 16.8 seconds at 82 mph in the standing quarter. "There's absolutely no trouble in shifting. Just grab the lever and move it. No matter how fast you do it, it's impossible to beat the clutch or the synchronizers."

In effect, Sportomatic was a compromise solution to the perennial problem of Americans lugging along in high gear at low rpm, fouling plugs and otherwise loading up engines because they were loathe to stir the gearbox. It was also likely a nod to the perennial preference of most Americans for easier, more convenient driving than they'd found in previous Porsches. The 911's high torque peak meant lots of shifting with manual, but *R&T* observed that Sportomatic allowed staying "in 4th gear down to ridiculous speeds like 20 mph and still accelerate smartly away with traffic. The 911 engine likes revs, and the converter lets it rev." Unhappily, it also made for more engine noise at low rpm, a sound *R&T* said was "very much like a GM city bus."

Viewed objectively, Sportomatic was a typical, well-thought-out Porsche response to a perceived need, and it didn't much hurt performance or mileage. Declutching by a mere touch on the shifter was disconcerting (one wag suggested Porsche put burrs on the knob, to be removed after 500 miles), but the driver adapted with experience.

Still, this wasn't the sort of thing

The 1969 B-Series 911 debuted for 1969 with a wheelbase stretched from 87.0 to 89.3 inches. This allowed for a much improved ride and better weight distribution, although the 911 was still tail-happy with 57 percent of its weight over the rear wheels. The S returned to the model lineup, while the E replaced the L, and the T was new for '69. Respective horsepower ratings were 125, 160, and 190, all SAE. All models received flared wheel openings, and the Targa (*left*) traded its zip-out plastic back window for a fixed glass unit.

likely to appeal to Porsche owners, even the American ones for whom it was created. Sure enough, it didn't. By the early Seventies, U.S. demand for Sportomatic was practically nil. Not widely appreciated, however, is the fact that the option would be technically available all the way through May 1979, when Porsche finally admitted defeat and dropped it.

Though "unhappy" with Sportomatic in its March 1968 road test, *Car and Driver* was pleased to note the adoption of inch-wider (5.5-inch) wheels for all 911s. "Racing seems to have improved the breed here, and Porsche, which stormed off with the under 2-liter championship in the '67 [Sports Car Club of America] Trans-Am series, has obviously paid attention to how they accomplished that. Ride harshness suffers, but what the hell. It's a Porsche, and Porsches are cars." *C/D* liked the 911's handling more than ever, but still recommended that "a newcomer...approach [the car] with great respect. The transition

A 1969 Porsche 911T (*above left*) poses with a trio of 1970 models. Porsche-Audi Public Relations described that year's 911 as "a race-bred sports car that's at home on the street or track." Top horsepower from the flat-six increased by 10 to an even 200 (SAE) for 1970. Models shown are the 911S coupe (*above right*), the 911S Targa (*top*), and the 911T (*opposite page*).

from initial understeer to mild oversteer can be disconcerting to the novice."

For 1969, the 911 line was sorted out on both sides of the Atlantic with a three-model B-Series that entered production in August 1968. (The 912, to be replaced in 1970 by the "Volks-Porsche" 914, continued to evolve in parallel, though its engine was unchanged.) This new trio would continue for the next three model years. The initial U.S. versions were as follows:

911T: 125 bhp DIN (145 SAE) @ 5800 rpm, 128 mph official top speed; base price (coupe): $6430.

911E: 155 bhp DIN (175 SAE) @ 6200 rpm, 137 mph official top speed; base price (coupe): $7895.

911S: 180 bhp DIN (200 SAE) @ 6500 rpm, 144 mph official top speed; base price (coupe): $8675.

Only the T used carburetors (dual

In 1971 the bottom-line Porsche—if there ever was any such thing—was the 911T. Still quite moderately priced at $6500, it was a bargain among exotic sports cars. It did cost more than an E-Type Jag or a Corvette, but was $1000 below the Mercedes 280SL. The Fuchs five-spoke alloy wheels had come on stream in 1967.

Weber 40 IDTs); the new E (replacing the L) and the reintroduced S sported fuel injection, the intelligent way to reconcile high performance with low emissions. Transmission choices comprised Sportomatic and four- or five-speed manuals for T and E; the S now came with five-speed only.

Developed by Porsche and Bosch, the injection system was a mechanical setup similar to that of Mercedes, with a squirter for each cylinder (making this a port or multi-point system in today's terms) and a double-row six-plunger pump driven by toothed belt from the left camshaft. Tubes carried mixture to the ports just below them. An electric fuel pump fed the injection pump; check valves in the injectors opened at a set pressure from the injection-pump plungers. The ram tubes and a richer mixture improved power at higher crank speeds while reducing pollutants at lower rpm. Capacitive-

discharge ignition on both models helped combat the old plug-fouling problem.

Fuel injection permitted other power-boosting engine changes. The E reverted to the original 911's cam profile, which was wilder than the L's. The S had slightly higher compression and reshaped inlet passages, plus an extra oil cooler for greater reliability with the higher power. All 911 crankcases now switched from aluminum to cast magnesium construction, supplied by Mahle of Stuttgart.

Bodily, the only apparent change was slightly flared wheel openings, necessitated by wider brakes that expanded E and S track by 0.4-inch. The S also got six-inch-wide wheels, up half an inch from '68. Less obvious was a 2.25-inch (57-mm) wheelbase stretch (to 89.3 inches/2268 mm) via longer rear semi-trailing arms (drivetrain position was unchanged), resulting in more even fore-and-aft weight distribution (from 41.5/58.5 percent to 43/57). At the same time, the previous Nadella axle shafts gave way to Löbro assemblies with Rzeppa constant-velocity joints, and the shafts were now angled slightly rearward from the inner joints.

Another new suspension wrinkle was Boge self-adjusting hydropneumatic front struts, standard on E and early S models, optional on the T and later S's. Replacing the normal front struts, torsion bars, shocks, and sway bar, they maintained the nose at a specified ride height regardless of weight distribution or load in the (forward) trunk. Unlike Citroën's oleopneumatic system, Porsche's pump was not engine driven but pressurized by suspension movement.

The Boge struts were part of a 911E Comfort Package, optional in Europe but standard in the U.S. The rest of it comprised smaller, 14-inch-diameter wheels and tires, aluminum brake calipers, a more strident "highway" horn, bumper rub strips, bright-metal rocker-panel trim, gold deck script, velour carpeting, leather-covered steering wheel, and gauges for oil pressure and oil reservoir level.

Fuel injection and the CD ignition wrought terrific improvements in 911 driveability. The E, for example, could lug down to 35-40 mph and still accelerate smoothly away, yet was almost as fast as a '67 S. *Road & Track*'s example did 0-60 mph in 8.4 seconds, the standing quarter in 16 seconds, and topped out at 130 mph while averaging near 20 mpg overall.

The longer wheelbase shifted static weight distribution about 1.5 percent toward the front, but this was balanced on strut-equipped cars by lack of the front anti-roll bar. Oversteer remained the 911's terminal handling trait, but was never an unruly surprise to the skilled, knowledgeable driver.

Completing 1969 refinements were a new three-speed heater fan, flat-black wiper arms, and electric rear-window defroster. The last was standard, not just for coupes, but Targas too, as Porsche abandoned the leaky, noisy zip-out rear window for fixed wraparound glass. It made for a less open Porsche, but was far more practical. In all, the '69s were the most tractable and pleasurable Porsches since the 356C.

With 1970's C-Series, all 911s became incrementally quicker, thanks to a 4-mm bore increase that brought total displacement to 2165 cc (132.1

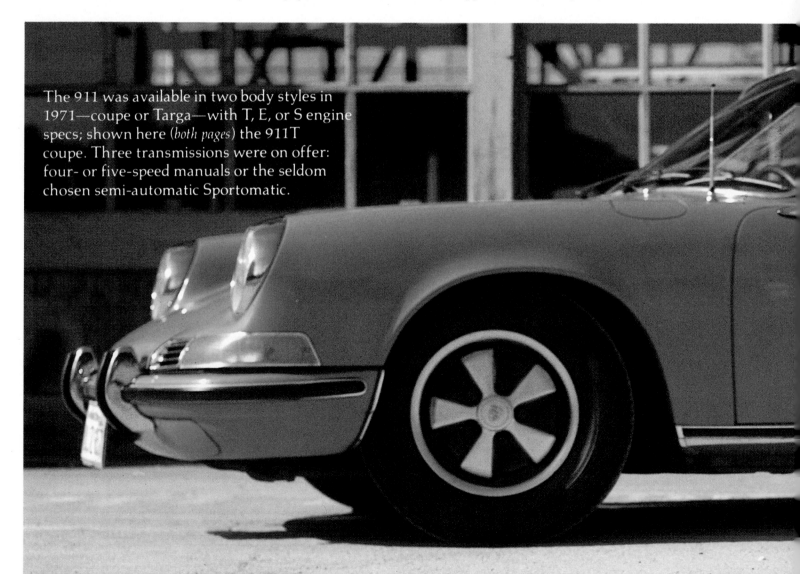

The 911 was available in two body styles in 1971—coupe or Targa—with T, E, or S engine specs; shown here (*both pages*) the 911T coupe. Three transmissions were on offer: four- or five-speed manuals or the seldom chosen semi-automatic Sportomatic.

CHAPTER SEVEN

The '72 Porsche, here a 911T Targa (*top left and below*) saw numerous changes, including a wheelbase stretch to 89.4 inches. The engine was stroked 4.4 mm, bringing the displacement to 2341 cc, although Porsche optimistically gave it a 2.4 badge (*top right*). A one-year-only change placed the *oil* tank filler flap on the right fender (*top center*), an invitation for disaster that service station attendants pumping *gas* just couldn't seem to pass up.

cid). Compression ratios stayed the same, but the T switched to Zenith carbs (40 TIN) and horsepower and torque were higher across the board. Clutch diameter was accordingly increased 10 mm (to 225 mm) on all models. Thoughtful chassis changes involved front-strut upper attachment points moved forward 0.55-inch (14 mm), which reduced steering effort and kickback, and first time availability of limited-slip differential, at extra cost. The 1970 U.S. lineup:

911T: 125 bhp DIN (145 SAE) at 5800 rpm, 128 mph official top speed; base price (coupe): $6430.

911E: 155 bhp DIN (175 SAE) at 6200 rpm, 137 mph official top speed; base price (coupe): $7895.

911S: 180 bhp DIN (200 SAE) at 6500 rpm, 144 mph official top speed; base price (coupe): $8675.

Porsche took advantage of the extra cc's to make the S engine a little more composed, resulting in still better low-end flexibility and, of course, cleaner exhaust. "As impressive as the fact that it meets smog laws is the way the 911S runs," said one tester. "It idles smoothly at 800-1000 rpm and runs without any of the common symptoms of mixture leanness found in today's emission-control[led] high-output engines at moderate speeds."

Good though it was, the S remained too much car for speed-limited U.S. driving. It displayed "very little torque until about 4500 rpm, and one did not wisely use fifth gear under 50 mph.... But going up through the gears to the redline brings out noises that will warm hearts even of those accustomed to exotic V-12s. Glorious noises!"

While the S was still in the same performance league as the Jaguar E-Type and big-inch Corvette, not to mention Detroit's fast-fading muscle cars, it was built better and achieved its exciting ends through finesse, not brute force. It was, however, becoming frightfully expensive, rarely leaving the showroom for under $9000, though perhaps this was part of its appeal. As *Road & Track* quipped, the 911S offered "performance on the order of an American Supercar but without the stigma of low cost."

By contrast, the bottom-line 911T

was still quite moderately priced in 1970-71 at only $6500, a bargain among exotic sports cars. It did cost more than an E-Type or Corvette but was $1000 below the 280SL—fortuitous, as the prospective 911T buyer was more likely to consider the Mercedes as an alternative rather than the Jaguar or Chevy.

In any case, the 911T beat all these rivals in a 1969 *R&T* comparison test, rating the most "bests" and the fewest "worsts." Though the editors allowed that "the conclusion is too obvious to need saying," but they said it anyway: "We found the Porsche to have more that was good and less that was bad than the other cars...."

After a little-changed group of 1971 D-Series models came the E-Series 911s for 1972, again showing increases in displacement and wheelbase. A longer stroke (to 70.4 mm, up 4.4 mm) on an unchanged bore (84 mm) brought the flat six to 142.9 cid/2341 cc, though engine-lid badges optimistically proclaimed "2.4" liters. Wheelbase lengthened a mere 3 mm to 89.4 inches (2271 mm), a change for which no explanation has ever been offered. It wasn't easily noticed.

The extra engine capacity was more easily explained, prompted not by any demand for higher performance but Porsche's desire to maintain existing performance in the face of fast-stiffening U.S. emission standards. California, always demanding lower pollutant levels than other states (mainly because of the Los Angeles Basin's unique smog-producing topography), passed a law requiring that cars sold there be operable on low-lead 91-octane gasoline beginning with model year '72. U.S. automakers responded by simply reducing compression—and thus performance—while the Europeans turned to different pistons, heads, and head gaskets. Thus began the disappointing era of "Federal version" imports, characterized by an ever-widening performance/economy gap with home-market models.

Porsche also lowered compression for '72, but the greater displacement more than offset it. In fact, all three engines showed useful output gains, so 911 performance scarcely suffered, which was fairly rare that year. The specifics:

911T: 130 bhp DIN (157 SAE) @ 5600 rpm, 7.5:1 CR

911E: 165 bhp DIN (185 SAE) @ 6200 rpm, 8.1:1 CR

911S: 190 bhp DIN (210 SAE) @ 6500 rpm, 8.5:1 CR

Those figures weren't all that different from those of 911s sold in Europe (which was about to enact emission standards of its own), reflecting a corporate philosophy that Porsche would publicly declare a decade later: namely, one engine spec and one performance level for all markets. As if to signal this, the Bosch injection was now applied to the U.S.-model T.

Car and Driver put all three 911s through their paces in a 1972 comparison test, and the results bear scrutiny:

The 911T for '72 boasted 157 bhp. It scooted from 0-60 in 6.9 seconds and went on to a top speed of 125 mph. Only .9 second slower to 60 than the $2000-more-expensive 911S, it represented good value.

	911T	911E	911S				
0-60 mph (sec.)	6.9	5.8	6.0	Top speed (mph)	125	135	140
0-1/4 mile (sec.)	15.1	14.3	14.4	80-0 mph (ft)	271	234	280
1/4-mile mph	91.7	96.9	96.8	Curb wt. (lbs)	2425	2475	2455
				Base price	$8804	$10,506	$10,749

Two things emerge here: first, the T's continued status as a remarkable buy in Porsche performance; second, the performance similarity between the E and S, even though *C/D*'s E was the heavier Targa model (the others were coupes). Evidently, the E was improving at a faster rate.

But then, the same could be said for

all 911s. For starters, there were two small appearance changes for '72, both functional. The oil tank for the dry-sump lubrication system was resited from the right rear wheelarch to a position between it and the right door, hidden beneath a flap like the one for the gas filler on the left *front* fender. But it was abandoned after only one year because service station attendants tended to put fuel in the oil tank by mistake—with unfortunate results. The oil tank itself was now made of stainless steel, and the fuel tank was enlarged to 21.1 gallons by stamping its upper half to conform to a new space-saver spare tire (prohibited in Britain).

Aiding appearance as well as high-speed stability on this year's 911S was a small under-bumper "chin" spoiler up front. The result of aerodynamic work by Porsche engineers, it reduced front-end lift from 183 to 102 pounds at 140 mph—which, of course, was purely academic in an America headed for a 55-mph national speed limit. The spoiler was optional for the T and E, and became so popular that it was made standard wear for all models from 1974.

Chassis changes for '72 included larger-diameter anti-roll bars for the S, now 15 mm front and rear, and cancellation of the hydropneumatic Boge struts, which had garnered few orders. All models now came with standard four-speed manual gearbox. The optional five-speed was strengthened, made easier to shift, and—a welcome change—given a conventional gate with fifth on a dogleg to the right and first in the upper left of the normal H.

In its comparison test, *Car and Driver* noted that the 911T "has exactly the same acceleration in the quarter-mile as the 2.0-liter 911S of 1969 and is a whole lot less fussy about the way it's driven.... The E is easy to get along with too, and it turned out to be the fastest quarter-mile sprinter of the bunch [yet] doesn't even seem to breathe hard. It's smooth at low speeds, feels strong at 3000 rpm, and climbs up to its 6800-rpm redline with determination.

"On the other hand, the S is an altogether different kind of machine...a top-speed car more than anything else. The engine doesn't feel capable until about 5000 rpm, and you usually end up shifting there even in routine traffic [accompanied by] the furious sound of the sharp, hard-edge exhaust pulses rushing out the stubby tailpipe. It is rough at low speeds and wants to buck in traffic. The torque band is narrow, so much so that even though all of the 5-speed 911s have the same transmission ratios, they feel too wide only in the S."

After track testing at California's Riverside Raceway, the most affordable 911 emerged as *C/D*'s favorite: "The T was the lightest, it had the most forward weight distribution, and we liked it best because it was the most predictable. The E, whose Targa roof

Porsche pointed out that the 1972 models (*left top and center*) sported black grillework over the engine, now "rated" at 2.4 liters, and boasted that the external filler in the right rear fender made "checking and topping up the oil supply easier." The '73s (*below*)—S, T, E—featured big, black-rubber bumper guards and steel reinforcing door beams, as per federal mandate.

probably give it a fractionally higher center of gravity, had slightly more steady-state understeer and more vigorous tail-wag in transients. Its most conspicuous trick, however, was its three-legged dog stance in turns. Typically, 911s lift the inside front wheel, but few to the dizzying heights of this Targa....

"The S was much like the E. Perhaps a little less understeer and an extra increment of twitch. Like the T, the S was a coupe, but its electric sunroof alters its weight distribution somewhat.

There were extra pounds in the roof and the electric motor was back in the engine compartment. If handling is your goal, it's best to stick with the plain coupe."

Plain or fancy, the 911 continued its winning ways for 1973. There were few changes in that year's F-Series models: big black-rubber "baby buggy" bumper guards and steel reinforcing door beams per federal mandate, plus distinctive "cookie-cutter" alloy wheels on the E. Engines stayed the same through mid-model year, when

the T-type received Bosch's new CIS fuel injection.

The 911 was now a decade old, yet seemed hardly to have aged a day. It was, of course, getting better each year, evolving through steady, thoughtful development in time-honored Porsche tradition.

But 1974 would be a Big Year for the 911 and automakers the world over. The first Energy Crisis was at hand, an upheaval that, ironically, would only underscore the amazing design durability of the classic Porsche.

The 1973 911RS Carrera (*above*) was a *Rennsport* model, specially lightened and sans emission equipment. It was not U.S. street legal, but it *did* race here. The 911T Targa (*below*) continued its winning ways, whether out for fun in the sun (*left*) or facing the elements (*right*).

1974-77
Type 911 & 930
Turbo:
Challenge and Change

F ew car companies—and as few car enthusiasts—like to remember model year 1974. It was a pretty grim season. In what was becoming an annual event, stricter-than-ever U.S. emission limits made engines less efficient than ever. Meanwhile, a bumper crop of heavy, power-sapping—and ugly—battering rams sprouted front (1973) and rear (1974), having been seeded by Washington's 5-mph impact standards. Inflation continued to push prices up and sales down, while soaring insurance rates devastated the ranks of the few remaining performance machines.

Adding insult to these injuries was a heretofore little-known cartel called OPEC (Organization of Petroleum Exporting Countries), which in late 1973 decided to make "black gold" as precious as real gold by shutting off Middle East pipelines. Waiting lines soon formed at gas stations and prices for petroleum-based products from double-knits to diesel fuel went out of sight. The winter of 1973-74 was longer and colder than usual for the world's industrial nations as rationing and other energy-conserving measures threatened to become a way of life.

Against this bleak backdrop stood a refurbished trio of Porsche 911s that remained uncompromising high-performers in utter defiance of what passed for logic that year. They, too, had "crash" bumpers, but so beautifully integrated that they looked like part of the original decade-old basic design.

And while many automakers turned to smaller engines, the 911s had a larger one that met all the latest "smog regs" while sacrificing little in performance or fuel efficiency.

Of course, no one could have predicted the events of model year '74, so these changes were pure coincidence. Nevertheless, these design *tours de force* offered proof—if any be needed—that when the going got tough, Porsche knew how to get going.

The '74s deserve more than a casual look because much of their styling and engineering survives in today's 911s. And much of that goes back to 1973 and a very special European model: the Carrera RS.

RS (meaning *Rennsport*, "racing sport") signified a competition Porsche—in this case, a 911 trimmed and tuned for easy homologation in the Group 4 GT class. Regulations specified that a minimum 500 be built, and Porsche deliberately held the price to about $10,000 in Germany to insure they sold.

There was little to fear. Demand proved so strong that production had to be upped to 1000 units and, ultimately, 1636. One result was that the RS ended up in Group 3 (series production GT cars), which it stood to dominate because allowable race preparation was minimal. Another was that Porsche happily raised the price by several thousand dollars to more closely approximate the car's true worth. Marque expert Dean Batchelor

records that approximately 600 RS's were trimmed *a la* 911S for road use in Europe. None came to America, though: "dirty" engine, you know.

But powerful. All RS's carried a new 2.7-liter version of the Type 901 flat six (designated 911/93), achieved by boring out the 2.4 from 84 to 90 mm. This required deleting the Biral cylinder liners and coating the bores with Nikasil, an alloy of nickel and silicon carbide that brought a happy bonus in reduced internal friction. Retained were the 2.4's valve sizes and timing, 8.5:1 compression, and Bosch/Porsche fuel injection. All this yielded an extra 20 horsepower for a total of 200 DIN/230 SAE at 6300 rpm in road-going trim.

As a homologation special, the RS 2.7 was lightened drastically and, in places, ingeniously. For instance, the body was made of thin-gauge steel, and fiberglass was used for the engine cover and rear apron (the latter found only on racing models). There was no insulation for the cockpit, which was predictably spartan: rubber mats instead of carpeting, pull-cord releases rather than door handles, thin-shell bucket seats, no clock, passenger sun-visor, or superfluous trim. Without all this, curb weight came in below a ton and about 300 pounds less than a stock 911S. The chassis was beefed up with gas-pressurized Bilstein shock absorbers, super-stiff anti-roll bars, and aluminum wheels of familiar S-type design. The last were an inch wider at

119

the rear (six inches versus five) than the 911S's.

Outside, RS 2.7s were unmistakable. All were finished in white, and Zuffenhausen designers played up the return of a production-based Carrera by putting an outsize version of the traditional script (in blue) above the rocker panels. Rear fenders were flared to accommodate the wider wheels (also blue), and a small "bib" spoiler appeared beneath the front bumper.

But the most obvious distinction was the RS's skyward pointing rear spoiler, molded into the engine cover. Nicknamed "ducktail," it looked weird but worked beautifully, reducing lift from 320 to 93 pounds to keep the back end firmly planted at speed. It also improved airflow through the engine-cover grille and moved the car's effective center of pressure about six inches rearward, which also aided high-speed stability.

The Carrera RS was greeted with

high enthusiasm, and the full-fledged RSR track version wrote a brilliant record in Group 4 (detailed in Chapter 13). Porsche upped the ante for '74 with the RS/RSR 3.0, needing to build only 100 for homologation as an "evolution" of the 2.7. Incorporated were a wider, horizontal rear spoiler, quickly dubbed the "whale tail"; a bulkier front spoiler with large, rectangular air intake; even wider wheels (8 × 15 fore, 9 × 15 aft) and tires (215/60VR-15 front, 235/60VR-15 rear); die-cast aluminum

The 1974 Porsche 911 sported beautifully integrated five-mile-per-hour crash bumpers that looked like they were part of the original design that had appeared at Frankfurt some 10 years earlier. The engine was enlarged to 2687 cc and developed 143 horsepower at 5700 rpm, this despite stiffer emissions rules.

crankcase; and the huge cross-drilled disc brakes from the mighty turbocharged 917 Can-Am racer. The '73 RS had needed a special road permit in Germany because the ducktail was deemed hazardous to pedestrians. Porsche avoided this by supplying the '74 with two engine covers: one with a large racing spoiler, the other with a smaller whale-tail edged in protective black rubber. Several wild body colors were newly available, all set off by black-finish window moldings, tail-light housings, door handles, and outside mirror.

Despite retaining all the '73's weight-reducing mods, the '74 ended up about 400 pounds heavier. But that was more than offset by another 5-mm bore increase, bringing total capacity to 2993 cc and net roadgoing horsepower to 220 at 6200 rpm.

In testing a 3.0 RS for *Road & Track* magazine, journalist/race driver Paul Frère averaged 124 mph on 78 miles of Italian autostrada. "This is one of the fastest road cars we have ever timed," he wrote; "60 mph is reached in a staggering 5.2 seconds with the help of superlative rear-wheel grip, and the ½-mile mark comes in 14 seconds.... The car understeers, though lifting off at the limit of adhesion will swing the tail out sharply. On the Casale track, near Torino, I found that fast bends must still be approached with some power on and that getting the car around fast and safely still calls for a certain amount of delicacy."

Like the 2.7, the "street" 3.0 wasn't sold in the U.S., though Roger Penske gave the RSR a lot of publicity by ordering 15 for his inaugural International Race of Champions series of driver showdowns. Another 49 were built, and continued to dominate competition like the SCCA Trans-Am and IMSA Camel GT series. A final 60 were finished as roadgoing RS's.

But it scarcely mattered that these race-and-ride 911s weren't sold over U.S. counters because their influence was plainly evident in a new top-line '74-model 911 looking very much like the 3.0 RS—"whale tail," bulged fenders, big graphics, and all. It, too, was called Carrera (no suffix letter, though), returning the name to American Porsche showrooms for the first time since the last 356 Carrera 2s. Inevitably, it was slower than its European cousin but somewhat more civilized.

Porsche continued with three 911s for '74, but specs and model designations were juggled. The base offering was now just plain 911, equivalent to the previous T. With the new Carrera,

the 911S became the middle model, roughly equivalent to the former E in trim and performance.

All shared the 2.7 engine from the '73 RS, though much more mildly tuned. Carrera and S packed 167 bhp (SAE net) at 5800 rpm, the base 911 "only" 143 bhp. The extra displacement was yet another timely Porsche response to tightening emissions limits, complemented by switching to Bosch's more sophisticated K-Jetronic fuel injection, sometimes called CIS (Continuous Injection System). This same lineup also appeared in other markets, albeit with less restricted breathing and commensurately more horsepower: 150 bhp (DIN) at 5700 rpm (911), 175 at 5800 rpm (911S), 210 bhp at 6300 rpm (Carrera 2.7).

Regardless of where they sold, all '74-model 911s boasted the new front and rear bumpers mandated by American law, good-looking and universally fitted as a production economy. *Road & Track* noted that, in customary overkill fashion, "Porsche went beyond 1974 requirements for sports cars and did a major redesign to put the bumpers' ef-

fective heights at the 16- and 20-in. level already required for sedans and to be [required] for sports cars next year." This involved simply pulling the bumpers out from the body and putting them on aluminum-alloy tubes that collapsed when struck at 5 mph or above—and thus had to be replaced. Still, the new setup afforded superior body protection. The bumpers themselves were aluminum, again to save weight. Hydraulic shock-absorber attachments that *didn't* need replacing post-impact were standard for the UK market and extra-cost elsewhere—in the U.S., a $135 "mandatory option." Accordion-pleat rubber boots neatly filled the gaps twixt body and bumpers, which were overlaid in color-keyed plastic with black rubber inserts.

It was a typical Porsche solution to a problem no one could have foreseen when Butzi Porsche penned the 911, and it made most other "crash" bumpers seem clumsy. Not that Zuffenhausen didn't have an incentive to do it right: the U.S. now accounted for more than 50 percent of its total pro-

In addition to the safety bumpers with their accordion pleats at the ends, a new chin spoiler and flared rear wheel arches came standard on all versions of the 911 for '74. The base 911 (*opposite page*) looks much tamer than the 911 Carrera (*above*) with its flashy side graphics and bold rear spoiler.

duction. (By contrast, U.S. sales for BMW and Mercedes were still well below 20 percent of their annual volume.)

There were other changes for '74, most functional. Out back were a full-width taillight lens bearing the Porsche name, and a black-finish engine grille with chrome "2.7" legend. Inside were new high-back bucket seats, safety control knobs, tiny fresh-air vents at each end of the dash, and new steering wheels. Adopting the new space-saver spare tire made room for a larger fuel tank (21.1 gallons, up 4.7 gallons) and Targas exchanged their fold-up roof panel for a more convenient one-piece affair.

On the chassis front, forged alumi-num alloy replaced welded steel for the rear semi-trailing arms across the board, and there were greater differences in sway bars and wheel/tire packages among the three models. The base 911 rode the usual 5.5 × 15 rims and 165HR-15 tires; the 911S had forged-alloy 15 × 6 wheels with 185/70VR-15 tires (optional on the base car). Both sported a 16-mm-diameter front anti-roll bar and could be ordered with an 18-mm rear bar. The Carrera used the S wheel/tire combo in front and 215/60 rubber on 15 × 7 rims at the rear. It also came with the rear bar as standard plus a larger, 20-mm front bar.

Road & Track tried all three '74s, and its results were about what you'd ex-pect despite non-stock tires on the test 911 and S that made handling comparisons difficult. The Carrera, on its wider rear tires, exhibited more stick and less understeer on the track, but equal-size tires made the base model faster and more agile through the slalom. Interestingly, *Car and Driver* also found that the 911 generated higher cornering forces than the Carrera: 0.83g versus 0.80. Of course, neither of these figures was exactly shabby. In fact, they still pass muster today.

As for performance, *R&T* observed that "all our '74s would beat [a '73] 911S soundly in the ¼ mi despite having taller gearing. The basic 911 is plenty quick, getting to 60 mph in 7.9

In spite the major revamp of '74, the 1975 Carrera
(*both pages*) received a deeper front spoiler and a
larger IROC-style rear spoiler. Opening side rear
windows, intermittent wipers, and rear anti-roll bar
were standardized across the board for 911s, and the
Carrera was treated to leather upholstery.

sec and covering the ¼ mi in 15.5 sec; its top speed is limited by power to 130 mph. The 911S and Carrera accelerate identically to 100 mph and beat the 911 to 60 or the ¼ mi by 0.4 sec; the margin widens to 2.6 sec by 100 mph. There's quite a difference to be felt by the driver, too: whereas the less powerful 911 pulls evenly toward its rev limit (all three . . . stopped at 6400 because of their rev limiters) the S/Carrera unit comes 'onto the cam' strongly at about 3500 rpm and shoots toward 6400 at a dizzying rate. All our test cars, by the way, had the optional 5-speed gearbox—which we think you can jolly well do without, so strong is the low-speed response of either engine."

Alas, the high-power engine suf-

fered "a good old-fashioned case of temperament" at low speeds, "bucking just like the more highly tuned older S unit." At least fuel economy was "still reasonably good. At 17.5 mpg overall, the 911 is a bit more thirsty than last year's 911E and the S/Carrera does another 1.5 mph less but remains more economical than the old S."

R&T carped about prices, and with good reason: They were up 20 percent from '73—to a minimum $10,000 and close to 14 grand for the Carrera. "The Porsche people also have the nerve to charge you extra for opening rear-quarter windows in all but . . . the Carrera, and the air conditioner costs $1125!" At least the Carrera came with electric lifts for the front windows.

Still, *R&T* rightly concluded that "they've got you over a barrel: a Porsche is like no other car, and if you want one there's no substitute."

Speaking of 911 options, they'd proliferated greatly. The five-speed, still an across-the-board extra, cost a reasonable $250. A new two-stage electric rear window defroster added $70, and there was such miscellany as Koni shocks (to replace the standard Bilsteins), deluxe steering wheel, and contrasting colors for 911S road wheels. Also on the "long and intimidating" list by now was paint and upholstery "to sample," which meant that Porsche would finish a 911, inside or out, in hues and/or materials to match anything a customer wanted. Al-

most unnoticed, Porsche was becoming a builder of "boutique" automobiles with fast-rising prices, no surprise given the inflation of these years.

Two external distinctions marked the '75 Carrera: a deeper front spoiler and an IROC-style rear spoiler. The base 911 disappeared, while the 911S was visually unchanged. But Porsche, perhaps responding to *R&T* criticism, expanded standard equipment to include those opening rear side windows, plus intermittent wipers, rear anti-roll bar and, on Carrera, leather upholstery. Having bowed in Europe the previous year, high-pressure headlight washers (developed jointly with Hella) appeared as a U.S. option for '75. The heating system gained separate

left/right controls, and a higher-capacity alternator was specified along with a single battery (replacing the two smaller cells used since '66).

News from the engine room was less heartening, as both Carrera and 911S lost 10 horses (15 in California) to detuning for 1975's lower pollution levels. The Carrera's 0-60 mph time was up a second (to 8.4), its official top speed down 10 mph (to 132), yet fuel consumption was no worse (but no better, either). Still, Porsche had so far avoided the worst maladies of the emissions-control era—just exhaust-gas recirculation on 49-state cars, plus twin thermal reactors for Sunny Cal. And the '75s had better driveability than the '74s: still easy to start from

cold but better behaved in the city grind and blessed with abundant low-end torque.

The Carrera now cost $1700 more than the 911S, but made up for it with the standard bodyside graphics in special colors, the opening rear-quarter windows, electric door windows, RS-type black exterior trim (chrome was still available), wider wheels and tires, the big spoiler, plus a three-spoke steering wheel. Interiors were funereal in this period, as matte-finish black or silver replaced the shiny stuff now banned by the Feds. All things considered, though, the '75 remained "one of the world's best sports cars," in *R&T*'s widely shared view. "If an automotive bargain still remains in our in-

Opposite page: The American edition of the Turbo Carrera (*top*) arrived for '76. Its engine (*bottom*) cranked out 243 SAE net horsepower, good for 0-60-mph times of around six seconds. *This page*: The 1976 911S (*top*) yielded more standard equipment, cost more. The 912E (*bottom*) was a new model for 1976.

flation-ridden world, the Carrera, or any 1975 911, is it."

Honoring 25 years of Stuttgart production, Porsche issued a limited-edition Silver Anniversary 911S in 1975. Only 1500 were built, half coming to the U.S. Each was painted diamond silver metallic, had custom interior trim of woven silver-and-black tweed, and bore a numbered dash plaque with Ferry Porsche's facsimile signature.

America celebrated its bicentennial in 1976, and Porsche joined in by unleashing the mightiest 911 yet: the Turbo Carrera. This was yet another creation of the prolific Ernst Fuhrmann, who became Porsche chairman in 1972 (after the Porsche and Piëch families relinquished control of the company and Porsche became a joint-stock corporation—today's Dr. Ing. h.c. F. Porsche AG—with a board of directors). Fuhrmann, it will be recalled, had designed the original 356 Carrera quadcam four, and also directed development of the 1972-73 Carrera RS/RSR.

Fuhrmann knew and appreciated good engineers, and hired many of them himself. Like Ferry Porsche and his father, he knew that racing really does improve the breed. He also knew a great deal about turbochargers from Porsche's work on the tremendous hyperaspirated flat 12 in the racing 917. What could a turbocharger do for the 911? Shortly after taking the helm, he set up a program to find out.

One of its first fruits was a "911 Turbo" displayed at several European shows in 1973—but without comment on possible production. The following year, the Martini & Rossi team had mixed results with a turbocharged 2.1-liter Carrera RSR packing 333 bhp (one was doing 189 mph on the Mulsanne Straight at LeMans when it threw a rod and retired). Nevertheless, that experience encouraged Fuhrmann and company to develop a production turbocar: a smooth, quiet, very fast coupe with a blown version of the 2993-cc Carrera 3.0 RS engine.

It bowed in prototype form at the 1974 Paris Show as the 911 Turbo, later changed to simply Porsche Turbo. So extensive were the modifications that the Turbo got its own internal type number: 930. Motive power was stupendous: 260 bhp (DIN) at 5500 rpm and 245 pounds-feet torque peak-
continued on page 130

Opposite: The '76 "race-and-ride" Turbo Carrera
RSR was—borrowing a phrase from Chevy—"a
meaner hombre." Porsche said the '77 911S
Targa (*this page, above*) was "one of the few
remaining convertibles in America" and that the
Turbo Carrera (*top*) did 0-60 in 5.5 seconds.

ing at 4000 rpm. An American version, emissions-tuned to 234 SAE net horsepower (245 DIN) arrived for model year '76 as the Turbo Carrera.

Enthusiasts should thank Fuhrmann and his team for persisting with the roadgoing Turbo in spite of the OPEC oil embargo and all that it seemed to imply for the future of high-performance, high-thirst cars, European and American. They did defeat the sales department's campaign, as Karl Ludvigsen records, to price the 930 artificially low. Fuhrmann felt that if they were going to do it, they should go all out.

They did. As the ultimate 911 to that point, the 930 arrived with most every luxury and convenience the factory could squeeze in. Air conditioning,

AM/FM stereo (U.S. version), electric antenna and window lifts, leather upholstery, tinted glass all-round, headlamp washers, rear-window wiper, oil cooler, and Bilstein shocks were all included in the initial East Coast base price of $25,880. (That seems a bargain now, when you can't get much more than an upscale Japanese sedan for that sum, but it was a bundle of bucks back then—proof of just how much our dollars have shrunk in the intervening decade.) The U.S. options list was short: electric sliding sunroof ($675), limited-slip differential ($345), heavy-duty starter ($50), "Turbo" graphics ($120), and custom paint ($250). The 930 came only as a coupe and was never offered with Sportomatic (though several factory test cars

were so equipped and worked well).

The 930 engine (produced in /50, /51, and /52 versions) revealed anew the amazing adaptability of the basic 911 flat six. The 3.0-liter size was chosen for the best possible off-boost performance with the lower compression then required for turbocharging, which was 6.5:1 for all markets. The blower itself was placed on a cast-aluminum manifold studded to the heads. Ultramid plastic tubes for the Bosch K-Jetronic fuel injection sat between manifold and intake ports. Boost pressure was set at 11.5 pounds per square inch. Even in emissions-legal U.S. trim, the 930 packed a prodigious 246 lbs-ft torque (SAE net) at 4500 rpm, which Porsche thought sufficient to pull a wide-ratio four-speed

The Porsche 911S for 1977 changed only in detail: two
additional air vents graced the dash, heater controls
were altered, inside door locks became more thief-proof,
and carpeting now ran up the lower door panels.

transaxle instead of the 911's close-ratio five-speed.

Still, the 930 engine was predictably less torquey than the 911 unit below 3000 rpm, though things started to happen quickly above that. Yet there was "no sudden urge of power as there is with the cammy S," said Road & Track. "Rather, the buildup is . . . strong and silent as the turbocharger muffles the usual raucous-sounding Porsche exhaust to a dull roar. It takes the driver a moment or two to realize [that] some awesome, unseen force is pushing him back into his seat and thrusting the Carrera forward at an incredible rate. And another brief moment to realize that the engine is starting to stumble because it's reached its 6950-rpm rev limit. Then it's shift into

the next gear and prepare for the same heavy loads and fireworks to start all over again."

R&T allowed that a slipping clutch made its test car a bit slow, so it's interesting to compare results with those of Car and Driver's 1976 Turbo test:

	C/D	R&T
0-50 mph (sec.)	3.7	5.2
0-60 mph (sec.)	4.9	6.7
0-80 mph (sec.)	7.9	9.9
0-100 mph (sec.)	12.9	15.3
0-1/4 mi. (sec.)	13.5	15.2
top speed (mph)	156	156

Though 930 dynamic behavior was basically routine 911, R&T judged the Turbo more stable at speed because of its larger rear tires and wider track. Not everyone agreed. NASCAR ace Bobby Allison, testing the similar-

chassis '75 Carrera for Car and Driver, described the handling as "almost squirrelly." But R&T claimed the Turbo "far and away the easiest Porsche to drive near the limit that we have ever tested." Its 62.8 mph through the magazine's slalom test broke a record held by Ferrari's mid-engine Berlinetta Boxer—by 2.4 mph. And driver Sam Posey, who happened by while R&T was testing at Lime Rock, hopped in and unofficially broke the track record for production cars!

Like the normally aspirated Carreras, the 930 had stiffer springs and shocks in addition to its fatter aft footwear, so it didn't ride as well as lesser Porsches. Its steering was heavier, too, and tire noise was considerable. There were no complaints about the brakes, however: fade-free, impossible to lock, and capable of 60-0 mph halts in under 160 feet—excellent given the fairly hefty curb weight (2825 pounds).

In all, the 930 was remarkably civilized and undemanding for an ultra-performance car. "It can be pottered around town all day in top gear and a bit of second without bother," said Britain's *The Autocar* magazine. "And when the town limits are past, there is all that ocean of surging performance under your right foot, immediately, with not the slightest need for tiresome plug-clearing first."

Paul Frère, driving a Turbo prototype for *R&T*, put it another way: "All you note when you push the accelerator is a tremendous surge of power that goes on and on and on ... but with added immense flexibility, incredible silence and the luxury of the plushest Porsches. And driving the car on the Weissach track certainly confirmed that even with a [comparatively] softly sprung road car, the Porsche development people certainly know how to get all the benefits (mainly remarkable traction) of the overhung rear engine without having to accept its usually re-

cognized limitations....This Turbo Carrera certainly offers the finest blend of ultimate performance and refinement I have ever come across."

A year later, the same magazine, anticipating an earlier end for the 911 and its derivatives than has proven to be the case, opined that technological achievements would assure the Turbo's place in history. "In one fell swoop, Porsche engineers have not only proved that turbocharging and low emissions are totally compatible, but have also silenced the critics who say racing doesn't improve the breed.

True, such clever engineering doesn't come cheaply, but then Porsche has never before offered a 911 with the [Turbo's] luxury, performance and technical sophistication...."

R&T was correct. The day would come when production turbocars met emission standards as a matter of course. Like many technical breakthroughs, Porsche had pioneered it.

Though ousted by the Turbo from the 1976 U.S lineup, the normally aspirated Carrera continued in Europe, along with a base 911. In this form it offered 200 bhp (DIN) at 6000 rpm—still pretty impressive—and sold in Germany for DM44,950.

Little change attended the '76 American-market S aside from a $1000 bump in base price, but at least you now got most of the previous Carrera's standard equipment, plus remote-adjustable body-color door mirrors and (a yet further) improved climate system with optional automatic temperature control (also available on the Turbo). A new extra for both '76s was Porsche's first-ever cruise control, developed mainly for long-distance U.S. driving.

Responding to buyer concerns about durability in the face of rapidly rising prices, Porsche now galvanized all 901-series bodyshells on both sides, and backed it up with a six-year no-rust warranty. It was only fair. If Porsches had to cost the world, they could at least outlast the loan payments.

A busy 1977 saw Porsche introduce its "heretical" new water-cooled front-engine models: the V-8-powered 928 in Europe (Chapter 11) the four-cylinder 924 in America (Chapter 10). The 911S and Turbo were accordingly little changed. An extra pair of air vents appeared in the middle of instrument panels, heater controls were jiggered again, interior door locks were reworked to discourage thieves, and carpeting was run up into the lower door panels. A bit depressing, but evidence of Porsche thoroughness, were a special speedometer and speed governor on U.S. models. These limited maximum velocity to 130 mph, the speed rating for the tires now specified. Sportomatic-equipped 911s (except with right-hand drive) and the U.S. 911S received an Ate vacuum brake booster, and softer-riding tires and shocks were optional as part of a $495 American-market Comfort Group that also included electric windows.

As with most everything else in these years, Porsche prices continued nowhere but up. The Turbo held the line for '77, but the 911S that had sold for less than $12,000 three years before now nudged $15,000—and its 1978 successor, the 911SC, would start at over $22,000.

Even so, the 911 was still something of a bargain. Throughout one of the most troubled periods in automotive history, when engineers and stylists everywhere bowed to the enforced wishes of politicians and bureaucrats, Porsche managed to keep the 911 within the law and as exciting as ever.

At that 25th birthday party in May 1974, Ferry Porsche confirmed that the old warrior was far from finished: "With all the regulations that are known to us now, we think the 911 can keep going for the next six years." As usual, the good Doctor was being modest. In the autumn of 1983, the 911—on balance, one of the all-time greats—had its 20th birthday. And by the time you read this, it'll be 25. Time *does* fly when you're having fun.

Although the '77 911S continued Porsche's policy of gradual refinement, prices didn't, going from $12,000 in 1974 to almost $15,000 in '77 to $22,000 for the '78 successor 911SC.

1970-76 Type 914 and 912: Back to Basics

Don't cry for the 914. Though criticized during its five years as a disappointing ersatz Porsche, it has lately been discovered as an interesting car that just happens to be the most affordable modern Porsche around. And therein lies an irony, for this recent surge in enthusiasm is pushing prices far higher than many would have predicted in 1975 when the 914 was abandoned like the star-crossed child it was.

Hopes were high when the 914 was unveiled at the Frankfurt Automobile Show in September 1969. It was very much a back-to-basics car, a literal return to Porsche's roots, much as the 356 Speedster had been nearly 15 years before. Of course, the 914 was a rather different package because of the way it came about and because of its mid-engine configuration, though Porsche was hardly a stranger to "middies" by that point. Yet, like the Speedster, the 914 was a more affordable, Volkswagen-based sports car, conceived to bring the pride and pleasures of Porsche ownership to a much wider audience in the face of steadily escalating prices for the 911 and 912.

But before telling its story, it should be noted that the 914 ousted the 912, which had been evolving in lockstep with the 911 Series through 1969. "Generally speaking," writes Porsche expert Dean Batchelor, "all running changes made to the 911 (with the exception of the engine) were made to the 912 at the same time. This was a

production economy, but one that was beneficial to the buyer...." Among the more salient interim improvements were addition of the Targa body style and optional availability of the Webasto gasoline heater (1965); slightly wider track (1966); standard five-dial 911 instrumentation, safety door locks, upgraded carpeting, and new engine mounts (1967); and 1969's lengthened wheelbase and associated body/chassis changes.

Prices naturally kept pace. "The least expensive 912 cost more than $5000 by 1969," Batchelor notes, "and could top $6000 if all the available options were ordered. This seems like a tremendous bargain today...considering the buyer got the same quality and most of the [911's] handling and performance.... But there were problems related to the reduced horsepower in a car that looked faster than it was and had a reputation for performance that many 912 drivers seemed to feel obligated to maintain.... [They] had to push [their cars] harder yet couldn't begin to achieve the performance of a 911. And, if [they] tried it often enough, the engine suffered abuse that drastically shortened its life.

"Also, too many mechanics, and some owners, thought the 912 engine was 'just another Volkswagen' and this muddled thinking could prove fatal.... It was a Porsche design through and through, and needed good care and maintenance by a qualified Porsche

mechanic or a knowledgeable owner."

Aware of these problems, Porsche had begun planning in 1966 for a new four-cylinder model that would sell for somewhat less than the 912. The need to keep the price at least reasonable, plus production constraints at Zuffenhausen (owing to strong 911 sales), made it inevitable "that Porsche should seek a partner in the building of such a car," as Karl Ludvigsen records. A mid-engine design was almost as inevitable because it would "put Porsche in the position of being able to draw direct marketing parallels between the successes of its mid-engined racing cars...and the attributes of [its] production cars."

Then too, the mid-engine layout was beginning to look like the wave of the future for production sports cars by 1966. All the buff magazines said so, and Lotus introduced a roadgoing middie that year, the Renault-powered Europa. But though others would follow—Fiat X1/9 in the Seventies, Toyota MR2 and Pontiac Fiero in the Eighties, plus assorted Italian exotics—the mid-engine layout is still far from universal.

The reasons are well known. Though perfect for the race track, it's less than acceptable in a road car. Mounting the drivetrain immediately behind the occupants puts noise, vibration, and heat that much closer, requiring more heroic insulation efforts than in a front- or rear-engine design. No production middie has been entire-

Sold as a VW-Porsche in Europe, and as a
Porsche in the U.S., the 914 was the result of
a star-crossed joint venture. Widely
misunderstood in its time, the 914 is gaining
better acceptance as time goes by. Shown here
is a 1972 model with the 1.8-liter engine.

Rare then, rarer now, the 914/6 bowed in late
1970. It boasted a *real* Porsche engine, the
2.0-liter 110-bhp flat six from the 1969-model
911T, with capacitive discharge ignition and
two triple-choke Weber carbs. It also featured
5.5-inch-wide five-lug steel wheels, chrome
bumpers, vinyl-covered rollbar, and more
amenities. Only 3351 were built through 1972.

ly successful in this regard, nor in resolving the problems of over-the-shoulder vision, service access, and shift quality, all of which the configuration tends to compromise. A midships package is also more difficult—and expensive—to design and build than a conventional one. While it eliminates the need for a driveshaft (but so does front drive), it mandates a costly independent rear suspension and convoluted shift linkage.

But none of this seemed very important in the mid-Sixties. Mid-engine cars were dominating the tracks, and more adventuresome automakers expected a competition aura to do wonders for sales of showroom models. Porsche was no exception, but as it turned out the 914 was not destined to set buyers to beating down the doors.

In Ferry Porsche's words, the 914 project sprang "from the realization that we needed to broaden our [model]

program at a less costly level [and] that we couldn't do it alone." Accordingly, the chief of Zuffenhausen contacted the chief of Wolfsburg, Heinz Nordhoff, who had brought VW to the peak of success by making it America's dominant import car.

What emerged was an early example of what we'd now call a "joint venture." It was, of course, a natural. VW and Porsche had worked together for years, and both firms were German,

With its roof in place (*top left*), the Porsche 914/6 (and the 914/4) offered excellent weather protection. The roof could be stored in its own spot in the rear trunk (*above*). There was a second trunk up front, too (*bottom left*). Door handles were flush-mounted (*below*).

with all the clarity of understanding that implied. VW's expertise in volume production was as obvious as Porsche's in sports cars. And as luck would have it, Nordhoff wanted a sportier model to replace the slow-selling Type 3 Karmann-Ghia, not the winsome Beetle-based original, but a later, square-rigged model never sold in the U.S. (though closely related to the late-Sixties Fastback and Squareback "sedans"). A mid-engine two-seater designed around VW components by folks at Porsche might just fill both companies' needs.

In due course, Nordhoff and Ferry hatched an intriguing plan. Porsche would design the car to accept the powertrain from VW's forthcoming upscale rear-engine sedan, the 411, in which form it would be sold by Volkswagen as a "VW-Porsche." In return, Zuffenhausen could buy bodies for installation of its own engines and sale through its own dealers. An incidental benefit was giving the Wilhelm Karmann works something to build in lieu of the Type 3 Ghia.

Porsche was more than willing. Its dealers were clamoring for a less costly offering now that 911 and 912 prices were way above 356 levels. Even better, Porsche had recent mid-engine experience in a near-roadgoing car, the sports-racing Type 904 GTS (see Chapter 16).

Styling was deemed important, even critical. Nordhoff didn't want the new sports model to look like a VW, and Porsche didn't want it to resemble the 911. Again, luck was with them. Gugelot Design GmbH in Neu-Elm, about 50 miles from Stuttgart, had been working on a front-engine prototype to demonstrate a new body material comprising a foam core within layers of bonded fiberglass. This "sandwich" construction interested Porsche, VW, and Karmann, as well as BMW and Daimler-Benz, though tests showed it unsuitable for mass production. But the prototype's distinctive styling was just what Nordhoff and Ferry Porsche were looking for. A team directed by Ferry's son Butzi, who'd created the template for the 911, suitably revised it for a midships drivetrain and the desired image, and the 914 was born.

The result was unorthodox, though that was, perhaps, inevitable given the midships layout. To lend Teutonic rigidity to the open, all-steel monocoque, a

Targa-type rollbar (which some journalists dubbed the "basket handle") was devised; the roof consisted of a removeable fiberglass panel that attached to the rollbar and the windshield header. The body was devoid of ornamentation, but the bumpers, designed to meet pending U.S. impact standards, could hardly be called beautiful. Normally, they wore a body-color finish, but they looked better in extra-cost chrome. Because of the low nose, pop-up headlamps were used to meet minimum-height requirements.

These were a typical piece of *Porsche-arbeit*, with every contingency anticipated. Each headlamp had an electric motor *and* provision for manual operation in case of power failure. Both methods were designed so that either could easily break the thickest coat of ice the engineers could conjure in cold-weather tests. To prevent catching an unwary finger as the lamps flipped down, Porsche provided a safety panel that would give way before one's digit. It was the only correct approach to a feature then becoming fashionable.

Reflecting economic constraints, the cockpit contained all the essentials, but it exuded little warmth. Instruments maintained a Porsche-like look, featuring an upright binnacle that highlighted a large central tachometer, which was flanked by a speedometer on the right and a fuel gauge and warning lights in a matching circle to the left. Heat/vent controls came from the 911; door and dash hardware were cribbed from VW.

At least the cockpit was roomy, intended to accommodate the largest of American anatomies, although the bucket seats were criticized as too flat. *Road & Track* noted the hunkered-down seating position (the 914 measured four inches lower overall than the 911) but said "vision to the rear is the best of any mid-engine car (except roadsters) we've driven—the blind spot made by the basket handle is so far forward that it can't obstruct anything that needs seeing."

A pull-up handbrake mounted outboard of the driver's seat was one of the 914's more unusual touches. Ordinarily, this would have complicated entry/exit, but Porsche thoughtfully provided a double-jointed handle that could be folded down, out of the way,

once the ratchet engaged. It was a predictive feature: The later 928 and today's Corvette both have it.

Car and Driver observed that "since the [914's] structure is concentrated in the flat, platform floor . . . the door sills are low and the tunnel is no higher than what is required to house the shift linkage and a few electrical wires [so] almost the entire width of the car becomes available for seating. The designers like to think that, if you drop a cushion between the seats, there is a place for a third person and they've included an extra set of seat belts for just that eventuality."

However, only the driver's seat had fore/aft adjustment (and generous at that), another cost-cutting measure. The passenger's seat made do with a movable footrest anchored to the right kick panel by a plastic strap. *C/D* derisively described this as "a chunk of what feels like wood, shaped like a concrete brick, covered with mouse-fuzz grey carpet. . . . If you're tall enough so that your feet will reach the front bulkhead, the strap can be unhooked and the block stored in one of the trunks. Or heaved over the side."

Trunks? Yes, like some other midengine designs, the 914 had two. In front was a deep, main hold with horizontally stored spare tire; behind the engine was a wide but shallow compartment with its own lid (hinged for-

On its 1970 introduction, Porsche was quick to say that the "new 914 roadster is the world's first large volume mid-engine production car [with] its engine located ahead of the rear axle [for] outstanding driving qualities."

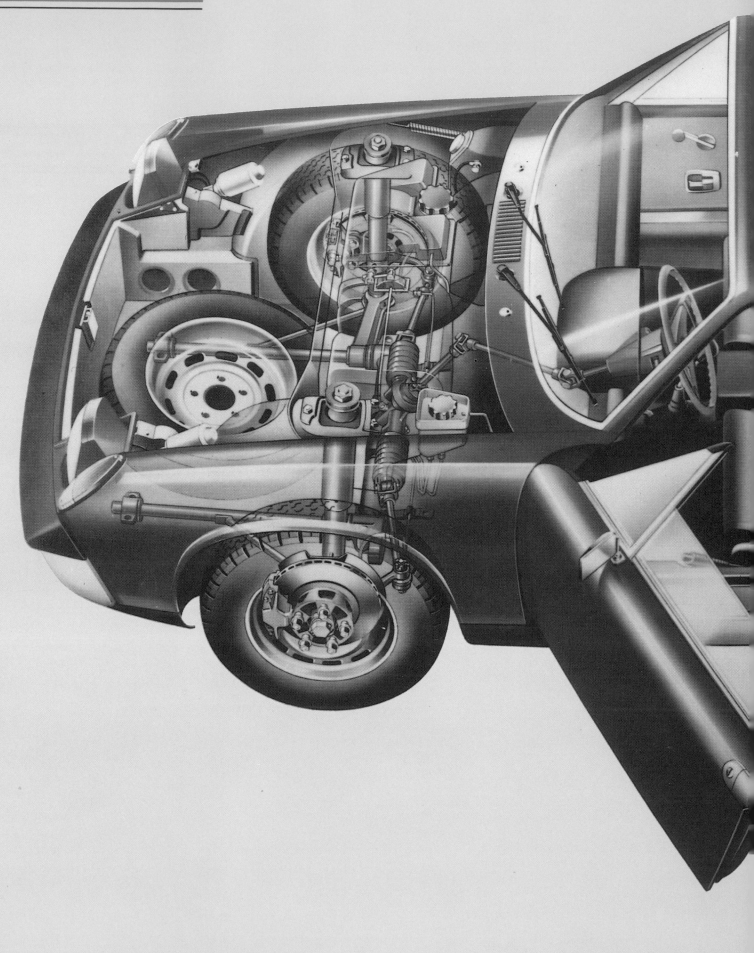

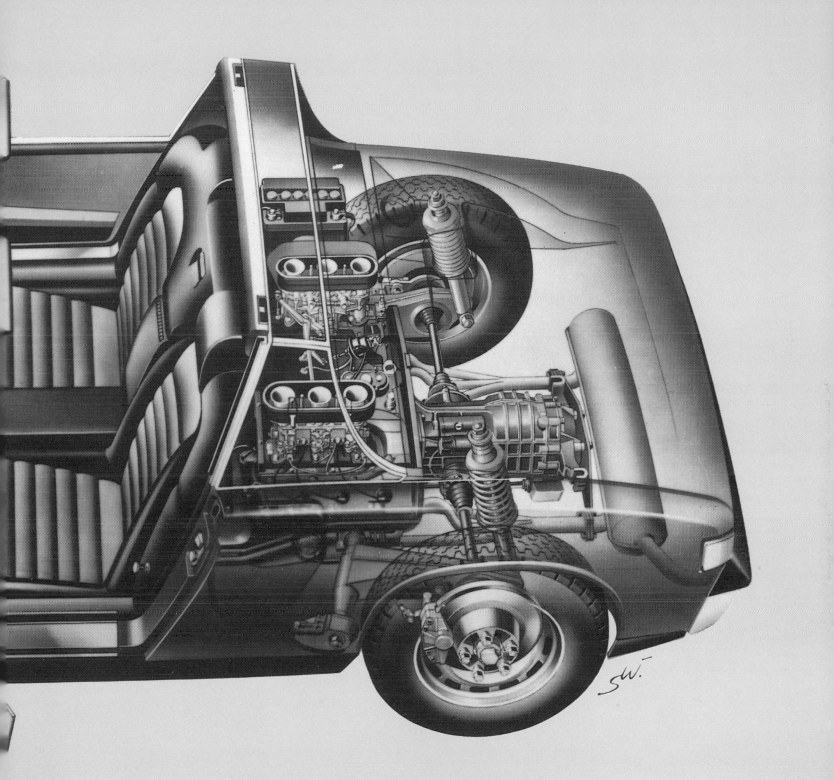

This cutaway drawing indicates that a lot of thinking
went into the 914/6 (and 914/4) in terms of engineering.
The mid-engine placement allowed for a roomy cockpit and
for two trunks, and it did not ruin rear vision.
Other features touted were the fully independent
suspension, five-speed transmission, four-wheel
disc brakes, and built-in roll bar.

Although critics panned the 914 for using a *VW* engine, the styling was probably the 914's most controversial aspect. The front end did not look Porsche-like, some said, and the proportions forced on it by the mid-engine location were not "right." Perhaps, but Porsche could honestly claim a kinship between the 914 and its mid-engine racing cars.

ward) and clips for carrying the roof panel. The engine was reached—none too easily—through a narrow lift-up hatch just behind the rear window.

Production economics naturally dictated shared chassis components, so front suspension—MacPherson struts, lower A-arms and longitudinal torsion bars—was lifted almost intact from the 911. The rear, however, had 911-style geometry but new pieces: semi-trailing arms and coil springs, the latter a first for Porsche. So little body roll occurred that anti-sway bars were deemed unnecessary at first, but the very stiff springing resulted in a hard ride. As a result, early 914s developed squeaks and rattles literally unheard of in a 911 or 356. The lift-off roof was mostly to blame; it also generated a lot of wind noise. Steering was rack-and-pinion, brakes solid-rotor discs all-round. VW also provided the wheels, skinny four-lug 4.5 × 15 rims from the 411. Boge telescopic shocks were standard, but gas-pressurized Bilsteins could be had at extra cost.

The 914 engine was a 1679-cubic-centimeter (102.4-cubic-inch) fuel-injected overhead-valve flat four, unchanged from its 411 application, though it would soon be modified. The injection system, devised by Bosch

under Bendix patents, allowed the 914 to clear U.S. emission limits without an air pump. Mild 8.2:1 compression yielded modest initial outputs of 85 SAE horsepower at 4900 rpm and 103 pounds-feet torque peaking at 2800 rpm. The standard and only transaxle was the 911 five-speed manual, complete with its awkward racing-style gear pattern. Sportomatic was advertised as an option, but never fitted.

On the road, the 914 was initially both more and less than enthusiasts expected. In acceleration, it was comparable with the antediluvian MGB, according to R&T, able to do 0-60 mph in about 14 seconds and the standing quarter-mile in a tick over 19 seconds at 70 mph. Car and Driver managed somewhat better times: 11.3 seconds and 18.1 seconds at 75 mph. Top speed came in at a respectable 105-110 mph—though at

near 2100 pounds, the 914 wasn't exactly light for its 96.4-inch wheelbase and an overall length two inches shorter than a VW Beetle's. Weight distribution was a reasonably good 46/54 percent front/rear.

Through the twisty bits, R&T observed that, for a middie, the 914 didn't have "great absolute cornering power—at least not yet," this despite testing the car on one-inch-wider wheels fitted

Opposite page: The 914's hidden headlights (*top*) popped up electrically, but could be operated manually as well. PORSCHE was spelled out in large block letters on the engine cover (*bottom*). The cockpit of the 914 (*above*) was roomy and featured Porsche-like instrumentation. The handbrake was mounted outboard of the driver's seat.

by the west coast distributor. By contrast, transient behavior was judged "excellent. Initial response to steering input is utterly without delay.... And what happens when the driver lifts his foot off the throttle in a hard corner—this is the trickiest thing about rear-heavy cars—is simply a mild tuck-in of the front or, at the extreme, a smooth breakaway of the rear."

C/D had a slightly different view: "It understeers...a lot. While you are making the transition from straight to curve, there is no real problem unless you have to slow down abruptly.... Here the 914 has the same trailing-throttle oversteer characteristics... found in the 911E.... Lift your foot off the gas as you enter a hard bend and

the tail tries to come around. An expert driver can use this to set up for a corner, but a novice will probably never try it twice."

Bearing VW-Porsche badges (on steering wheel and tail), the 914 went on sale in Europe in February 1970. It reached U.S. dealers a month later wearing the Porsche name in block letters on the engine cover, and a Zuffenhausen crest on the steering wheel (but never on nose or road wheels of the 914/4). This was deliberate—and about all that remained of the verbal agreement between Nordhoff and Ferry Porsche.

What had happened was this: Nordhoff had sadly passed away in April 1968, and his successor, Kurt Lotz, had

decided to change some terms of the deal. The results were three. First, a new company called VG (*Vertriebsgesellschaft*, "Motors Inc."), owned 50/50 by the partners, was formed to handle European sales and marketing for VW, Porsche, and Audi (the last part of VW by now) as well as the new Volks-Porsche. For the U.S., Porsche and Audi would be combined as a division of Volkswagen of America and the new middie sold as a Porsche through its freestanding dealer network. Second, Karmann, by this time a VW subsidiary, was to build complete four-cylinder 914s on a "turnkey" basis for VG in Europe and Porsche + Audi Division in America. Finally, Porsche could still buy 914 bodies, but at a much higher price than agreed.

Initial U.S. advertising for the 914 emphasized the advantages of its mid-engine design (lower center of gravity, better handling and braking, increased tire life) as proven in Porsche's competition cars: "If there's one thing we've learned from racing," said one ad, "it's where to put the engine.... So if you're thinking about a true two-seat sports car, think about this: When you don't get a back seat, you should at least get an engine in its place."

Yet neither press nor public were impressed. A big reason was price. Though announced in Germany for the equivalent of $3015, the 914 arrived in the U.S. at just five bucks short of $3500. At that, it competed not against the MGB (to which it was clearly superior), but the Triumph TR6 (cruder but quite a bit faster) and the Fiat 124 Spider (a prettier, full convertible). Most worrisome for Porsche, however—and rightly so—was the new Datsun 240Z from Japan, a conventional but sensationally styled and fully modern closed GT bargain-priced at $175 less.

Against these foes, the 914 seemed a dubious buy. *Road & Track* tested them in June 1970 (except the 240Z, then in a class of one and really better than the others), and the results were telling. The 914 was slowest off the line but marginally fastest all out, equalled the Italian car and handily beat the two Brits in braking, and outdid all three in fuel economy. But its styling was the most controversial, and neither workmanship nor materials seemed worthy of the Porsche name—or the price.

On considering the latter, *Car and*

Driver judged the 914 "an altogether underwhelming car. It offers less performance and less comfort than its competitors and has tricky handling in the bargain. It does have a midship engine (be the first on your block!) and it would allow you to tell everybody that you drive a Porsche [but] you'll have to make up your mind if it's worth it."

A lot of folks—over 100,000—would eventually say the 914 was worth it. But the VW engine made it hard for some marque fans to accept the 914 as a "real" Porsche.

Zuffenhausen didn't feel comfortable with it, either, and decided to make it a *real* Porsche. The result appeared in late 1970 as the 914/6 (at which point the four-cylinder model became informally known as the 914/4). Powered by the 2.0-liter 110-bhp flat six from the 1969-model 911T, with capacitive discharge ignition and two triple-choke Weber carbs, it came

The 914 received European-style bumper-mounted driving lights for 1972. An Appearance Group, a $311 option, gave this 1972-model 914 a bit of extra pizazz by trading the standard black bumpers for chrome units and adding a vinyl covered rollbar. Note also the chrome wheels.

with 5.5-inch-wide five-lug steel wheels (which included a Porsche crest on the hubcaps). Distinctive 10-spoke light-alloy wheels were also available to go with the suitably fatter tires and ventilated front brakes were fitted to all 914/6s. Amenities were also more generous: 911-style full instrumenta-tion (with 150-mph speedometer and 8000-rpm tachometer), three-speed wipers and electric washer (the latter replacing a foot-operated bulb type), dual-tone horn, and a vinyl covering for the basket handle.

Built entirely by Porsche (and badged as such in all markets) the 914/6 sold for over $2500 more than the four cylinder job—about $6100 in the U.S.—and was thus even harder to sell. To no one's surprise, it was quietly canned after 1972 and only 3351 examples.

Nevertheless, the extra cylinders made a world of difference. It was hard

to think of the 914/4 as anything but a VW; indeed, *C/D* allowed as how it would have made a fine replacement for the original Karmann-Ghia, surely damning with faint praise. But there was no escaping the flat-six engine's exciting wail or that seat-of-the-pants feeling that the 914/6 was a Porsche.

It certainly performed like one. *Road & Track* recorded 0-60 mph in 8.7 seconds, the standing quarter in 16.3 seconds at 83 mph and a 123-mph maximum speed, plus 21.3 miles per gallon—in all, typically balanced Porsche performance. Nevertheless, *R&T* said they'd "probably pay the extra $431 for a 4-speed 911T, with its handsomer body, better detailing, extra years of development, slightly better performance and +2 seating. For those who insist on open-air driving, the 911T in Targa form is $675 dearer or more than a grand above the 914/6. This differential, plus the technical novelty of the mid-engine package, will assure the new car plenty of buyers [obviously, it didn't]. What we all hoped for was a true Porsche nearer to $5000, but that's asking a lot."

One thing made any 914 less than a true Porsche: it just didn't get the intensive yearly development accorded the 911. This might also have been expected for a car that fell between corporate stools, but "it indirectly led to the demise of the 914," in Dean Batchelor's view.

Still, the four-cylinder cars would see a few changes. The '71s had virtually none, but the '72s gained a revised engine (designated EA-series, replacing the original W-series unit) with recalibrated fuel injection that let it run on 91-octane fuel, as required in California that year. Unusually, it delivered about 10 percent better mileage with no harm to performance.

Also new were fresh-air vents at each end of the instrument panel, a wiper/washer control incorporated with the turn-signal lever (as on the 914/6), and a fully adjustable passenger seat that eliminated need for the footrest. The most drastic—and unwelcome—change was a near $700 hike in list price.

As before, one could pop for a $311 Appearance Group on top of that. Included were the 914/6's vinyl rollbar trim and dual-tone horn, plus the aforesaid chrome bumpers, foglamps, upgraded carpeting, 165-15 radial tires

on 5.5-inch rims, and leather-rim steering wheel.

More energetic tweaks followed for '73. The 1.7-liter engine was retained, with an even more anemic 69-bhp setup for smog-plagued California, but Zuffenhausen added spice to the recipe with an optional 2.0-liter four. Rated at 91 SAE net horsepower, it was a simple bore-and-stroke job (from 90×66 to 94×71 mm) that gave performance about midway between that of the original 1.7 and the 914/6. In fact, the 914 2.0, as it was badged, was in effect a replacement for the Porsche-powered model. Its base price was a less lofty $5599 (East Coast POE), and that included the Appearance Group and alloy wheels plus a center console mounting clock, volt-

meter, and oil temperature gauge. Also new were bulky front bumper guards, a response to the 5-mph front impact protection rule imposed by the Feds. Still, the 914 remained a tough sell.

At least the 2.0-liter four offered better tractability along with its extra performance, being an easy starter and revving quickly to its 5600-rpm redline. With it, the 914/4 now roughly equalled TR6 performance. The five-speed gearbox was particularly useful here, allowing the driver to extract the maximum from the gutsier powerplant. Porsche had evidently changed its mind about anti-roll bars, for it fitted one at each end of the 2.0. This, in turn, permitted lower spring rates for a slightly softer ride.

As a result, the 2.0-liter seemed

The 916 (*both pages*) was a swoopy evolution of the 914 that sported wildly flared fenders and body-color bumpers. A fixed roof for extra structural strength was necessary to handle the 190 bhp from the 911's 2.4-liter flat six. Alas, it never made it to production.

completely bereft of the dreaded Porsche oversteer. Said *Road & Track*: "The relative stiffness of the front and rear anti-roll bars seems to have been chosen to provide understeer at all times and under all conditions. When driven around a curve, the front end slides and the back end sticks. Apply full power and the front end pushes toward the outside of the turn. Let up on the throttle and the front end tucks toward the inside of the turn. This is very safe...but the sporting driver may wish sometimes for the freedom of, say, a 911S, in which an occasional 'nasty' trait can be provoked and exploited with skill. Perhaps the not-quite-Porsche 914 isn't allowed to provide that sort of test and perhaps that's why the 914/2 [*R&T*'s designation]

isn't allowed to be the 914S" [the 2.0-liter's proposed designation, turned down by the factory].

For 1974, 914s were treated to a bored-out (to 93 mm) 1.8-liter engine as standard power; it came from the 411's upgraded 412 replacement. With modified rockers, combustion chambers, and ports, plus larger valves, the 1.8 almost held the line against the drain of desmogging, delivering 72 bhp (SAE net) at 4800 rpm, 4 horsepower below the 1.7. The European version (with twin carburetors instead of fuel injection) was down a like number of DIN horses (76 versus 80). A jazzy U.S. model, prosaically called Limited Edition, was issued with front spoiler, side stripes, alloy wheels, choice of black or white paint, and special in-

terior. It was supposed to perk up languishing sales, but nothing seemed able to turn that trick.

After grafting bigger bumpers onto American-market '75s, Porsche gave up on the 914. Production stopped at 118,947, including 914/6s—not inconsiderable, but not what the partners had hoped. Their "people's Porsche" was a good idea, but a half-breed image and the altered marketing arrangement defeated it. As Karl Ludvigsen wrote, the "VW-Porsche [marque] had neither image nor tradition. At the same time it was both VW and Porsche and neither VW *nor* Porsche."

Dean Batchelor notes that the 914 was also likely hurt in the U.S. by persistent hot-weather driveability woes, mainly vapor lock that made for

Although the 914 was never restyled, it changed to keep
up with federal mandates. Note that the 1973 (*above*)
lacks the rear bumper rubber blocks of the '74 (*right
bottom*). The '74 Limited Edition (*right top*) came with
front spoiler, side stripes, alloy wheels, choice of
white or black paint, and special interior.

hard—sometimes no—starting, plus chronic engine overheating. These bothers were slow to be rectified, which was curious for Porsche, though the engine was, after all, VW's. Regardless, Batchelor says that "many 914 owners feel the demise of the car could partly have been Porsche's lack of a cure for vapor lock from 1970 to 1975, when the fuel pump was moved [from near the right heat exchanger] to a cooler position up front."

But mediocre value for money was always the biggest problem. Because VW had directed Karmann to charge more per body than originally agreed, Porsche was never able to exploit the intended economies of scale that could have made for a less costly and more saleable 914/6, something that would have helped the four-cylinder cars too.

This wasn't deliberate VW sabotage, however. Ludvigsen quoted Ferry Porsche as saying, "They calculate costs differently in a big firm. They couldn't consider the advantages of having a sports car in the line, the way it can attract people into the showroom." VW looked mainly at tooling amortization, which meant a high per-body price at the 914's modest volume. Porsche, by contrast, never applied the true cost of an individual model to that model alone. "We put them all together and divide by our total volume," said Ferry.

There's no telling what the 914 might have become had it been better received—or treated more seriously by Volkswagen—but the potential was certainly there. Porsche demonstrated that by fitting a flat eight, the wonder-

ful 3.0-liter unit from the Type 908 racer, into an experimental called 914/8. Packing 310 DIN horsepower, it could do 0-60 mph in six seconds and reach 155 mph. *Road & Track* reported on another "914/8," a conversion with 283 Chevy V-8 power conceived by Californian Ron Simpson. This "Porschev" did 60 mph from rest in 6.3 seconds and the standing quarter-mile in 14 seconds flat at 90.5 mph.

Several other specials were based on the 914. Among them: a trio of GTs by Louis Heuliez in France, a study by Albrecht Goertz of BMW 507/Datsun 240Z fame, one by Frua, and the sensational gullwing Tapiro show car from master stylist Giorgio Giugiaro.

But the development that came closest to production was the factory's own 916, a swoopy 914 evolution

powered by a 2.4-liter 190-bhp 911 engine. As Porsche's ultimate mid-engine road car, it would likely have sold at $15,000-$16,000, directly competitive with Ferrari's Dino 246GT. And with a curb weight of almost exactly a ton, its performance was competitive, too. Porsche said 0-60 mph took "less than seven seconds," though there was reason to believe that claim was conservative, as usual.

The 916 differed considerably from 914 appearance, sporting flared fenders and body-color bumpers front and rear, plus a fixed roof for extra structural strength, no doubt required with the muscular engine. Inside were leather trim, 914/6 instruments, even a radio. The suspension incorporated heavy-duty Bilstein gas/oil shocks, stiffer anti-roll bars at each end, 911S vented brakes, and 185/70-15 Michelin XVR tires on S-type alloy wheels. The five-speed gearbox followed the new gate arrangement Porsche was moving to at the time, with the four lower gears in the H and fifth to the right and up.

Unhappily, the 916 was nipped in the bud, just after the first press pictures were distributed. Only 20 were built (all prototypes); one escaped to America and Brumos Porsche in Jacksonville, Florida. Again the problem was price. The factory had grave doubts about sales volume at $15,000, especially since both 914/4 and 914/6 had been roundly criticized as overpriced. In retrospect, Porsche was probably wise to cancel the 916, but it's a shame that a few more weren't built.

The last 914s quietly disappeared from dealerships in early 1976. In their place as the budget Porsches, pending release of the new front-engine 924, was a one-year 912 revival. Designated 912E (E for *einspritzung*, fuel injection), it was a fine car in its own right. The VW four from the 914 2.0 substituted for the Porsche engine of earlier 912s; also on hand were all the 911-Series body and chassis changes since '69. U.S. East Coast POE price was near $11,000, considerably more than

late 914s but far less than a 911. And, of course, it had Butzi Porsche's lovely 901 body.

"The 912E will obviously find favor with those who prefer a slightly more practical and tractable Porsche," *Road & Track* predicted. "It's a car with almost all the sporting virtues of the more expensive 911S, yet its simpler pushrod 4-cyl. engine should make for better fuel economy and less expensive maintenance than the 911's six," though the Bosch injection tended to misbehave in cold weather. SAE net horsepower was 86 at 4900 rpm, torque a useful 98 lbs-ft at 4000. Curb weight came in at 2395 pounds, which meant that the 912 had somehow picked up 400 extra pounds since '69. Still, *R&T*'s 11.3-second 0-60-mph time and 115-mph top speed looked good against the observed 23.0-mpg economy.

As a stopgap, the 912E was the single instance of "planned obsolescence" in Porsche history. Only 2099 were built, but this plus "one-year" status and all the desirable qualities inherited from the 911 have since made the 912E one of the more collectible four-cylinder Porsches.

And what of the 914? Surely it was hurt by being more "Vee-Dub" than Porsche. Had it been Zuffenhausen's own, with a Porsche engine and looks to match, more people would likely have paid the admission price. Remember how Ferry Porsche wisely insisted that the 911 look something like a 356? Granted a mid-engine car has different requirements, but at least the 914 could have had more of a Porsche face. Then too, four-cylinder U.S. 914s were supposed to have all the performance and quality implied by the Porsche name—which, of course, they didn't—and one can't help thinking they would have sold better as Volkswagens. Yet VW, then suffering financial hard times, couldn't justify spending much on development, not with the modest sales volume.

With all this, the dumpy styling was simply a final letdown. *Car and Driver* said the 914 had "all the fluidity of line

of an Erector set." *Sports Car Graphic* termed it "a pleasant eyesore." *Road & Track* suggested that maybe we weren't used to mid-engine sports cars: "There is not only an unfamiliar relation between the center section and the rear overhang but a difficult problem in getting adequate rear vision combined with decent esthetics. The 'basket handle' roof section...does indeed look strange, but to make the car more esthetically palatable (i.e. more like the beautiful mid-engine cars such as the DeTomaso Mangusta) would have meant accepting decreased rear vision or an exceedingly expensive expanse of glass."

That was what their heads said. Their hearts said otherwise. A year after that analysis, *R&T* noted that 1972 styling was unchanged "and that's a disappointment....We were hoping for at least a mild reworking of the uncharming front end." Even in its initial report, the magazine termed the 914 "a great big disappointment.... Undoubtedly the mid-engine is the coming thing, but...." Well, Porsche has never claimed to be perfect, though it sure tries to be.

Let's also not forget that for all its faults, the 914 did pave the way for a another Porsche/VW joint venture, one that would prove successful in both commercial and automotive terms. It was, of course, the 924, which would lead to the even better 944.

That story is told in another chapter, but a closing thought for this one. It's fitting that the 914 has a following now. We think a big reason for it is that, at current asking prices, the 914 enables thousands of folks to fulfill their dream of Porsche ownership without having to be one of the rich and famous. That may not always be true (as we said, collector values are on the rise), and it doesn't make the cars more virtuous in any case. But it does suggest that 914s are likely to be pursued and preserved well past the millennium, and that's not a bad fate for any car—even a "not-quite" Porsche.

The 914, "the most popular mid-engine sports car ever built," Porsche claimed, received self-restoring bumpers and a new choice of interior fabrics for '75 (*opposite*). Engines were either the 1.8- or 2.0-liter flat four.

1976-88
Type 924 and 944
Series:
Troubles and Triumphs

I t was the first front-engine, water-cooled Porsche to reach production, but the 924 actually followed the 928 in Zuffenhausen design chronology. It also followed the 356 in using contemporary VW components: suspension, brakes, steering, and engine. Aside from engine position and cooling medium, the big difference was that the 356 had been designed *as* a Porsche, while the 924 was designed *by* Porsche to be a Volkswagen and ended up a Porsche.

One other parallel is that both led to something better. As 356 sired 911, so 924 begat 944. Yet here, too, there's a difference. While the 911 eventually superseded the 356, the 944 hasn't ousted the 924—at least not yet.

But we're getting ahead of the story, which begins back in 1970 with two key developments. The first was the arrival of Rudolf Leiding to succeed the controversial Kurt Lotz as managing director of Volkswagen. Leiding was a sports-car advocate and racing-minded, but he was also budget-minded.

A good thing, as he took over a financially troubled company. Wolfsburg's prime profit-maker, the Beetle, was waning, and there was no replacement in sight despite numerous attempts. The big 411/412 was proving a costly flop, the Type 3 range (Fastback and Squareback in the U.S.) had never lived up to expectations, and acquiring Audi/NSU from Daimler-Benz in 1969 brought problems of its own while

further draining capital reserves. To ease the budget crunch, Leiding quickly handed much of VW's developmental engineering work to Porsche, whose expertise was as obvious as was VW's need for inspired new products.

To that end, Leiding set VW on a new product-planning course: *Baukastenprinzip*—literally, building-block principle. It was, of course, a GM-style approach, with cars of different sizes, shapes, and prices derived from a relative handful of components, thus reducing development costs and capitalizing on production economies of scale. This led to two spinoffs of newly planned front-drive models. The Audi 80/Fox spawned the VW Passat/Dasher to replace the 411/412, while the Golf/Rabbit, the Beetle's heir apparent, became the basis for a Karmann-Ghia successor, the sporty Scirocco.

It was also in 1970 that VW-Porsche *Vertriebsgesellschaft*, the jointly owned marketing firm for Porsche-designed cars using VW components, realized that the 914, as Porsche historian Dean Batchelor put it, "was not going to become the lasting favorite that the 356 had been. Management, therefore, began planning a new car to be designed *by* Porsche *for* VG to sell as a VW/Audi—no more 'VW-Porsche' in Europe and 'Porsche' elsewhere, as the 914 had been conceived." Coded EA425, this project marked the birth of the 924.

It would not be an easy delivery.

Batchelor records eight separate requirements for the new sports car: interior space comparable to the 911's, 2+2 seating, "useful" trunk volume (presumably more so than the 914's), greater comfort than 914, all-independent suspension, maximum use of high-volume VW components and—the most interesting—a *front*-engine design with some technical and stylistic similarity to Porsche's new 928 luxury GT, then under development (see next chapter). "Once the parameters had been agreed to," says Batchelor, "components...were selected by a process of logical application....It was understood that air-cooled engines were nearing the end of their production at both Porsche and Volkswagen [the 911 has since proven otherwise], so one of the new water-cooled units under development would be used. The one selected was a Volkswagen design, built by Audi, used in carbureted form in the VW LT van...." It was also destined for the forthcoming Audi 100 and, of all things, the American Motors Gremlin.

Things were well along in 1973 when VG was disbanded and EA425 became VW's own project. It was only fair: VW had been paying the bills, which then totaled $70 million. But then Leiding announced that EA425 would be built *only* as a VW or Audi, mainly so it could be sold through 2000 West German VW dealers instead of the 200 VW-Porsche outlets that handled the 914. Zuffenhausen was stunned because that meant EA425 was a potential competitor for its own four-cylinder 912.

The situation seemed resolved when Leiding suddenly departed in 1974, his expansion program having left VW/Audi even more overextended. But his replacement, former Ford Europe executive Tony Schmucker, promptly told Porsche that VW now saw no need for EA425, not with the sports-car market reeling in the aftermath of the OPEC oil embargo.

Porsche nevertheless had faith in the car and decided to save it by buying the production rights. The price: $60 million, a slight "discount" on VW's investment, though Porsche would spend that much and more on further development. A sweetener for VW was Porsche's willingness to build the car as planned at the Audi/NSU plant in Neckarsulm, a half-hour north of Stuttgart. This was more or less a necessity, as Porsche's Zuffenhausen facilities were completely occupied by the 911 and the forthcoming 928.

By then, the only remaining matter to settle was where to put the transmission. Despite what one might think, front-wheel drive *was* a possibility. Though admittedly a stranger to it in production cars, Porsche never wore technical blinders; besides, the great Ferdinand's first car, the Lohner electric, had had it, so front drive wasn't exactly outside Porsche's heritage.

Like the 356, the Porsche 924 used VW components. It was the first Porsche—but not the last—to use a water-cooled front-mounted engine. Introduced in 1976, it lives on, but like a true Porsche it has undergone constant development over the past dozen years.

But with all the requirements, including VG's original notion that space be allowed for a larger engine from some future VW project, front-engine/rear-drive seemed most appropriate—more specifically, a rear transaxle. Porsche's experience there was plentiful, management thought the configuration "technically interesting," the 928 was going to use it. Engineer Jochen Freund thought he could produce a good rear transaxle within EA425's cost constraints. Most important, the layout would provide near even fore/aft weight distribution, thus minimizing the feared oversteer of previous Porsches.

Thus did VW Project EA425 evolve into the Porsche Type 924, a designation chosen to signify a complete break with the 914. (Porsche never used project numbers between 917 and 924 save 923, the internal code for the four-cylinder 912E engine.)

The front-engine/rear-transaxle concept wasn't new, having appeared on such diverse machines as Pontiac's "rope-drive" 1961-63 Tempest compact and the Ferrari 275 GTB, but Freund's layout was carefully designed with *Baukastenprinzip* in mind. The driveshaft was a tiny, 20-mm-diameter splined affair, straight and without U-joints, encased in a tube and running in four bearings strategically placed at points of greatest torsional stress. At its ends were the gearbox and clutch, the latter bolted up directly to the engine. Both engine and transmission were supported by a pair of rubber mounts. Another "clutch housing" was provided in back for the torque converter from Audi's forthcoming fully automatic three-speed transmission, which would be a 924 option and something new for Porsche. The manual transaxle initially offered had but four forward ratios (using non-Porsche baulk-ring synchronizers), but a five-speed would come along later.

Conventional but contemporary described the engine, an overhead-cam inline four with aluminum head and cast-iron block. Slightly oversquare bore/stroke dimensions of 86.5 × 84 mm gave a displacement of 1984 cubic centimeters (121.1 cubic inches). The cylinder head was a crossflow design with Heron-type combustion chambers (dished pistons, flat-face head). Unlike its VW applications, the 924 engine sipped fuel via Bosch's reliable K-Jetronic (CIS) injection (as did the Audi 100 unit). Other features included toothed-belt cam drive, double valve springs, and exhaust-valve rotators (for reduced heat and wear). Installation was at 40 degrees to starboard, making this a "slant four" technically speaking. It also made sparkplugs hard to reach, as they were located on the right (along with alternator and exhaust manifold).

Initially, the 924 was tuned for 125 DIN horsepower, but arrived in America with only 95 bhp (SAE net), the difference coming from lower compression—8.0 versus 9.3:1—and smaller valves. At least power was the same for all 50 states; California models used a catalytic converter to meet emission standards while "federal" cars relied on an air pump. The clutch was a single-plate diaphragm-spring unit.

Per *Baukastenprinzip*, the 924's chassis pieces also came from the corporate bins, but were carefully selected. The front suspension was comprised of lower A-arms from the Golf/Rabbit and coil-sprung MacPherson struts from the Super Beetle. Out back were torsion bars and Beetle semi-trailing arms; halfshafts came from VW's Type 181 utility vehicle, a.k.a. "The Thing." Bilstein shocks, cast-aluminum road wheels, and anti-roll bars would be optional. Steering was Golf/Rabbit rack-and-pinion with a slower ratio (19.2:1). Brakes were front discs from the Beetle and rear drums from VW's K-70 sedan (inherited from NSU).

These disparate pieces worked together remarkably well, as did the en-

Opposite page: "Phantom" drawings highlight the 924's front-engine/rear-transaxle chassis. *This page*: Porsche trotted out a "Championship Edition" in 1977 (*above left*) after winning the 1976 World Championship of Makes and Sports Cars. The 1977½ 924 (*right*) could be had with an automatic transmission, a first for Porsche.

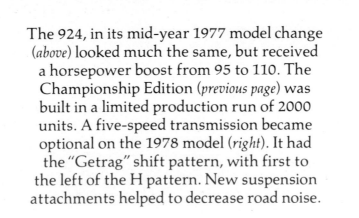

The 924, in its mid-year 1977 model change (*above*) looked much the same, but received a horsepower boost from 95 to 110. The Championship Edition (*previous page*) was built in a limited production run of 2000 units. A five-speed transmission became optional on the 1978 model (*right*). It had the "Getrag" shift pattern, with first to the left of the H pattern. New suspension attachments helped to decrease road noise.

tire package. The 924 was certainly more a "corporate kit car" than the 914. Yet as *C/D* concluded: "The 924 may have its engine in front and a hatch in back but it's still a non-conformist in the best Porsche tradition."

Except, happily, on the window sticker. Thanks to high-volume engineering and all the borrowed parts, Porsche now achieved the production economies it had missed with the 914, and buyers reaped the literal reward. The 924 arrived in the U.S. for model year 1977 with a base price of just $9395, versus $15,000+ for the 911.

As with the 914, styling was deemed all-important, but it was more competently handled this time. Credit Harm Lagaay, supervised by Porsche's American-born design chief Anatole "Tony" Lapine. Despite the order for a familial resemblance to the 928, the 924 was its "own car." Its classic teardrop shape would have pleased Paul Jaray and the first Dr. Porsche, and Lagaay reinterpreted certain traditional Porsche elements, notably the grilleless nose and a strong increase in visual mass toward the rear. The smooth front fenders swept from hidden headlamps past a beautifully raked windshield and on back in an unbroken line, terminating in a neatly rounded tail. Above was a large compound-curve rear window that doubled as a hatch for access to the luggage compartment. All 924s wore color-matched bumpers, but the 5-mph aluminum units on American models mounted further out from the body on hydraulic struts.

Overall, the 924 was quite distinctive—and influential. Its nose, for instance, was aped by Mazda's RX-7, introduced in 1978, and the new-for-'84 Chrysler Laser/Dodge Daytona sports coupes were unabashedly cut from the 924 pattern (as their G-24 project designation implied).

Aerodynamics wasn't a major concern in the early Seventies, but the 924's coefficient of drag (Cd) was a reported 0.36, then the lowest in the world and not bad even today. Here again, the "heretical" 924 hewed to Porsche tradition and was quite predictive in doing so. Back in 1977, *C/D*'s Pat Bedard felt some would "denounce the styling as antiquated. Molded Jello-O shapes went out with the Volvo PV544, they'll whine." Little did they know . . .

At 94.5 inches, the 924 was some 10 inches longer than the 911 between wheel centers, yet had a similarly close-coupled 2+2 cockpit. The driving position was appropriately low and sporty, so outward vision wasn't the best despite Porsche's claim that "at no point is more than 63° of the driver's full 360° obscured." As in the 914, furnishings were spare but functional, and there were some obvious signs of component sharing: Rabbit/Scirocco auxiliary gauges (riding above the heat/vent controls in a vertical extension of the tunnel console), VW steering-column stalks, Beetle door handles.

There were also a few lapses. The steering wheel, for instance, was not only oval but mounted slightly off-center, presumably to increase under-rim thigh clearance, though most testers thought it did just the opposite. Directly ahead was a large central speedometer, flanked by a tachometer on the right and a fuel-level/coolant-temperature dial on the left—fine, except that their conical lenses distorted the gauge faces and picked up unwanted reflections.

As the budget Porsche, the 924 had fewer standard features and more options than the 911, but it could be quite plush if the buyer spent enough

The five-speed manual was made standard for the 924 for 1979, and an extra-cost sport package, as on this 924S (*left*), utilized the four-wheel disc brakes of the European Turbo model. The 944 was introduced in May 1982 as a *1983* model (*right*), according to Porsche. It featured a *real* Porsche engine and flared fenders.

money. Among U.S. extras were air conditioning ($548), leather upholstery, the aforesaid automatic transmission (for Europe in late 1976, for America from March '77), stereo radio, metallic paint ($295), removable sunroof panel ($330), front and rear anti-roll bars ($105), headlamp washers, rear-window wiper, tinted windshield and side glass (a tinted backlight was standard), and a radio prep package (three speakers plus antenna, $105).

Two option groups were also offered. Touring Package I ($345) delivered 185/70HR-14 tires and 6.0-inch-wide alloy wheels (versus 5.5-inch rims with 165-14 rubber), the radio prep kit, and a leather-rim steering wheel. Touring Package II ($240) added headlamp washers, right door mirror, and rear wiper.

Early 924 road tests showed 0-60-mph times in the 11-12-second range, top speeds of around 110 mph, and fuel economy of 20-22 miles per gallon. These weren't sensational figures by any means, but they weren't bad for a well tuned 2.0-liter four in a modern, adequately equipped small 2+2. In a comparison test with the rival Alfa Romeo Alfetta GT and Datsun 280Z, *Road & Track* gave first place to the Por-

sche even though the Z went for $3000 less in base trim—strong recommendation indeed. They loved the 924 on the track, praising its beautiful balance, flat cornering response, and light, fast steering. But their car had all the chassis options; the editors didn't think as much of the standard issue. R&T found two, more serious problems: a rather buzzy engine, and a jouncy ride with lots of thumping over rough surfaces. With time, Porsche would, as usual, ameliorate both.

European 924s were considerably quicker and more flexible than American versions, particularly after the five-speed option, a Getrag gearbox, arrived for '78. By mid-1977, Porsche had partly attended to lackluster U.S.

performance, bumping output to 110 bhp (SAE net) via higher-lift cam, larger intake valves, modified pistons, advanced timing, and higher 8.5:1 compression (as used with automatic on U.S., Canadian, and Japanese versions). Of course, none of this affected running on 91-octane fuel.

Alas, there was still a terrific amount of engine noise, but R&T felt sure that the '78 would yet beat the Alfetta and 280Z: "The Porsche's overall design, its interior layout and its handling are better. [It] looks great (especially with the optional alloy wheels), its seating is as comfortable as a well worn Gucci loafer and the car sticks to the road like chewing gum on the bottom of a theater seat."

Still, R&T repeated that the 924's noise, buzziness, and milquetoast performance were simply unacceptable for a $10,000 car—especially a Porsche. This it underscored in a later comparison test with the even more formidable Datsun 280ZX, Mazda RX-7, and Chevrolet Corvette. Here, the 924 finished third (ahead of the 'Vette) despite winning six "firsts" (braking, handling, visibility, exterior finish, interior and exterior styling). "When it's good, it's very good," said the editors, "but when it's bad, watch out."

"Very well," the Zuffenhausen folk seemed to say. "We will fix those problems—and we will give you a turbocharged 924 for good measure." That they did, introducing it to Europe in

Opposite page: Porsche often offered special models to celebrate its various successes, one of them a limited edition 924, the "Sebring '79" (*top*). The '80 model (*bottom*) received a "trap-door" for the gas filler and standard-equipment power windows, and got 32 EPA mpg on the highway. The Turbo (*below*) sported four aggressive-looking air slots on it nose.

The 924 Turbo spawned the Carrera GT (*opposite page*), which was sold only in Europe and was intended partly as a customer race car. Its plastic flared wheelarches provided inspiration for the 944, which used all-steel construction. The air scoop on the hood differed from the NACA duct on the Turbo model. The coefficient of drag was rated at 0.35.

1979, to America for model year 1980.

This time, Porsche built both car and engine. The Turbo's powerplant retained the basic 2.0-liter block (shipped from Neckarsulm) but hardly anything else. There was a new Porsche-designed cylinder head, still cast aluminum but boasting larger valves, modified hemispherical combustion chambers, and new water seals (copper gasket and silicon rings). Sparkplugs now had platinum tips and sat on the intake (left) side. So did the starter, displaced by the turbo mounted low on the right.

The blower itself, made by the German firm KKK (Kuhnle, Kopp & Kausch), fed a huge cast pipe that sent boost pressures of up to 10.15 psi (7 psi on U.S. models) up and over the head to the intake manifold; the charge then went down to the ports on the engine's upper left. Compression was suitably lowered, as was then necessary with turbocharging, landing at 7.5:1 for all versions. The Bosch K-Jetronic injection was recalibrated to match, and there were two fuel pumps to assure full system pressure at all times. A standard oil cooler helped deal with the extra heat of pressurized power. As on the 930, a wastegate prevented boost from exceeding the specified maximum. Porsche also fitted a blow-off valve as "fail-safe" backup.

The result of all this was 125 DIN horsepower at 5500 rpm and an abundant 181 pounds-feet torque at 3500 rpm for the European version. American-model figures were 143 bhp (SAE net) at 5500 and 147 lbs-ft at 3000 rpm, the latter still a worthy improvement. Weighing 2780 pounds at the curb, the Turbo was considerably heavier than the normally aspirated 924 (and even the 911), but its performance advantage was relatively enormous. At around 7-8 seconds, it was 4 seconds faster from 0-60 mph, and its top speed was almost 20 mph higher. Simi-

lar gains were seen in Europe, where *The Autocar*'s test Turbo reached 60 mph from rest in 6.9 seconds and did 144 mph all out.

To handle this new-found urge, Porsche took its typical pains with the 924 chassis. Driveshaft diameter went from 20 to 25 mm to reduce the chances of whipping, rear halfshafts were strengthened, and rolling stock upgraded to 15 × 6-inch rims with 185/70 rubber. Gear ratios, spring/shock rates, and anti-roll bars were also revised, and a larger servo boosted the brakes, which were now ventilated four-wheel discs for Europe; American Turbos retained the previous disc/drum combo. The standard and only gearbox was the five-speed Getrag unit, complete with the awkward racing-style shift pattern that once plagued the 911.

Most early "turbo-era" cars were prone to poor low-rpm (off-boost) performance and turbo lag, the delay in response to throttle changes caused by turbocharger inertia. Both were apparent in the 924 Turbo but not irksome. Boost on the U.S. version began at a low 1600 rpm and peaked at just 2800 rpm. (The larger, slower-revving European turbocharger began boosting at 1800 rpm.) Observed *Car and Driver*: "As the turbo comes in, you can feel the zooming wheel of the crossover point and, with it, the character change in propulsion.... The boost is right there, coming aboard quickly with a firm punch that rushes you forward, picking off normal traffic and predictably defining the correct arc through every corner."

Internal gearbox ratios were altered to match this power and torque delivery, and were the same for all Turbos save fifth, which was somewhat taller on the U.S. model—0.60:1 against Europe's 0.71:1—though this was offset by a 4.71:1 final drive (versus 3.17:1). Said *Road & Track*'s John

Dinkel: "Even though 5th is an over-overdrive (60 mph is only 2280 rpm), you can let the revs drop to below 2000 rpm in top gear, tromp the go-pedal and the engine pulls smoothly, albeit slowly. Try that with a stock 924 and you'll be greeted with a chorus of shakes, shudders, buzzes and groans of protest that won't stop until you downshift at least two gears."

In all, the 924 engine had undergone a satisfying—if not miraculous—transformation. Much of the old noise and harshness was gone. The turbo helped quiet things somewhat, though its high-pitched whistle added a new note. Porsche merely added sound-deadening material at strategic places in both 924s. That also helped, if not enough to satisfy *C/D*: "[It] does little to hide the thrumming, hissing, gurgling and sucking that come through the firewall like the sounds of plumbing in a cheap apartment...." Still, the editors felt that "once you begin to associate the aural effects with the performance they accompany, you warm quickly to your little sound-effects symphony under the hood."

Visually, the Turbo differed just enough to be noticed, with lovely "spider web" alloy wheels (optional on normal 924s), a functional NACA hood duct, and a quartet of nasal cooling slots, plus Turbo tail script and a spoiler rimming the big back window. The last, Porsche said, reduced the drag coefficient to 0.35, which in America made this 1980's slickest car. There were fewer differences inside, a leather-trimmed 911 Turbo-style steering wheel and shift boot being most obvious. Speedometers read to 160 mph (later to only 85 mph, per federal edict), but a boost gauge was nowhere to be found. Porsche evidently had much confidence in the blown engine's strength and reliability.

Considering its performance, the

Porsche had so much confidence in its 924 Turbo
that it didn't even bother to put a boost gauge
on the dash. The Turbo sported "spider web"
alloy wheels, a functional NACA hood duct, and
a spoiler that rimmed the big back window.

924 Turbo was remarkably frugal, most early tests reporting averages of around 25 mpg. But there was a price for all this: a little less than $21,000 for the 1980 U.S. model. Yet, as the sort of exciting evolution expected of Porsche, the Turbo was just the image boost the 911's baby brother had needed so badly. "Here is another real Porsche," said *The Autocar*, "a superb high performer...."

Interim changes to the normal 924 were less dramatic, but welcome nonetheless. The Getrag five-speed became standard for '79, along with a space-saver spare (except in Britain), pressure-cast alloy wheels, tinted glass, passenger's visor vanity mirror, and stereo speakers.

The '80s received a non-Getrag five-speed, basically the old four-speeder with an extra gear and—praise be—a conventional gate. Emissions control and driveability improved as three-way catalytic converters arrived during the year on both 924 and Turbo, making them 50-state cars. Porsche also attended to the occasional severe judder and hop of previous 924s via tighter driveline tolerances, revised rear suspension mounts, and new hydraulic transaxle mounts. The result was a better, if still rather hard, ride. Finally, U.S. 924s gained a little performance via altered camshaft and ignition timing, plus lower final-drive ratios with manual transmission (5.00:1 against the previous 4.11:1). Horsepower now stood at 115 SAE net and 0-60-mph acceleration at 10.5-11 seconds, yet mileage stayed the same.

Another new 1980 U.S. item was Sport Group, a package option priced at $2045 for the normal 924 and $1960 for the Turbo. This bought you the ventilated all-disc brakes previously restricted to Europe, five-bolt "spider web" wheels wearing beefy 205/55VR-15 Pirelli P7 high-performance tires, higher-rate shocks, and a 14-mm anti-roll bar to go with the stock 23-mm front stabilizer.

All 924s were curiously little changed for '81—just standard halogen headlamps, rear seatbelts and, belatedly, rear disc brakes. This might have signalled that Porsche had something better in the pipeline. It did: the thoroughly overhauled 944. With that, both 924s were temporarily withdrawn from the U.S. but continued in production for other countries.

Opposite page: Visually, the 924 Turbo
(top) differed just enough from the
regular 924 to be noticed, and the KKK
blower gave the engine *(bottom)* new life:
143 SAE horsepower at 5500 rpm and 147
lbs·ft torque at 3000 rpm. A 0-60-mph
run took but 6.9 seconds. The interior
(above) featured a leather-trimmed 911
Turbo-style steering wheel.

Meantime, rumors were spreading of yet another "budget" Porsche, the so-called 918. A decade of inflation and falling dollar/DMark exchange rates had pushed the 924 way upmarket by 1980, and the betting was that Porsche would counter with a new, lower-priced, 914/924-style "cocktail" model. Most reports mentioned a Targa-roof two-seater bearing 924 styling hallmarks and based on the VW Scirocco chassis. Power would allegedly be supplied by the 1.8-liter VW four from the European Golf GTI (and the new-for-'83 U.S. Rabbit GTI), while the body would mix aluminum and steel panels with polyurethane bumpers.

In the end, Porsche resisted the "918." True, the mass exodus of British sports cars had left a tempting market gap at the $12,000-$15,000 level, but Zuffenhausen concluded there was no point in competing there again. Undoubtedly influenced by American-born Peter Schutz, who succeeded Ernst Fuhrmann as company chairman in late 1981, it was a logical decision given the market of that day. Porsche was selling every car it could build, even at inflated prices growing more so every year, so it had no need for anything new—let alone a less expensive car on which it would be tougher to turn a profit. As ever, Porsche's future success seemed to rest with its time-tested formula of steady improvements to existing products that were already superb.

But not perfect, though no car ever is—which brings us to the motivation for the 944. Though the 924 had been a commercial success, it was nevertheless not widely perceived as a true Porsche. It may have been more of one than the 914, but even the Turbo couldn't shake the VW/Audi heritage of the basic 924 design—especially the engine, which still left something to be desired. And the fact that Porsche, not Audi, built the Turbo never got through to enthusiasts and critics.

Pride is a strong motivator, and Porsche has always been very motivated. Since the image problem seemed to rest with the engine, the obvious answer was to give the 924 a new engine—an all-Porsche engine. Then there'd be no doubt that this was a Zuffenhausen car, even if everyone had apparently forgotten that the basic package had been designed there. Almost as obvious was the new en-

The Porsche 944, like the 924, achieved good weight balance because of its rear-mounted transaxle (*right*). The 1983 model (*bottom left*) was rated at 143 bhp. This cutaway car (*bottom right*) shows that the 924/944 was well built; to prove it Porsche offered a ten year rust warranty and a 50,000-mile drivetrain warranty in 1986.

gine's source. The 924 had a slant four. The big 928 had an all-aluminum Porsche-designed 4.5-liter V-8, and a V-8 is basically two slant fours put together. Why not slice the 928 engine in half? And of course, they did.

The result was an altogether superior car that lived up to its badge in a way the 924 never could. More important, the 944 reassured Porsche partisans that Zuffenhausen was still on course. Don Vorderman, a critic not known for liberal praise, called it "the best small sports car ever made."

It was certainly a much-improved four-cylinder Porsche—starting with muscled-up styling predicted by the European 924 Carrera GT, a short-lived Turbo variation never sold in America. Fenders were aggressively flared to enclose broader 15 × 7J alloy wheels and 215/60VR-15 tires, a deep airdam was integrated with the lower front sheetmetal, and there was a new polyurethane nose cap. The 924's under-bumper air intake was retained, a pair of standard foglamps was flush-mounted in the airdam, and a 924 Turbo-style rear spoiler continued. Unlike the Carrera GT, whose fender flares and other panels were plastic, the basic 944 body was made entirely of steel. Despite what Porsche claimed was extensive wind-tunnel work, the "aero" mods lowered the drag coefficient to only 0.35, barely better than the original 924's.

The engine was far more effective. Being derived from the 928's then-current 4.5-liter V-8, it was a single-overhead-cam design with silicon-aluminum alloy block and crossflow aluminum head. Stroke was the same, too—78.9 mm—but a 5-mm bore increase, to 100 mm, brought 944 displacement to a little more than half the V-8's: 2479 cc (151 cid). And for all the similarities, there were no interchangeable parts, though Porsche saved quite a bit of development and tooling money compared to a clean-sheet design.

The 944 engine parted company in two more important respects. First, the 928's relatively simple Bosch L-Jetronic fuel injection gave way to the same firm's new state-of-the-art Digital Motor Electronics (DME) system with integrated computer management of injection and electronic ignition. Second, the 944 employed twin counterweighted balance shafts in the

Porsche debuted the 944 Turbo (*left*) for 1986. Perched atop Porsche's sawed-off V-8, the KKK turbocharger (*bottom right*) contributed to a top speed in excess of 150 mph, but the fun came in at a heady $29,500. The 944's interior (*bottom left*) featured 928 seats with electric height adjusters.

block, turning at twice crankshaft speed and in the opposite direction, to dampen the vibrations (technically termed "coupling forces") inherent in plus-2.0-liter inline fours. (A Gilmer-type cogged belt drove the camshaft; a second belt, with teeth on each side, drove the balance shafts.)

The balancer idea was novel but hardly new, dating from 1911 and Frederick W. Lanchester in England. Moreover, Mitsubishi of Japan had recently resurrected—and patented—it. Porsche tried to avoid infringement by running its balancers in three bearings each instead of Mitsubishi's two, but ultimately decided to pay a royalty estimated at $8 per car. Dean Batchelor quotes one Porsche execu-

tive as saying at the time, "There's no need to reinvent the motorcar." With this feature, there wasn't.

On 9.5:1 compression, U.S. 944s delivered 143 bhp (SAE net) at 5500 rpm and 137 lbs-ft peak torque at 3000 rpm. The Euro version had 153 (160 DIN) thanks to a tighter 10.6:1 squeeze. The factory claimed the former would run 0-60 mph in 8.3 seconds, slightly slower than its transatlantic cousin. However, both beat the 924 Turbo and were nearly as fast all out (130 versus 134 mph)—all without the blower's complexity. Strict weight control helped. The 944 engine weighed just 340 pounds dry, while curb weight was initially 2778 pounds, slightly higher than the Turbo's.

Porsche claimed no sweeping chassis alterations in turning 924 into 944—just the usual honing of spring/shock rates and anti-roll-bar diameters, plus attention to steering and transaxle mounts. The aforementioned beefier wheels and tires were standard equipment, as were the 924 Turbo's all-disc brakes. An optional sport package offered even stiffer shocks, limited-slip diff, and 16 × 7 alloy rims with 205/55VR-16 rubber.

The cockpit was much the same too, though instrument markings went from white to yellow for easier reading, and a nice new tweed-cloth upholstery option made the ambience less sterile. No-cost amenities were abundant, running to air conditioning,

175

In line with Porsche's policy of building
the same car for all markets, the Euro-spec
944 Turbo (*above*) differed little from the
American market models. Note, however, the
side marker light *behind* the "telephone
dial" front wheel, four of which came with
each Turbo. The Porsche drivetrain (*right*)
has proved remarkably durable.

removable sunroof, tinted glass, three-spoke leather-rim steering wheel, electric door windows, and heated power-remote door mirrors.

A discouraging word was seldom heard—or rather seen—in early road tests. Batchelor remarks that a number of publications wrote about the 944 "as if employed by Porsche's advertising agency," and *Road & Track* was typical in judging it "worthy of the marque."

Perhaps predictably, the engine earned the highest and most frequent praise. *R&T* reported that "it fires up immediately and runs smoothly, even when cold. And Lordy, does it rev— right up to redline in every gear except 5th. There are no stumbles, flat spots or resonance points. Furthermore, there's low- and mid-range flexibility that allows you to drop the revs as low as 1000 rpm in top gear and the engine pulls without protest."

The 944's handling was simply "terrific," according to *Car and Driver*: "You can drive like a hero without sweat popping out on your brow. The 944 is great because it responds crisply and decisively to every command, and it builds up to its limit in perfectly linear fashion. You won't find killer understeer here. And you won't find any nervousness at the limit." With standard tires, the 944 rounded *C/D*'s skidpad at an excellent 0.81g. *R&T*'s like-shod car did 0.818g.

And now *R&T* said the junior Porsche was *more* than a match for the rival Datsun and Alfa. In fact, the editors picked it over the all-new Corvette, Ferrari's 308GTBi Quattrovalvole and even the 928S in a 1983 comparison test. "The 924 won simply by having so few weak points. Balance again.... The 944 produced the fewest complaints while being fun to drive and proving itself a useful, fine-handling, well built all-around car."

In "sibling competition," said *R&T*, the 944 "more than holds its own with the 924 and even the 911SC. However...it was not quite as good as the 924 Turbo because [the test car had] the standard-issue 60-series tires and not the 55-series Pirelli P7s....But given a similar wide-footprint, sticky tire pairing, we'd bet the 944 would surpass the Turbo in both [skidpad and slalom] tests."

Arriving in the U.S. at under $20,000, the 944 was another bargain in Porsche performance, praised because of it, and well nigh irresistible. Sales were strong from the start, and the good folk of Zuffenhausen began breathing easier.

But they didn't rest, for the usual yearly refinements—and a couple of significant evolutions—were on the way. The first appeared for 1984, when the original welded A-arms were replaced by alloy castings. Mid-1985 brought a handsome new 928-

style instrument panel with more readable instruments, plus a smaller, round steering wheel to replace the never-liked oval unit. The fuel tank swelled to 21.1 gallons at the same time.

As if to answer speculation about the return of a blown junior model, Porsche released the 944 Turbo for 1986. Aside from the turbo and correspondingly lower compression (8.0:1), its engine was basically stock but delivered a healthy new wallop: 217 bhp (SAE net) at 5800 rpm and 243 lbs-ft at 3500 rpm in U.S. trim at the maximum 10.9-psi boost. It should be mentioned, though, that American-market Porsche engines were by now almost identical with Europe's, reflecting Zuffenhausen's "one spec, one performance level" policy.

Typical of Porsche, the 944 Turbo was not a halfway job. For example, new ceramic inserts in the exhaust ports kept exhaust gases hotter to provide more energy for the turbo and faster catalytic converter warmup for minimum emissions. The turbocharger itself (again by KKK) was not only water-cooled for longevity, but provided with a small electric pump that circulated coolant through it after engine shutoff, thus avoiding oil coking of the turbo center bearing and possible damage. A boost-limiting bypass valve supplemented the usual wastegate, as on the 924 Turbo, and

A "bargain basement" Porsche, the $18,900 924S, arrived
in the U.S. in '86 (*above and opposite*). Basically a
recycled 924 with a 944 engine (*bottom left*), it ran
sans flared fenders and had a simpler interior and the
old 924 dash (*bottom right*). It was actually a bit faster
than the 944, but by 1988 the "bargain" cost $25,910.

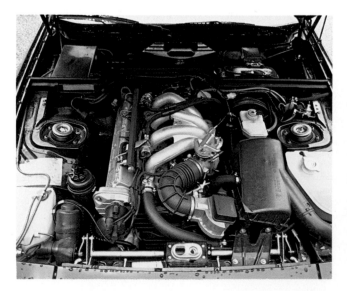

DME electronics took on the duty of varying boost with rpm, providing more pressure at low crank speeds where it's safe, less at higher speeds. DME also varied ignition timing in response to signals from engine sensors of incipient knock (detonation), a traditional problem in turbomotors.

Like newer 911s, the 944 Turbo had wider rear wheels and tires: 16 × 8 and 225/50VR-16, versus 16 × 7 and 205/55VR-16 front. Brakes were fortified with light-alloy four-piston calipers, and spring/shock rates were adjusted to suit the higher engine performance. Outside were distinctive five-hole "telephone dial" type wheels similar to the 928's, a revised nose with wide cooling slots and reprofiled bumper/spoiler, rear underbody pan (to smooth airflow leaving from beneath the car, again for better high-speed stability), and a more prominent rear spoiler. C_d was now 0.33, a useful if not startling reduction.

With all this, the Turbo had to cost more than the unblown 944: a minimum $29,500 on introduction. That

represented quite a hike, but Porsche anticipated "sticker shock" by fitting 928 seats with electric front and rear height adjusters as standard, along with headlight washers and more uptown cabin trim. Options now included a power sunroof ($695).

The Turbo didn't overwhelm magazine types as much as the original 944, perhaps because it cost so much more and wasn't as easy to drive. Car and Driver, for instance, lauded "acceleration to match its impressive top speed," but noted that in low-speed driving "the Turbo feels more muscle-bound than powerful. Unless you punish either the tires or the clutch by starting hard enough to keep the turbo on the boil, the boosted 944 feels sluggish off the line; flooring the throttle after a normal clutch engagement produces little response for at least a second. And in top [fifth] gear, the Turbo requires 14.7 seconds to accelerate from 30 to 50 mph, versus 12.0 for the standard car."

Nevertheless, C/D judged the 944 Turbo as "not only fast but well

rounded ... very competitive with the 911 Carrera and 928S. [While it] makes its driver work harder to generate the straight-line performance that the others produce effortlessly ... the Turbo delivers much of the 928S's comfort and refinement for about $20,000 less. And it demands less skill to drive quickly than the slightly more expensive Carrera."

A rather obvious price-and-performance gap between the two 944s suggested the need for something in between, and Porsche obliged in late 1986 with the 944S. The attraction here is not a turbocharger, but a new twincam head with four valves per cylinder. Though similar to the head on the latest 928S 4, again, no parts interchanged.

Valvegear was unusual. A single toothed belt drove the exhaust cam, which in turn drove the intake shaft via a chain between cylinders two and three. Other changes included larger-than-944 ports and beautifully cast manifold runners for both intake and exhaust. The result was not only

That the Porsche 924/944 series—now a dozen years old—
remains vibrant is a tribute to constant development,
as seen in the 944 (*below*) and 944 Turbo (*right*).

more power and a fatter torque curve compared with the two-valve 944, but smoother power delivery than the Turbo and almost as much go. The specific outputs: 188 bhp (SAE net) at 6000 rpm and 170 lbs-ft torque peaking at 4300 rpm.

Model year '87 also brought Bosch's four-channel anti-lock brake system as a 944S and Turbo option— surely one of the most worthwhile contributions to "active safety" ever devised. For passive safety, airbags for both driver and passenger became standard for the Turbo and optional for other 944s, making them the first cars available with a passenger airbag at any price. It sounds anti-performance, but only reflects Porsche's longstanding concern for safety.

More pleasant '87 developments were higher-tech sound systems and a standard split rear-seat backrest to enhance cargo carrying versatility. A noteworthy suspension change was switching from slightly positive to slightly negative steering roll (or "scrub") radius, claimed to improve driver control in a front-tire blowout or with one side of the car running on a lower-friction surface.

Conceptually, the 944S was a mixture: Turbo-type wheels, normal 944 bodywork and features, in-between price. But while twin cams and 16 valves is neat stuff, the 944S generated more mixed reactions than even the Turbo. In a September 1987 test, *Automobile* magazine founder David E. Davis groused that "in the mountains, the 944S wants to be driven between 4000 and 6000 rpm in order to strut its stuff. The 944 Turbo is lazier.... In traffic, however, the Turbo becomes finicky—it won't be lugged—and requires just as much shifting as the S."

But the S avenged itself on the track. "It is forgiving, neutral, pitchable," said Davis, "maybe the easiest car in the world to drive fast. It scrubs off speed obligingly, using both ends.... Any tendency for the tail to come around is mild and controllable.... The Turbo, on the other hand, became a mittful.... It requires both experience and finesse to be driven well at the limit." Davis put this down to tire differences: 215/60VR-15s on the S versus the Turbo's unequal-size rubber (but an S option). "The two cars, so much alike to the casual onlooker really define their quite different personas the moment a serious driver sits down behind their respective steering wheels."

Davis' sum-up strikes us as accurate and thus worth repeating: "The 944S is a true next step in the evolution of the original 944. It's lively, quick [7.7 seconds 0-60 mph] and responsive. It has no vices. At $30,850, it is expensive, but we reckon it's money well spent. The 944 Turbo is lower and meaner-looking...and it transmits an entirely different set of signals to its

driver. It feels heavy, but it is also very fast in everyday driving [6.1 seconds 0-60 mph, 10 mph faster than the S all out at 152 mph]. The combination is an exciting one, but it really isn't a 944 anymore. It ought to have its own type number."

Zuffenhausen, meantime, had been wrestling with a long-time problem: namely, how to keep at least one model reasonably affordable with a declining dollar/DMark ratio it could do nothing about. There was also a need to perk up 924 sales in Europe, which had fallen off of late. Again, the answer was about as obvious as the 944 solution had been previously.

It materialized for '87 in all markets—including the U.S.—as an upgraded 924 carrying the S suffix. Except for wheels, it retained the original 924's basic design (dash included) but carried 944 chassis hardware and running gear, plus a good many standard extras (air, tinted glass, heated power-

remote door mirrors, and power steering, windows, and antenna). With its lighter-than-944 shell and the smoother, more potent eight-valve 944 engine, the 924S had a higher top end than the old 924 Turbo and nearly matched its acceleration. It also proved quicker than the base 944, to Porsche's embarrassment. Still, the 924S was just what Porsche fans of lesser means had craved. And by late-Eighties standards, it was a relative bargain at $19,900.

For 1988, the U.S. 924S/944 shifted to a higher-power catalyst version of the eight-valve 2.5-liter four previously restricted to Europe, gaining 11 horsepower (for a total of 158 bhp) and 15 lbs-ft torque (to 155). Tighter compression (10.2 versus 9.7:1) and recalibrated DME did the trick. The factory said the manual-shift 924S was now 0.3-second quicker to 60 mph (8.0 seconds) and 3 mph faster all out (137 mph). Comparable 944 figures were

8.2 seconds and 136 mph (up from 131).

Otherwise, the four-cylinder series was little changed, though options proliferated: CD player, 10-speaker sound system, "soft look" leather upholstery. A new marketing tactic was evident in a Special Edition 924S and 944; only 500 of each were planned. These were mainly the standard issue with specific paint and interior, plus certain options from the regular list. A similar treatment called "S package" was applied to 470 Turbos, though Porsche also threw in a "Club Sport" engine with a larger turbocharger and 30 extra horsepower, plus 928 brakes. And so it goes.

The 924s and the 944s it sired were part of a new direction for Porsche, both technically and commercially. They weren't always successful in those terms, but their record of troubles and triumphs to date suggests that there's still room in this world for

four-cylinder Porsches—*provided* they're built like Porsches, drive like Porsches, and don't cost the world.

Alas, relentless price escalation—not to mention a new Japanese onslaught led by the second-generation Mazda RX-7, a 944 look-alike—has been lately been taking its toll in sales of the four-cylinder models, both in Germany and the U.S. As of December 1987, U.S. prices stood at $25,910 for the 924S, $30,325 for the 944, $35,930 for the 944S, and $38,795 for the 944 Turbo. With prices at those levels, perhaps it not surprising that in late 1987 Porsche announced a cutback in 924/944 production, ostensibly to concentrate on the more profitable 928 and 911 models. Rising prices and falling sales are the big reasons why the 944 Cabriolet has taken over four years to materialize (now due in 1989).

But enthusiasts will rejoice when it appears, for it will be a sign of Zuffenhausen's continued commitment to four-cylinder cars, and these in particular. The 924/944 may not be perfect or even "budget models" anymore, but not everyone likes the 911 and not everyone can afford a 928.

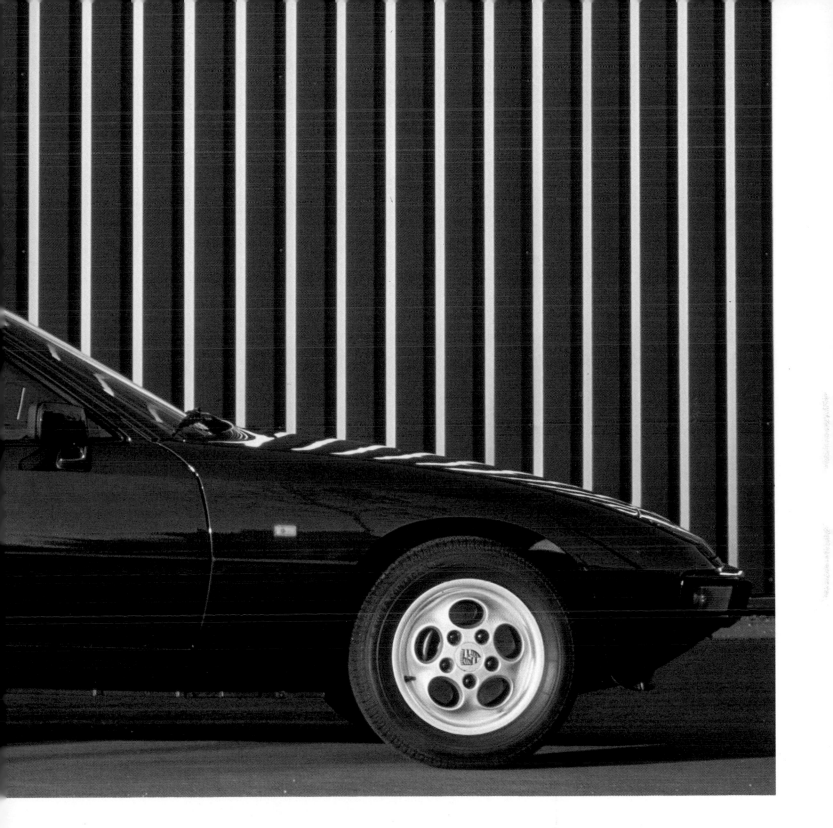

For 1988, the 924S and 944 models were further
refined, as is usual for Porsche. Prices went
up, of course, and the competition was tougher.
But, as CONSUMER GUIDE® noted, "Unlike
Japanese rivals...the four-cylinder Porsches don't
have a lot of bells and whistles. They're for
serious drivers who don't mind paying lots of
money for good performance."

CHAPTER ELEVEN

1977-87
Type 928:
Upward Bound

Thomas Alva Edison would have understood the Porsche 928. Remember his definition of genius as "one percent inspiration and 99 percent perspiration?"

Porsche chairman Dr. Ernst Fuhrmann, no small inventor himself, sweated along with his Zuffenhausen colleagues in the early Seventies, not about what was going wrong (nothing much was) but what *could*. Mainly, they worried that the 911 just might stop selling—perhaps suddenly—before they'd readied a replacement. Their concern was not unjustified. The 911 was then nearing its 10th birthday, no successor was in sight, and Porsche knew better than anyone that no car lasts forever. Why, even the evergreen 356 had run "only" 15 years. Time was running out!

It wasn't, as we now know. The 911 is still with us, eternally popular, better than ever, and showing every sign of continuing into the next millennium. But Fuhrmann and company couldn't know that back then and we can be glad. Perspiration and no little inspiration spurred their genius to produce a fabulous new Porsche unlike any that had gone before.

Other concerns prompted thoughts of a 911 successor. Most immediate was the trend to increasingly stringent emission, safety and noise standards not only in the U.S.—Porsche's most important export market—but Europe as well. This led to the idea that the air-cooled/rear-engine concept might not be able to keep pace, that it could, in effect, be legislated out of existence.

There was also the feeling that perhaps it was time for Porsche to try per-fecting a different sort of car: a "non-911." Last but not least, Porsche was envious of Swabian rival Mercedes, next door in Stuttgart, and BMW in neighboring Bavaria, both of whom were doing good business with large, luxurious GT coupes. Porsche wanted some of their action.

All this came together in project goals for a new model that, in the beginning at least, was seen as a 911 replacement. As Dean Batchelor records, it first had to have "all the quality and performance of previous Porsches" and "be capable of meeting any and all government regulations that might be conceived in the foreseeable future." The latter seemed to imply a water-cooled engine in front, which by now was seen as a given for all future production Porsches.

The new car would also have to be more refined, comfortable and luxurious than any prior Porsche so as to compete with Mercedes and BMW. And it would have to play well in America where more than half of all Porsches were sold. Of course, a long production run was assumed—at least 10 years—which meant styling that just wouldn't date.

Adding significance to these requirements was the fact that this would be Porsche's first "clean-sheet" road car. (The 356 had been VW-based, the 911 had evolved from it, and the 924 would be taken over from VW after this new project was started.) Considering that, it's amazing that the 928's basic concept was "worked out, deliberated, and decided within a few days," as Fuhrmann later told author Karl Ludvigsen.

By late 1973, Porsche had decided on a relatively large-displacement water-cooled V-8 up front, plus rear trans-axle, all-independent suspension, and all-disc brakes, the last two now long-standing Porsche traditions. Mounting the transmission aft would confer more even front/rear weight distribution with the forward engine, plus a high polar moment of inertia to aid handling and high-speed stability. A 90-degree V-8 might seem rather "American," but Mercedes had one. And it had certain advantages over the 60-degree V-6 that was briefly considered (and may have given rise to rumors of a new "911" with a front six): superior power potential and running smoothness, greater scope for future displacement increases, and compactness—important, as Fuhrmann wanted a characteristically low Porsche hood-line. Design chief Anatole Lapine deliberately planned the styling to be futuristic and a little shocking, reflecting his notion that if a car looks good right away, it soon looks old-hat.

Marque expert Batchelor notes that the decision to proceed with this "relatively thirsty and seemingly ostentatious car" now seems quite courageous, as it coincided with the OPEC oil embargo and the first Energy Crisis, events that cast rather large doubts on the commercial future of such cars. But again, Porsche needn't have worried.

Though Porsche usually premiered new models at Frankfurt, its biennial "home" show, it chose the Geneva Automobile Salon for introducing the 928, in March 1977. The choice was fitting, as the original 356 had debuted

In an unusual move, Porsche debuted the 928—its first true "luxury" car (shown as a 1983 928S)—at the Geneva Automobile Salon in March 1977. One of its unique features was the laid-back headlights.

there back in 1950. U.S. deliveries began in late '77, in time for model year 1978.

What people saw was a sleek if heavy-looking 2+2 hatchback unlike anything else on the road—a sort of German Corvette. That may seem an invidious comparison to Porschephiles, but it's logical, and not just because both cars have V-8s. For example, the 928 rode a 98.4-inch wheelbase, just 0.4-inch longer than the Chevy's. Overall size was broadly similar, though the Porsche measured 10 inches shorter (175.7 inches) and managed "+2" seating where the Vette couldn't. Both were obviously high-style high-performance sports cars, but the 928 was more weight-efficient, tipping the scales at just under 3200 pounds (versus 3500-plus). Undoubtedly, the 928's fixed-roof unit structure was lighter than the Vette's steel frame and separate fiberglass T-top body.

Efficient the 928 engine certainly was. It was not, as some thought, an adaptation of the 4.5-liter Daimler-Benz V-8. Displacement was close enough—4474 versus 4520 cubic centimeters (273 vs. 276 cubic inches)—but the Porsche unit was more oversquare, bore and stroke measuring 95 × 78.9 mm.

Pistons were iron-coated aluminum-alloy units running in linerless bores, made possible by casting the block of Reynolds 390 silicon-and-aluminum alloy like the 911 engine. Here too, the bores were electro-chemically etched to leave silicon crystals as the wearing surface. (GM tried the same thing with its Chevrolet Vega four, but it worked far better here.) The traditional forged-steel crankshaft ran in five main bearings, with forged connecting rods paired on common journals.

Naturally, there were no Detroit-style pushrods and rocker arms but a single overhead camshaft per cylinder

bank, driven by a Gilmer-type belt. Though the banks were set at right angles, their cam covers were situated to make the installed V-8 look much like the 911 flat six, which was possibly deliberate. The cylinder heads were also of alloy, again for lightness. Compression was 8.5:1, and Bosch's reliable K-Jetronic injection fed fuel from a 22.7-gallon plastic tank at the extreme rear.

With all this, rated output was 240 DIN horsepower at 5500 rpm and 257 pounds-feet torque peaking at 3600 rpm. U.S. models arrived with 219 bhp (SAE net) at 5250 rpm and 245 lbs-ft (also at 3600) thanks to a more restricted exhaust system with catalytic converter for emission control (making this a 50-state car from the first) and minor retuning for operation on lead-free fuel.

Joe Rusz of *Road & Track* rhetorically asked why Porsche built this relatively simple sohc engine and not an exotic one. The answer, according to Zuffenhausen press officer Manfred Jantke: "A Porsche is not a toy." Finance director Heinz Branitzki added that the engine was designed "with growth potential." As we'd learn soon enough, there was room for more displacement—and a second set of valves and camshafts.

A front-engine/rear-transaxle layout made as much sense for the posh, potent 928 as it did the lighter, less powerful 924. And it worked just as well: Weight distribution was a near-perfect 51/49 percent front/rear.

The standard gearbox was a specially designed Porsche five-speed manual mounted ahead of the differential (not behind like the 924's), and departing from past practice with a direct-drive (1:1) top gear. It also had a racing-style shift pattern just like early 911s, with first to the left and down, out of the normal H. Porsche engineers explained that the V-8's ample torque

would permit routine starts in second gear, so first wouldn't be needed that much and should thus be "out of the way." Most owners disagreed. Daimler-Benz did provide one major component: the no-extra-cost three-speed automatic, though Porsche designed the housing. Either transmission pulled a long-striding 2.75:1 final drive.

Power went through a special Fitchel & Sachs twin-disc clutch of fairly small diameter (200 mm/7 in.). This was chosen to match the extra rotary inertia of a thin, rigid driveshaft, which was carried in a torque tube. A helper-spring release kept clutch effort manageable (33 pounds). As heavy clutch action is common among high-performance GTs, this detail illustrates how thoroughly Porsche engineered the 928.

Nowhere was that more evident than in the suspension. Geometry looked ordinary, but wasn't. Up front were unequal-length lateral A-arms, with the lower one mounting a concentric shock absorber and coil spring that passed through the upper arm to an attachment point above. An anti-roll bar was standard.

Rear suspension was something else. *Road & Track* described it as "upper transverse links, lower trailing arms, coil springs, tube shocks, anti-roll bar," but there was more involved than that simple listing implies. Porsche proudly called it the "Weissach Axle," after the site of its Development Center not far from Stuttgart (and, incidentally, pronounced VEE-sock).

Britain's *The Autocar* noted that each lower arm "takes braking and acceleration torque loads as well as helping the ball-jointed single top link locate the wheel laterally. The bottom [arm] has its inboard pivot axis inclined outwards at the front, like a semi-trailing arm, to provide a measure of anti-squat. And at the front body pivot, it has a sort of double joint [actually an

Two views of the 928 in its initial European guise. The futuristic body design, created by American Tony Lapine, caused quite a stir then, and still turns heads today. Note the optional 16-inch-diameter "egg poacher" wheels and the smooth body-color nose with vestigial chin spoiler. The black "pips" on the bumper top are headlamp washer jets.

187

articulated mount]. The give of this in a corner under braking and decelerating forces [that ordinarily result in] an oversteer-inducing toe-out [instead] makes the outside rear wheel toe-in slightly [and] thus counters the usual accidental oversteering self-steer in the case where the driver who has entered a corner too fast lifts off, or, worse, brakes."

Like so many Porsche innovations, the Weissach Axle was an elegant solution to a thorny problem, and it marked a first for toe-compensating rear suspension in a production car. Other manufacturers have lately devised their own solutions (including full rear-wheel steering), but it took them at least a decade to follow Porsche's lead.

ZF supplied the 928's rack-and-

pinion steering which, unusually for a Porsche, was supplied with standard power assist. The latter was predictive in that it varied with vehicle velocity: minimal assist at highway speeds for proper effort and optimum control, maximum at low speeds for easy parking. Gearing was reasonably quick at 3.1 turns lock-to-lock. Again for better control, negative steering roll (or "scrub") radius was designed in to counter sudden changes in steering torque in situations like a front-tire blowout.

Speaking of tires, the 928 rolled in on low-profile 225/50VR-16 Pirelli P7s mounted on special "telephone dial" cast-alloy wheels. These state-of-the-art tires worked with the high-tech suspension to give the 928 uncanny cornering stick. "They hang on to ab-

surd limits," said *The Autocar*, "and combined with the drama-free way the car simply understeers ultimately, it is easy to dismiss the 928 as almost dull in a corner. And then you think about how fast you are going through the corner."

In fact, the 928 suspension was so remarkably compliant, absorbing most every kind of surface irregularity, that critics could hardly believe the race-car-like cling in hard driving. "True, those tires are harsh over sharp inputs," *Road & Track* pointed out, "and they're also noisy on all but the smoothest asphalt surfaces, but otherwise the ride is wonderfully supple and well controlled. The softness of the suspension on our California freeways had some drivers expecting a floaty, wallowy ride on fast, twisty undulat-

ing roads. Nothing could be further from the truth."

The big vacuum-assisted four-wheel disc brakes proved equally capable. They could reign in a 928 at up to 1g deceleration and, in *R&T*'s tests, a mere 139 feet from 60 mph. "One wonders how much the very handsome, wide-eyed wheels help in keeping the fade performance good," added *The Autocar*. "Few cars have such nakedly obvious discs . . . a piece of functional design that makes the car look all the more what it is—ideally functional." Then again, what else from Porsche?

How about performance, which was nothing less than brilliant. Despite its heft, a five-speed 928 would reach 60 mph from rest in 7-8 seconds; the automatic needed maybe a second more. Ditto the standing quarter-mile, which took 15-16 seconds with manual, by which time the speedo was reading some 90 mph. Top speed ranged between 135 and 145 mph, more than most owners would ever really need.

Of course, people had a right to expect super performance because the 928 was super expensive, arriving in the U.S. at a heart-stopping $26,000. "Hardly a bargain," sniffed *Road & Track* in 1978—when the price had ballooned to $28,500—"but clever engineering doesn't come cheaply, and few automotive design teams are more clever

Porsche described the 928 for 1978 (*both pages*) as "a sleek grand touring machine that combines exceptional roadholding and performance with luxurious accommodations for four passengers." Its maker claimed it could accelerate from 0-60 mph in 7.7 seconds and top 144 mph.

The 928's drivetrain (*above*) featured an all-aluminum, water-cooled overhead-cam V-8 with features such as hydraulic valve lifters, transistorized ignition, and CIS fuel injection. It cranked out 219 horsepower. The 928 listed at $26,000 in 1978 (*below*) and was backed by a 12-month unlimited-mileage warranty.

than the one residing in Zuffenhausen, West Germany." *Car and Driver's* David E. Davis was more emphatic: *"This is a new car.* Not a rehash, not a copy of somebody else's successful theme, not a refined agglomeration of sedan components, this new Porsche is as fresh and exciting as the first Porsche 1300 Super I drove back in 1953, and it will have the same dramatic effect on the enthusiast world's notions and perceptions. It will be controversial, but it will become the standard by which other sports cars are judged for at least the next decade."

Much of that controversy involved styling. Porsche was a bit sensitive about it, taking great pains to explain its benefits to customers and dealers alike: "The 928 was designed to have as many Porsche styling points as possible and to be clearly different from other sports cars," said a 1978 dealer training booklet. "Then there was the safety legislation [to consider].... And, of course, acceptable aerodynamic values had to be reached....

"The 928 styling with a fastback is an intentional continuation of Porsche tradition in that it is aerodynamically superior, because of the comparative short front end and a gently tapered and rounded tail, guaranteeing low air turbulence. As well as improving directional stability, the large-surface tail end also means a large passenger compartment and an outstanding amount of headroom for rear seat passengers in a sports car. We also believe that rounded forms are more interesting than clean-cut lines, which can be absorbed immediately and do not have anything new to offer the observer. The 928 looks different from each angle and remains interesting."

Porsche suggested its sales people offer this retort to prospects expressing doubts about the looks: "Naturally, every observer will need a certain amount of time to get accustomed to the unusual styling of the 928; but a car which is technically different from other cars has the right to look different, don't you agree?" Styling director

Porsche proudly pointed out that the 928 was voted
European Car of the Year shortly after its debut, the
first sports car to be so honored. The '79 (*above*) was
touted as the "best car ever" by some U.S. auto writers.
A leather interior became standard for 1980 (*opposite*).

Lapine later allowed that even Dr. Fuhrmann didn't like the 928 when he first saw it, though he later came to appreciate it.

So have many others. The 928 no longer seems strange 10 years later. As Lapine intended, time and tastes have caught up with it: "worn-bar-of-soap" shape, curvy flanks, body-color bumpers, flared wheelarches and all. Even the unusual side-window shapes have been rendered commonplace by imitators, notably the Chrysler Laser/ Dodge Daytona.

One element remains unique: the ex-posed headlamps that "stand up" when switched on and "sit down" (in re-cesses) when switched off, resting just below hood/fender level. This seemed curious a decade ago, especially since headlights on the cheaper 924 were fully concealed (via rotating panels) in an ostensibly more modern and costly style. Porsche still claims the lay-back arrangement enhances aerodynamics while ensuring that the headlights are cleaned every time the car is washed. Fine, but we'll bet the idea was lifted from the Lamborghini Miura. Some-thing else not found on the 924—or

most other cars—were separate driving and fog lamps, catering to most every sort of nighttime condition.

The 928 cockpit was the most sump-tuous ever seen from Porsche, with all the usual luxury-car features and a few that weren't. Among the latter were a standard tilt-adjustable steer-ing wheel that moved the entire in-strument cluster with it, thus insuring good gauge visibility at all times, and air conditioning that cooled not only the interior but the glove compart-ment. Teutonic thoroughness? How else to explain back-seat sunvisors

(which also make perfect blinders for worried occupants at 125 mph).

Those seats, by the way, were individual buckets and definitely of the "occasional" sort for adults; small children were a better fit. As on previous Porsches, the backrests folded down for extra cargo space. Between the rear seats was another large glove (mitt?) locker, and there were map pockets in each door concealed beneath armrests that could be pulled out four inches laterally for close support in spirited driving (an idea from R&D director Prof. Helmuth Bott). Nobody liked the op-art checkerboard cloth on seats and door panels, but it wouldn't last, and hide upholstery was available from the start.

Instrumentation was Porsche-complete, with large, central speedometer and tachometer flanked by oil pressure/voltmeter and fuel/coolant tem-perature gauges. A vertical extension of the tunnel console swept gracefully into the main panel, with a small clock at its base, surmounted by radio, climate controls and, topmost, a large air vent. Additional vents were provided in the upper front portion of the armrests (which also flowed into the dash). R&T complained about their meager airflow, but said "the heater, like the 911's, will practically fry eggs and burn toast."

Left of the center vent was a bevy of warning lights for a central monitoring system. This kept track of the usual items plus fluid levels, exterior bulb failures, and brake-pad wear. A malfunction illuminated the appropriate lamp, which spelled it out in words (like "wash fluid"), plus a large red master light simply labelled "!". Pressing a button turned off the master, which lit up when you next switched on the ignition. If the fault was serious, the master wouldn't extinguish until the problem was corrected.

Also on the 928's lavish list of standards were vacuum-operated central locking system, power windows, rear wiper, headlamp washers (activated with the windshield washer when the lights were up and lit), cruise control, wire-element electric rear-window defroster, electric remote-adjustable and heated door mirrors, and four-speaker stereo radio/cassette. Options included leather seating (which would be progressively expanded over time to include door panels and headliner), electric sliding sunroof, limited-slip differential, and factory-fitted burglar alarm.

Porsche initially made much of 928 structural safety, even claiming the stout B-pillars functioned like the 911

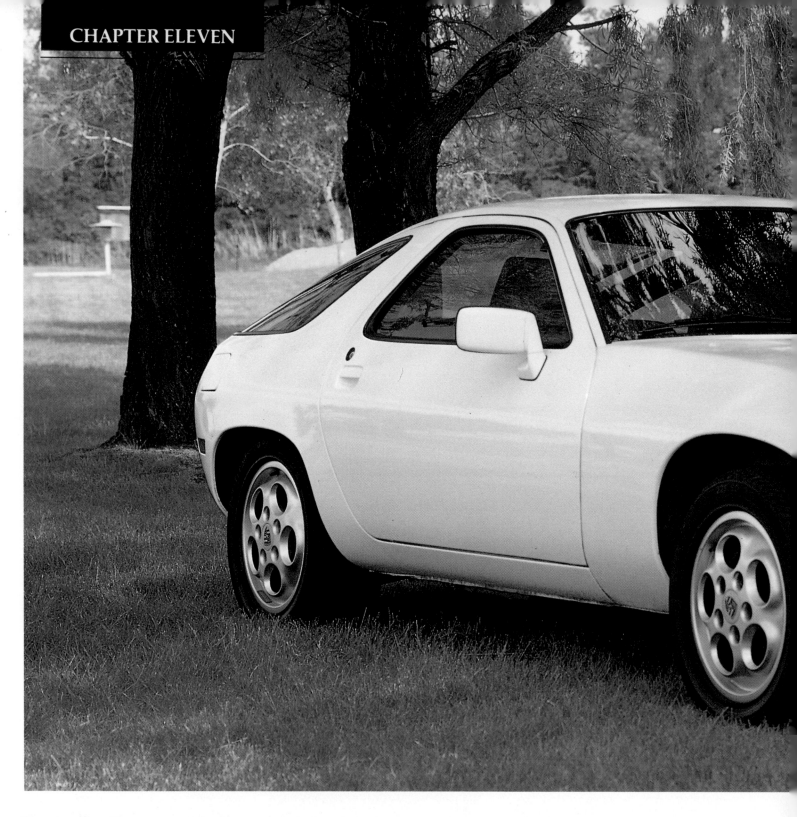

Targa's rollbar. The 928 was indeed robust but, as noted, a little portly despite the use of aluminum for doors, hood, and the detachable front fenders. (The weight of the large hatch window no doubt offset that.)

No matter, the 928 was built to go the distance. Reflecting Porsche's early-Seventies research into "long life" technology, the steel body/chassis was protected on both sides via the

unique hot-dip galvanizing process recently applied to 911s (see Chapter 8). Moreover, brake lines were sheathed in copper-nickel iron alloy and fuel lines were treated with chrome and then plastic-coated. By 1980, Porsche would offer a six-year warranty against lower-body rust on top of its normal new-car warranty for all U.S. models, following a program inaugurated in Europe a few years before.

The only requirement was that the car be inspected annually at a participating Porsche dealer. The coverage remained in effect even if the car changed hands during the six years. It was yet another expression of Zuffenhausen's commitment to top-quality craftsmanship.

For 1979, the 928 began the predictable Porsche process of logical, progressive evolution to higher levels of

In 1980, the ever-practical Porsche people boasted that the 928 had improved fuel economy: 15 city/24 highway, according to EPA. This was due to an oxygen sensor integrated into the electronic fuel injection system and a three-way catalyst. The 1981 edition went largely untouched, but the '82 (*above*) received an economy gauge. Mileage was now 16/25 EPA.

comfort, performance and refinement. The monitor warning lights moved to the instrument cluster on all models, but the big news was a more potent new 928S for Europe. A 2-mm-bore stretch (to 97 mm) brought the V-8 to 4664 cc (284.6 cid); with an interim compression boost (to 10:1) and dual exhausts, horsepower swelled to 300 (DIN) at 5900 rpm and torque to 283 lbs-ft at 4500 rpm. Also new were flat-face wheels with circumferential slots for better brake cooling, a "chin" spoiler beneath the big front under-bumper air intake, a small black-rubber spoiler at the base of the rear window, and bodyside rub strips.

The Autocar had found the original 928 slightly lacking in the "real raw performance which the 911 Series had taught us to expect," but had "no doubts now." The S's 0-60-mph time was just 6.2 seconds, top speed 152 mph, and the standing quarter-mile a 14.3-second, 97-mph trip. Noting that Britons had choice of 300-bhp Porsches that year, the magazine advised: "If you

Porsche said it didn't cover the headlamps even in the down position because left exposed they would be cleaned when the car was washed (*far left*). By 1982, the styling of the 928 looked less radical to most eyes.

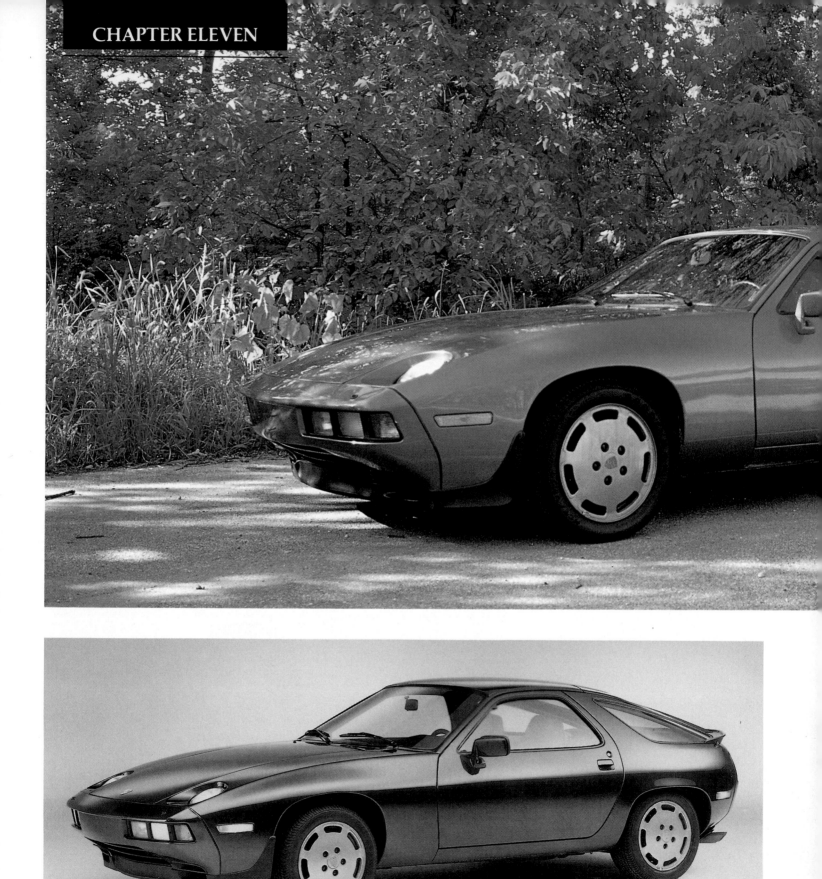

The 928 for 1982 (*bottom*) boasted larger brakes. The 928 became the 928S for 1983 (*left*), compliments of a larger 4.7-liter engine with 9.3:1 compression and an output of 234 horsepower SAE at 5500 rpm. A 0-60 run could now be made in seven seconds flat and top speed increased to 146. Rich Ceppos, of *Car and Driver*, was impressed with the big Porsche's "killer instinct coupled with luxocar civility" and concluded: "Here is one car that can do it all, friends."

want raw excitement...there is still nothing to touch the [911] Turbo—a truly fantastic car.... If it's refinement that matters, then there is no alternative to the Jaguar XJ-S. If refinement doesn't matter too much, and you can bear the road noise, then the 928S offers a tremendous amount of marvelous motor car which has restored our faith in Porsche's abilities to adapt their formidable skills to the ways of the front-engined Grand Tourer, for that is what the 928S most certainly is."

The action shifted to America for 1980. A half-point compression increase, improved emissions control (via oxygen sensor and three-way catalyst), revised valve timing, repositioned sparkplugs (4 mm closer to the combustion chamber centers), and adoption of more sophisticated L-Jetronic injection yielded only one extra horsepower but 20 more lbs-ft

torque: 265 at 4000 rpm. Top speed was harder to measure on the feds' new 85-mph speedometer, but *Road & Track* estimated 140 mph for its automatic-equipped test car. It also reported small gains in economy and off-the-line performance (0.3-second faster 0-60 mph, for instance)—nothing to write home about, but at least they weren't losses. Some 220 pounds were lost via a lighter, aluminum torque tube and hollow (instead of solid) transmission mainshaft and front anti-roll bar.

The 1980 U.S. equipment list also lost something as several items became optional: radio/cassette unit, rear wiper, headlight washers, and the big wheels and tires (replaced by five-inch-wide rims with 215/60VR-15 rubber). New extras included six-way power driver's seat (with a pair of rather hard-to-reach rocker switches

on the cushion's outboard side) and automatic temperature control for the climate system. Base price was close to $38,000 now, though that included leather seating and a pliable cargo-area cover that raised with the hatch. Late that season, Porsche offered an extra-cost Competition Group that brought over all the goodies from the European S, save its engine. U.S. emissions regulations precluded that.

There was also a second U.S. offering for 1980: the Weissach Edition. Sales were deliberately limited to 205 copies, all with Champagne Gold metallic paint, matching alloy wheels, the electric sunroof, fore/aft spoilers, and two-tone leather interior plus a matched three-piece luggage set valued at over $1000. Electronic-tune radio/cassette and automatic climate control were also included, as was a small commemorative plaque ahead of

To keep gas mileage reasonable with the enlarged 4.7-liter engine (*above*), Porsche lowered the final drive to 2.27:1. In 1983, the 928S (*right*) had escalated in price to a towering $43,000—and that was a minimum.

the shifter or automatic transmission lever. The Weissach would continue through mid-model year 1982.

The 928 took a breather for '81, though further emissions fiddling brought another incremental mileage gain on U.S. models. Not that fuel efficiency was a 928 strength (Porsche never intended that), but the addition of an economy gauge for 1982, the year's only significant change, was a telling admission in the wake of "Energy Crisis II" (1979-80). It registered instantaneous mpg in normal driving or fuel use in gallons per hour at idle or very low speeds.

Car and Driver's Pat Bedard termed the magazine's all-black 1981 test 928 "the triple distillation of evil, the baddest machine on any block.... But contrary to appearances, the 928, even with the so-called Competition Group, is a mannerly device lacking all the frenzy that characterizes rear-engined Por-

sches.... It's also a graceful performer on the track, something I wouldn't say about the 911 or any other road car in its class. In fact, I can't think of another car that offers as happy a combination of road comfort and ultimate handling." In short, the 928 was still everything Dr. Fuhrmann intended—and more.

During 1982, Porsche discontinued the original 4.5-liter 928 in Europe. This left only the 4.7-liter S, which finally got to America for 1983. On higher, 9.3:1 compression, horsepower rose to 234 (SAE net) at 5500 rpm and torque to 263 lbs-ft at 4000 rpm. Alas, price rose too—to a minimum 43 big ones—but the Competition Group was now standard. To maintain a semblance of fuel economy, Porsche lowered final drive to 2.27:1 with both transmissions. The optional automatic was now a four-speeder, again from D-B, with a better spread of ratios for performance; the five-

speed's four lowest cogs were more closely spaced for the same reason. A happy sign of an improving national economy was the return of 160-mph speedometer scales.

In U.S. trim, the manual 928S dropped to about 7.0 seconds in the 0-60-mph dash and climbed to 146 mph top speed; the automatic's numbers were 8.5 and 143 mph. As usual, magazine test results tended to bracket the official figures. Here's what *Car and Driver* and *Road & Track* reported on their five-speed S's:

	C/D	R&T
0-60 mph (sec.)	6.2	7.0
0-100 mph (sec.)	17.8	19.3
0-¼ mi. (sec.)	14.7	15.4
Mph at ¼ mi.	94	92
Top speed (mph)	144	136
Lateral accel. (g)	0.80	0.818

It hardly needed saying that despite such discrepancies, this was real Cor-

vette and Ferrari stuff. But *C/D*'s Rich Ceppos rightly observed that mere numbers couldn't capture the 928S's "double-agent personality: a killer instinct coupled with luxocar civility and the kind of bulletproof solidity you'd normally associate with a Mercedes.... The feeling around these parts is that the 928S actually gives you your money's worth in today's inflated market. Here is one car that can do it all, friends."

Road & Track mostly agreed: "The 928S is simply a marvelously competent car...as close as anything to being the complete automobile as understood in the year 1983....It's a judgment call to say a car this expensive is worth it, but at least the 928S gives you a good deal of substance to go with its costly image."

And Porsche was about to add new substance. While the U.S. 928 was all but unchanged for 1984, Europe was treated to a Series 2 version fortified in more ways than one. Bosch's advanced new LH-Jetronic injection teamed with electronic ignition and sky-high 10.4:1 compression to lift the 4.7 V-8 to 310 bhp (DIN) and 295 lbs-ft, gains of 10 bhp and 12 lbs-ft. Porsche claimed 10-12 percent better fuel economy, though you couldn't prove it by *The Autocar*, whose test S2 proved "patently" thirstier than previous 928s. But who cared? Top speed was now a thrilling 158 mph. "Even with all that luxury, you think the car is still too expensive?" asked *The Autocar*. "Get behind the wheel of the 928S Series 2, drop the clutch, floor the accelerator... and think again."

Even better was the arrival of an anti-lock braking system (ABS) as standard equipment. Since adopted by a number of other manufacturers, ABS does what any good driver would at the first sign of a skid: "pump" the brakes to get a locked wheel rolling again. The difference is that ABS does this more rapidly than any human could—up to 15 times a second—and only at the affected wheel (via electromechanical means in response to signals from wheel-mounted sensors), something no driver can. The result is a virtual absence of skidding (except on hard-packed snow or gravel) no matter how hard the brake pedal is pushed, thus preserving steering control. As past 928 brakes had been occasionally criticized for front and/or rear lock sensitivity, ABS was a very

Opposite page: The 928S offered the 1983 buyer every
conceivable luxury, such as a driver's power seat,
automatic climate control, and a cassette holder (*top*).
The back seat, while roomier than some 2+2s, was
still a bit of a squeeze for adults, and thus best left
for younger children or the family dog.

worthwhile addition, mating beautifully with the Weissach Axle to set a
new standard of active safety.

The 928S continued its upward
bound for 1985. Porsche stretched
bore another 3 mm and—the big attraction—doubled the V-8's valves and
cylinders. The result was a superb
4957-cc (303-cid) engine, with 10.0:1
compression made possible by the
four-valve head with sparkplugs centrally located above new pentroof
combustion chambers. SAE net horsepower came in at 288, while torque
swelled to 302 lbs-ft and peaked at the
lowest crank speed yet, 2700 rpm.

Wonder of wonders, America got
the revised 32-valve 928S before
Europe—and a lot of new thrills. *Car
and Driver* timed it at just 5.7 seconds to

60 mph, a mere 13.5 seconds to 100
mph, 14 seconds at 102 mph in the
standing-quarter, and 154 mph flat
out. "These are amazing figures for a
car with extremely tall economy-
oriented gearing....,"*C/D* observed
dryly, "A substantial improvement
over its predecessor."

Braking was somehow better too,
even though ABS had been left Over
There (it became standard for '86).
C/D termed the system "reassuring,
thanks to linear performance, well-
proportioned front-to-rear balance,
and excellent modulation. These characteristics contribute to the 928S's
ability to stop from 70 mph in just 175
feet. Perhaps even more impressive is
[its] ability to absorb triple-digit speeds
without fading or emitting any discon-

certing squeals, groans or odors."

There were few other changes for
1985, though Porsche's rust warranty
was up to an impressive 10 years. Inevitably, price was up too: now a cool
$50,000. Still, only a few, much cost-
lier Italian exotics were in the same
performance league, and the 928S was
far more reliable, comfortable, and
practical.

But an even better 928 was on the
way. It arrived for 1987 in all markets
save Australia as the new S 4 (denoting fourth series). "Porsche raises the
price and rewards of automotive he-
donism one more time," said *Car and
Driver*.

And how. Emissions-legal horsepower was now 316 at 6000 rpm,
torque 317 lbs-ft at 3000 rpm. Credit

The 928S 4 was the 928's first significant facelift, and was aimed at reducing aerodynamic drag. Both the front and rear ends were smoothed out and incorporated flush-mounted lamps and a wing-type rear spoiler appeared.

revised cylinder heads with larger valves, shallower (by 3 mm) combustion chambers, a narrower valve angle (27.4 degrees versus 28), altered valve timing, and a more compact new two-stage intake manifold. The last comprised twin resonance chambers or tracts—one long, one short—feeding air to the intake pipes via a Y-shaped passage from the throttle body. Below 3500 rpm, the engine breathed only through the long tract; above that, depending on throttle position, a butterfly valve in the second tract opened to increase airflow. Porsche claimed this setup ensured at least 300 lbs-ft torque from 2700 to 4750 rpm, a "fat" curve indeed.

Putting it to the ground more effectively was a larger-diameter single-disc clutch instead of the previous dual discs. The ABS all-disc brakes also got attention, with a shorter-travel

booster and larger pistons for the front calipers.

Further bolstering S 4 performance was the 928's first significant facelift, a minor one aimed at reducing aerodynamic drag. It did. Fog and driving lamps were newly flush-mounted in a smoother nose cap that added 2.3 inches to overall length, and the chin spoiler was now fully integrated with it. A revised cooling system brought thermostatically operated radiator shutters that opened only when needed as to minimize drag in high-speed driving, and twin variable-speed electric fans replaced a single engine-driven fan that consumed more power. A "detached" wing-type spoiler flew above a smoother tail, again with flush-mounted lamps. Also reducing turbulence were deepened rocker panels, a new belly pan beneath the engine, bonded-in windshield, and

windshield wipers that parked 20 mm lower.

All this added "down" to a drag coefficient of 0.34, versus 0.41 for the original 928 and 0.38 for the previous S. That was commendable considering that, in Porsche tradition, the rear tires had grown wider than the fronts: 245/45VR-16s versus 225/50VR-16s (respective rim widths were eight and seven inches).

The S 4 cockpit remained familiar 928. Body-hugging sports seats were still available, but there were two new options for the standard power seats. One was electric lumbar-support adjustable for vertical position as well as firmness. The other was "Positrol," a memory system that stored the positions of seat, lumbar support and even the door mirrors for recall at the touch of a button. Both were available for either the left or right seat which, as in

205

'86, could be fitted with optional heating elements as a separate extra.

As before, and as with recent 911s, Porsche would decorate a 928 interior to special order in any materials and/or colors the customer wanted. One example was done completely in ostrich leather for Jordan's King Hussein.

In all, the S 4 was the kind of thorough, timely update expected of Porsche, and made the 928 even more of what it always had been: a luxurious, supremely comfortable high-speed tourer capable of astounding performance on straights and curves alike. Porsche said the manual S 4 could do 0-60 mph in 5.7 seconds, but *Road & Track* reported 5.5 seconds. And though claimed top speed was no less than 165 mph now, Al Holbert, long-time Porsche racer and chief of Porsche Motorsport in the U.S., took a virtually stock S 4 to 170 mph his first time out in a series of USAC-certified speed runs at the Bonneville salt flats in August 1986. He eventually coaxed it to 171.110 mph through the flying mile and 171.296 mph in the flying kilometer, both new world records for normally aspirated production cars.

With that, the 928 surpassed the vaunted 911 Turbo as the fastest production Porsche, and not just in acceleration. The S 4 achieved truly incredible stopping distances in *Road & Track*'s March 1987 test: 137 feet from 60 mph and 234 feet from 80 mph. "That's shorter than any production car we've ever tested save the Ferrari 412, which does [80-0 mph] in 230."

The 928 is celebrating its 10th birthday at this writing. Changes for 1988 are confined to standard three-point rear seatbelts and driver's-seat Positrol, plus newly optional factory cellular-telephone preparation and warmer-looking "Supple Leather" upholstery. Alas, a weakening dollar has pushed base price to a lofty $66,710—actually some $7,390 less expensive than the 911 Turbo Targa and $15,075 below the 911 Turbo Cabriolet—but there's still nothing quite like Zuffenhausen's flagship in appearance, performance, and endurance. The latest styling successfully updates the futuristic original design, and surely no other car offers the S 4's kind of speed and solidity.

All of which suggests that the 928, like the 911, will survive into the 21st century at least. What developments can we expect in the meantime? An extended-wheelbase four-door version has been recently rumored, along with an even larger V-8.

Whatever Porsche comes up with, you can bet it'll be spectacular. Some things never change.

By 1987, the 928s had evolved into the 928S 4, the "4" denoting fourth series. Horsepower was now 316 at 6000 rpm, with a wide torque curve to back it up; putting the power to the road was a larger-diameter single-disc clutch. The ABS all-disc brakes were also improved.

1978-88 Type 911/ 930/959: Modern Maturity

I n an industry where "generation" means five years and not 15 or 20, the Porsche 911 is an octogenarian, a relic from a distant age. Except for the Alpine-Renault in France and John Z. DeLorean, nobody's designed a rear-engine car in decades. Air cooling? Ancient history.

So why does the 911 survive in today's front-engine, front-drive world? As we've seen, its basic design was inherently "right" to begin with, and Porsche has managed to keep it right for nearly a quarter-century despite unforseen developments, testimony to the firm's relentless pursuit of perfection. As a result, the 911 has been able to simply outlive most all of its original early-Sixties contemporaries, becoming more unique—and desirable—with each passing year.

And that's the heart of the matter: consistently strong sales. Also as noted, the 911 is still widely regarded as the one "real" Porsche, the one that "keeps the faith." It has thus usually been the best-selling Porsche, confounding those in Zuffenhausen who've wanted to let it die a natural death—and many observers who thought they should have. Through sheer staying power, then, the 911 has become too valuable to discard—and it won't be so long as it sells well enough to satisfy Zuffenhausen's accountants.

Not that Porsche has ever been run by bean-counters, which is why it's never stopped improving the 911. Still,

this classic-in-its-own-time got a new lease on life when Peter Schutz replaced Dr. Ernst Fuhrmann as company chairman in late 1981. Since then we've seen Porsche's first full cabriolet in two decades, the return of the mighty turbocharged 930 to America, and the best standard 911 ever, today's Carrera. We've also lately been awed by the 959, the ultimate evolution of the species—at least so far—the Porsche that "rewrites all the supercar rules."

It all makes you wonder whether the powers-that-be ever really wanted to kill the 911. Benign neglect is all that would have been required. But of course, that's never been Zuffenhausen's way.

And so it was with the 911SC, unveiled at the Frankfurt show in September 1977 alongside a virtually unchanged 930 Turbo. Essentially, this new 911 was the old Carrera 3.0 in everything but name, with the same basic specifications, styling, and features. (*The Autocar* accurately termed it "a Carrera with a broader market appeal.") Displacement was 2993 cubic centimeters (182.6 cubic inches) on identical bore/stroke dimensions of 95 × 70.4 mm (3.74 × 2.77 inches), but 8.5:1 compression and other tuning differences brought DIN horsepower from 200 down to 180 at 5500 rpm (172 bhp SAE net). However, that was slightly more than the previous 2.7 had, and a flatter, fuller torque curve with a peak 189 pounds-feet at 4200

rpm (SAE net) made the SC a lot easier and more enjoyable to drive.

In line with Porsche's move toward a single "world" specification and performance level, a U.S.-style air pump and Bosch breakerless electronic ignition (with rpm limiter) were adopted for all 1978-model 911s regardless of market. The American SC differed, however, in having the more efficient catalytic converter instead of thermal reactors as the main emissions-control device, which also improved driveability. Other mechanical changes included a stronger crankshaft with larger bearings, and the return of an aluminum crankcase (as on 1964-67 models, after which a pressure-cast magnesium piece was used).

Outside, the SC sported the Carrera's wider rear wheels and tires and flared fenders to accommodate them. A new Sport Group package option added the well-known Carrera "whale tail" and front air dam.

The 911 engine wasn't always known for tractability, but it was now. Said *Road & Track*: "The formerly finicky 911 drives like a big V-8-powered Detroit car. There's lots of torque, so constant downshifting isn't necessary even in slow traffic. No Porsche owner is going to let the revs fall to 1000 rpm in 5th gear and then attempt to accelerate. But to prove a point, we did this with the SC and the engine accepted the treatment with never a judder of protest....In the early 911s, particularly the 2-liter ver-

The Porsche 911, here a 1983 Cabriolet, has
survived for a quarter of a century because its
design was "right" from the beginning, and
because it has been continually updated.

The Porsche 911SC was unveiled at the Frankfurt Auto Show in September 1977. Shown here as a 1978 Targa, the SC was essentially the old Carrera 3.0 in everything but name, with the same basic specifications, styling, and features, among them a business-like instrument panel (*above*) and a plaid cloth interior (*below*).

sion, it takes some deft clutching to make a smooth start, but in the SC you just roll your foot off the clutch pedal and glide away. From then on you work your way up through the gears like a proper Porsche driver or cheat and slip into the appropriate cruising cog." *The Autocar* reported that in fourth gear "there is scarcely more than half a second's difference between the times for every increment between 30-50 mph [6.5 seconds in their test] and 80-100 mph [6.3 sec].... Even in fifth gear the same pattern emerges."

Some testers still complained about notchy shift action, though it usually disappeared after a few thousand miles. The linkage was made stiff on purpose (though less so starting with the '87 models, suggesting some recent rethinking in Weissach). Spring loading in the conventionally arranged gate is biased toward the far right plane (fifth/reverse), so selecting top demands conscious effort by neophytes; it's no problem for the experienced, however.

Like previous 911s, the SC tended to oversteer *in extremis* but was set up for more initial understeer, which it maintained through higher cornering speeds and forces. The bigger rear wheels and tires were adopted to ensure this, and optional Pirelli P7 tires (205/55VR-16 front, 225/50VR-16 rear) further aided what Jackie Stewart would call "traction management." Apply too much power through a hard bend and you merely got stronger understeer. Lift off the throttle in the midst of that turn, however, and the back end might try to catch up with the front. Still, it usually took a professional to elicit tail-wag now, and seasoned 911 drivers weren't bothered or surprised by it.

In all, the consensus was that the SC was a more manageable and forgiving 911. "The wide tyres have some demerits in wet weather," warned *The Autocar*. "We suffered occasionally from front-end aquaplaning under braking on water-covered roads, and understeer is also far more noticeable on wet surfaces. In these ... conditions the tail can sometimes be provoked out of line with the throttle, and understeer can also be killed by the traditional remedy of easing back on the throttle, being prepared to catch the resulting slide. Such intricacies of handling make the Porsche very much

For 1979, one could purchase the most powerful production Porsche yet, a fortified 930 renamed Porsche Turbo. Its engine, bored out by 2 mm, yielded 3299 cc and 253 SAE horsepower; a 0-60-mph run took only 4.9 seconds. This "whale-tailed" beauty listed for a towering $34,000.

a driver's car; experience with it constantly teaches new skills."

And we suspect that's part of the 911's ageless appeal: the challenge of driving it really well. Said *Car and Driver*'s David E. Davis in testing a 1978 SC Targa: "With less than 1000 pounds riding on the front wheels and about 1600 on the rear, the [911] has required increasing amounts of both science and magic...to keep it from punching holes in the hedges (backwards)....Their 30 years of experience with the rear-engine layout have made the people at Porsche very good at wringing all the very best out of [it]. But...the fast driver can still sense an angry, ill-behaved, oversteering Porsche trying to get loose. That the beast locked inside the [SC] hardly ever breaks its bonds is a tribute to Porsche engineering, but there is no doubt the beast is there....Whenever I pressed it hard, the Porsche would sort of warn me...with little twitches and flexings that combined to ask me if

I was really good enough to be doing what I was doing."

Even some professionals have never come to terms with the 911. Take Bobby Allison, who'd raced the IROC versions, as well as NASCAR stockers. His 1974 comments to *Car and Driver* still apply: "The most unnatural thing is, when you see that you are in a little bit of a problem and you lift off the gas, the problem increases. Then you're in trouble. What do you do next? With the race cars we found [that] you stomp your foot down and start steering like a wild man. But I don't think an inexperienced driver is going to do that.... The car has unique characteristics and some people may like it, but I don't."

So the overriding criticism history will register of the 911 is handling that can surprise the unwary. A defense lies in Allison's reference to *inexperienced* drivers, something most Porsche owners are not. As ever, there are cars that adapt to your style and those that

force you to adapt to theirs. The 911 has always been in the latter category, and drivers who can't—or won't—learn its ways won't ever feel truly at ease with it. As they say, "You pays your money and you takes your choice."

Design-by-decree wasn't much evident inside the SC. The cockpit was still awfully somber but free of ticky-tacky, exuding practical, high-quality functionalism as always. The steering wheel remained nearly vertical, the bucket seats "grabby" and comfortable, the five-dial instrumentation clear and informative, the steering-column stalk controls logical and within fingertip reach. Climbing into the SC was "like putting on a well broken-in pair of shoes," said *Road & Track*.

Only two real quibbles persisted. One was insufficient ventilation, especially now that opening wind-wings and rear side windows weren't available anymore. Offset pedals sprouting from the floorboard also be-

213

trayed the 911's elderly design. "The clutch is about where you'd expect the brake pedal to be," observed Davis, "and your first tentative stab at the throttle is apt to produce Stop instead of Go. As a first-time Porsche driver, you will get the pedals wrong a lot before it all begins to feel natural."

The SC marched into 1979 with standard servo-assisted brakes and a new clutch-disc hub that eliminated gear chatter at low speeds. The latter necessitated moving the engine back 30 mm (about 1.2 inches), but no handling difference was noticeable ex-

cept on the track. Porsche engineers also decreed that rear tire pressure be elevated from 34 to 43 psi. The optional Sportomatic transmission was dropped for lack of interest, and U.S. base price jumped by some $3500.

Up at $34,000 sat the most powerful production Porsche yet, a fortified 930 renamed Porsche Turbo. Widening bore 2 mm brought total displacement to 3299 cc (201.3 cid), and a new air-to-air intercooler squeezed more oxygen into every intake stroke to extract more energy from each power stroke. The intercooler was a squeeze itself,

shoehorned into the engine compartment, pushing the A/C condenser to the right side of the whale-tail's air intake. Compression remained a mild 7.0:1, but the intercooler and extra capacity sent horsepower to 300 bhp (DIN) at 5500 rpm (253 SAE net) and torque to 303 lbs-ft at 4000 rpm.

Even so, Turbo performance improved little. The larger engine was mainly to keep pace with U.S. emissions limits and new European standards then creeping in. For the record, *Car and Driver* ran 0-60 mph in 4.9 seconds and 0-100 in 12.1—still pheno-

menal going by any standard. To cope, the Turbo received the huge, ventilated cross-drilled disc brakes with four-piston calipers from the legendary 917 makes-championship GT racer. *C/D* reported they'd stopped the car from 70 mph in an excellent 168 feet. Skidpad performance was equally impressive: 0.81 g.

But again, numbers weren't the whole story. After noting that five minutes on the skidpad was "the exercise equivalent of 50 pushups," *C/D*'s Don Sherman declared that "under/oversteer is just one of the many evil traits that must be wrestled into submission before you become the Turbo's master. Steep first-gear accel-

The overriding criticism history will register of the 911, shown here as a 1979 SC, is handling that can surprise the unwary. There are cars that adapt to your style and those that force you to adapt to theirs. The 911 has *always* been in the latter category.

eration will jerk one wheel right off the ground if you light the booster exiting a slow turn. The shift linkage occasionally binds up to add a little extra excitement. And there are hidden aerodynamic curves. . . . Speed lightens front wheel loading dramatically, so understeer goes up with velocity. This would be a marvelous safety device were it not for the Turbo's lift-throttle antics. Aerodynamic understeer tricks you into lifting off the throttle when the nose starts drifting wide in a high-speed turn. It's not the thing to do. . . because this reverses longitudinal forces in the rear suspension. The back wheels toe out, the tail swings wide. . . . The Turbo won't spin easily, but things can get very scary if

you don't hang in there with some throttle and lots of steering."

All of which only confirmed Bobby Allison's opinions. Perhaps that's why Sherman concluded that the Turbo wasn't so much a car anymore as a "valuable piece of auto-art"—understandable given its high price and the high skills demanded of its driver. But then, the Turbo was never intended for just anyone. "The rest of us can dream," sighed Sherman, "and maybe toss [a] hunk of raw meat into the garage once in a while as if we actually had one."

It would be hard for any American to own a Turbo for the next few years. Though the 930 would continue in this basic form through 1986, it was of-

ficially withdrawn from the U.S. market after 1979 as a public-relations response to a new energy crunch that began that year. Of course, there are always those with extra will, and the notorious "gray market" would provide the way for a handful of European 930s to reach determined (and wealthy) U.S. buyers.

With inflation still galloping, base price of the U.S. 911SC jumped $5000 for 1980, though part of that reflected optional features made standard: electric window lifts; air conditioning, leather-rim steering wheel, under-dash console, and matte-black exterior trim. The Targa continued about $1500 upstream of the coupe. Federal law now mandated speedometers

The Porsche 911SC received a more efficient three-way catalytic converter and higher 9.3:1 compression for '80, standard halogen headlamps and rear seatbelts for '81. The 1982 SC, pictured, added a heated right door mirror, headlight washers, and leather front seats.

reading no higher than 85 mph—absurd for a high-performance car like this—with emphasis at the 55-mph mark to make sure you observed the national speed limit. Like the starter interlock of 1974, this nonsense wouldn't last, and full speedometer scales would again be legal for 1985.

An even odder change appeared on the 1980 SC in deference to the "double-nickel": The accelerator rested considerably below brake-pedal level, Detroit-style, because the factory thought this would be more comfortable at 55 mph! Throttle travel was unaffected, though, and a degree of adjustment was built in so that, with an hour of wrench work, the pedals could be properly aligned to facilitate heel-and-toe shifting.

Road testers had long since called the 911 flat six "venerable," but this year's 3.0-liter felt quite youthful, thanks to a more efficient three-way catalytic converter that allowed higher 9.3:1 compression for improved driveability and fuel economy. Rated power and torque were unchanged, but there were no peaks, no valleys, no flat spots in acceleration, and the engine would still lug down to ridiculously low revs in the upper gears without protest.

As with the 928, Porsche issued a special Weissach Edition 911 coupe during model year 1980. It was limited to the U.S., and copies were limited to just 400. Priced at $32,000, it was perfect for those who felt the basic $27,770 coupe lacked status, being nothing so much as a Turbo without the blower and wide-body rear end. Standards comprised stiffer shocks, remote-adjustable electric door mirrors, power antenna, sealed-beam halogen headlamps, leather cockpit trim, wider wheels, and special paint. Porsche press blurbs said the Weissach offered a 15-percent savings over the cost of these items ordered individually, but the hype was unnecessary as there weren't enough cars to go around anyway.

Further SC upgrades appeared for 1981: standard halogen headlamps and rear seatbelts, plus an anti-rust warranty extended from six to seven years (perhaps as a palliative for "sticker shock"). Little else was changed. The '82 story was much the same, Porsche adding a heated right door mirror, improved sound system, headlight washers, and leather-covered front seats. (Vinyl remained in back, practical for the toddlers most likely to ride there.)

The happiest happening of '82 bowed at the Geneva show in March: the long-rumored 911SC cabriolet, Porsche's first factory-built convertible since the 356. (Because of its fixed rollbar, the versatile 911 Targa was not considered a true convertible.) As with its fondly remembered predecessor, the body was built by Porsche's Reutter division.

A warm reception greeted the revived cabrio on its 1983 U.S. debut despite a rather chilling $34,450 base price. There was obviously no Max Hoffman working here, but this new 911 was far more civilized than any 356 Speedster.

Though a manual top might seem needlessly cheap at that price, it kept Cabriolet curb weight the same as the SC coupe's and 30 pounds below the Targa's. Typical of Porsche engineering thoroughness, the top had three bows, spring-loaded self-adjusting steel cables, and a concealed steel panel in front to keep things taut and snug at high speed. Porsche claimed this design also afforded minimal heat loss in winter (air conditioning was available for summer) and low wind noise. *Road & Track* was divided on ease of opera-

The 911 began receiving new emphasis when Peter Schutz became company chairman, as evidenced by the appearance of a 911SC cabriolet at the 1982 Geneva Auto Show. Though a bit slower than the SC coupe (*both pages*), it added extra excitement and prestige to the 911 lineup.

The 911SC cabriolet (*both pages*), Porsche's first
factory-built convertible since the 356, made its
American debut for 1983. Although one might have
expected a power top for the $34,450 list price, the
manual top did help to keep curb weight the same as that
of the SC coupe and 30 pounds below the Targa.

tion, but at least the top was quite compact when folded, allowing retention of the normal back seats. A conventional boot covered the bits and pieces, and a tonneau was available at extra cost. Top down, the 911 was far more streamlined than any 356 cabrio. The rear window was plastic, broadly wrapped for good outward vision, and could be zipped out for copious top-up ventilation.

Peculiar for Porsche was its claim that "the aerodynamic lines of the Cabriolet made it possible to match the 140-mph top speed of the 911SC coupe." The drop-top was nowhere near as slippery, topping out at 124 mph in *R&T*'s test. In acceleration it could stay with the coupe up to 60 mph or so, then dropped back as air drag began to tell—and that was with the top

up. But it mattered little. Where else could one get open-air pleasure *and* traditional 911 virtues?

Speaking of which, the Cabriolet had several virtues of its own. For one, it was very tight for a convertible. CONSUMER GUIDE®'s auto editors didn't hear any rattles from body or top (in a pre-production prototype, no less), a tribute to the literal integrity of the 911 hull. In fact, the coupe bodyshell proved so rigid that little reinforcement was needed to restore the torsional stiffness lost in slicing off the roof. It also testifies to Zuffenhausen's painstaking workmanship. (A detachable Targa-type rollbar was optional but added nothing to rigidity.)

Another nice feature was that with the top down and windows up there was none of the uncomfortable buffet-

ing that plagues so many modern convertibles. *CG* drivers found this true even at modestly illegal speeds. But the crowning touch was that this was a Porsche 911 convertible, with all that implied for excitement and prestige.

It also implied that the 911 was getting new emphasis in the scheme of things at Porsche. The reason was recently installed company chairman Peter Schutz, who approved the Cabriolet for production. Unlike those who'd long since written off the rear-engine Porsche, Schutz felt it should be "back on the front burner," as *Road & Track* reported. His reasoning was sound. Despite ups and downs in 928 and 924 sales, the 911 was still good for about 9000 units a year, and it had a vast, loyal, and enthusiastic following. Under Schutz, the 911 would continue

to be upgraded, but more aggressively—and often—than before. The Cabriolet was a first step. A new Carrera would be the second.

Reviving the great name used off and on since 1953 was a grand way to announce a new lease on life for the 911. Aside from identification script on the engine lid and standard foglights in the front spoiler, the '84 version looked little different from the superseded SC, but different it was.

Reflecting both the times and Porsche philosophy, the long-running flat six was enlarged to 3164 cc (193 cid)—its fifth such increase since 1964—achieved by combining the Turbo engine's 74.4-mm stroke with the SC's 95-mm bore. That brought total capacity to more than 50 percent above the original 2.0 liters, eloquent testimony

to the engine's design durability. Fuel injection switched from Bosch's mechanical K-Jetronic to the same firm's sophisticated new Digital Motor Electronics (DME), or "Motronic," system, a computer-controlled multipoint setup with integrated electronic ignition.

Together with slightly higher 9.5:1 compression (via reshaped pistons and combustion chambers), SAE net horsepower returned to 200 at 5900 rpm, a gain of 28 bhp over 1983. "More useful," observed *Road & Track*, "are a 12 lbs-ft increase in torque [to 185 lbs-ft at 4800 rpm], sharply improved flexibility, and no less than a 4-mpg increase in EPA fuel economy." Brakes received thicker rotors, larger vent passages, and 928 proportioning control to match the higher performance.

That potential was fully realized. "Like every major 911 engine that has gone before, this one produces tangible improvements," said *Road & Track*. "At lower speeds the Carrera isn't a quantum leap ahead of its predecessor, nor does it need to be. But as momentum gathers, so does steam. With fewer than 400 miles on its odometer, the test car's 6.2 seconds for the 0-60 sprint beat the 1983 car by 0.7 sec; by the quarter-mile mark it had gained 0.9 sec...and was fully 8 mph faster [14.6 sec at 96 mph]."

A fully run-in Carrera gave *Car and Driver* even better numbers: 5.3 seconds to 60 mph and 13.9 seconds at 100 mph in the standing quarter-mile. Top speed? A blazing 146 mph. In Carrera trim "...the growling, thrumming flat six remains in the forefront of the

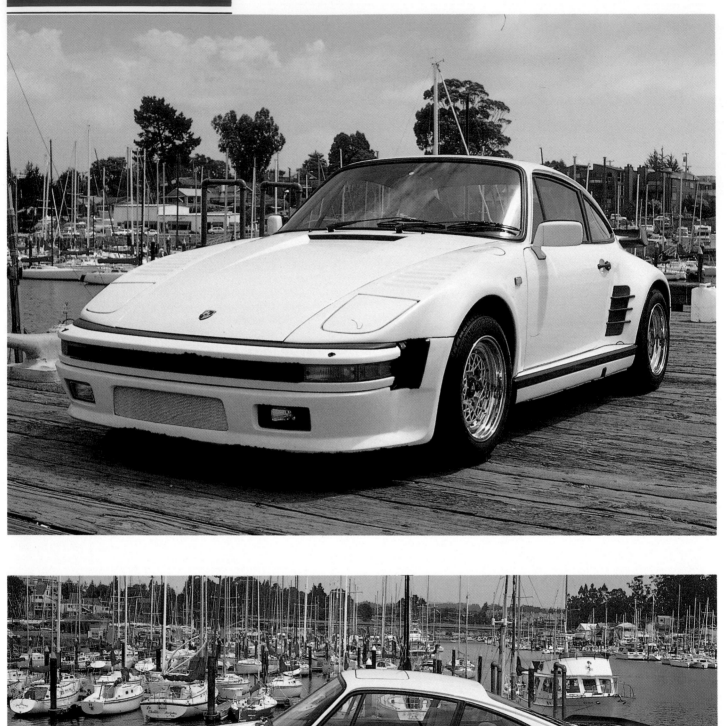

Porsche had originally developed the hidden-headlight "slant-nose" front end for the racing 935. It had been widely copied in the aftermarket, so Porsche decided to offer its own production version, the "Turbo slant-nose modification option," stupefyingly priced at $23,244.

world's grunt-and-git, instant forward rushers," waxed tester Larry Griffin.

"Just as impressive," countered *R&T*, "is the Carrera's newfound flexibility. With each enlargement the 911 engine has won low-speed torque, but this time it has reached the point where it can be driven 'like other cars.' It tugs lustily on the tires from 1000 rpm in 4th, and even at 40 mph in 5th—wonder of wonders!—there's enough acceleration for virtually any traffic situation on level ground." It was thus odd indeed that Porsche now fitted a warning light (in the tachometer face and hooked to the DME system) that advised the driver when to upshift for best economy. This was no econocar,

but the Carrera proved surprisingly frugal for its performance. *C/D* saw only 17 mpg, but *R&T* registered 24.5 mpg on a gentle highway run and 20.5 overall.

In short, the 911 had become better once more, no mean feat for an air-cooled rear-engine car in the mid-Eighties. "Not so long ago," recalled *C/D*'s Griffin, "911s were beginning to feel like a bad joke that had run much too long in the telling. Over the past five years, Porsche has turned the tables...."

Not that there wasn't room for improvement: poor ventilation and balky shifter (still!), too-lively steering, anachronistic ergonomics, and—as ever—

price. The minimum now started at $31,950, and options cost a bundle. Cruise control added a hefty $320, 16-inch rolling stock no less than $1580, AM/FM/cassette stereo another $600, electric sunroof $940, and the whale-tail plus a deeper front airdam $1325. Porsche even had the nerve to charge $70 for a black headliner and $40 for a closer-set (extended-hub) steering wheel.

Those who missed the 930 could order their Carrera coupes with a new package option called "Turbo Look." This gave the buyer the blown model's exterior sheetmetal and beefier chassis for a frightening $12,000. If Porsche hadn't been bleeding buyers before, it

223

certainly seemed to be now, and grumblings of discontent could be heard for the first time.

But the press and public still seemed willing to grin and bear it all. "The Carrera is a car to get down and wrestle with," said Griffin. "In exchange you will come away winded, exhilarated, and probably laughing out loud, sure of why it was that you first came to love the evil weevil, and sure that you still do."

There was even more to love for '85. The Turbo Look kit was extended to the Targa and Cabriolet, power front seats were offered (the driver's as standard, the passenger's at extra cost), the shift linkage was revised (though to no real effect), a "safety" windshield became standard, and central locking optional. Also new was an expanded warranty: two years/unlimited miles on the entire car (formerly one year/unlimited miles), 10 years on rust perforation (up from seven), and five-year/50,000-mile powertrain coverage.

During 1984, Porsche AG had taken over its U.S. sales, service, and marketing (from VW of America), creating Porsche Cars North America (PCNA), headquartered in Reno, Nevada. Zuffenhausen was also still moving toward common specifications and performance for all models regardless of where they were sold so as to sim-

Coinciding with Porsche's new distribution setup was its decision to reintroduce the fabled 930 to the U.S. lineup for '86. Now called 911 Turbo and priced at $48,000, it was almost the same as the European version, as shown. Though it had 29 more horsepower than the '79 Turbo, performance differed little.

plify production and eliminate bother-some gray-market traffic, particularly in the U.S.

Coinciding with the new distribution arrangement was Porsche's decision to reintroduce the fabled 930 to the U.S. lineup for 1986. Now simply called 911 Turbo and base-priced at $48,000, it was all but identical with the European version. Performance was little changed from the last 1979 U.S. model's despite an impressive 29 extra horsepower—a total 282 bhp at 5500 rpm—achieved via three-way catalyst, oxygen sensor, and computer control for the fuel injection (mechanical Bosch KE-Jetronic). Even better, the beast was more predictable and safe in really fast work, thanks to wider-than-ever 9-inch wheels mounting 245/45VR-16 tires front and 225/50VR-16s rear.

A real 930 stood to be a lot better than a Turbo Look Carrera, but *Car and Driver* wasn't so sure. Both the market and technology had changed a good deal since 1979, and with them, our perceptions. The Turbo hadn't changed as much, and that was the problem.

C/D's Rich Ceppos admitted that "in the last six years it's obviously been taught some manners. Antics that would have spun you out [in a 930] hardly faze [the 911 Turbo].... The 930 was deadly on the curves and awesome on the straights. The 911 Turbo is mellower in both areas.... Back in 1979, there really wasn't any other car in America that offered anywhere near the 930's kind of speed. Today, however, we're in the middle of a horsepower boom [and] the march of technology has produced a whole flock of turbo cars with much better manners.... Taking a cold, hard look at the 911 Turbo's vexing return, we get the feeling that fond memory may have been better left undisturbed."

Minor refinements attended this year's Carrera. Front seats were lowered for additional headroom and a heavy-duty windshield cleaning system became optional. Porsche again fiddled with the climate system and shifter, though testers felt neither was still really right even after all this time. Two more 911 complaints also persisted: wind leaks and minor rattles. These seemed downright odd for a design that had been around over 20 years, let alone a Porsche, and were big letdowns in light of towering prices

Porsche's 911 offerings for 1987 (*both pages*) received refinements, among them a 14-horsepower increase (to 214) and a new five-speed transaxle with cone-type synchronizers for the Carrera. The Turbo could be ordered as a Coupe, Targa, or Cabriolet, the last listing at $78,415 without options.

The 911 Carreras, here a Targa, received a few more options as standard for 1988: headlight washers, heavy-duty windshield cleaning, central locking, and electronic cruise control.

that in part reflected a fair degree of hand craftsmanship—which, come to think of it, may have produced these problems.

More encouraging was more power for the '87 Carreras. Thanks mainly to recalibrated DME electronics, horsepower rose by 14, to 214 (SAE net) at 5900 rpm, and torque by 10 lbs-ft, to 195 (still at 4800 rpm). A separate thermostatic electric fan was added for the secondary oil cooler in the right front fender, and the clutch switched from mechanical to hydraulic actua-

tion. But the most telling change was a new five-speed transaxle with cone, not Porsche ring-type, synchronizers. More positive shifting was again claimed, but the improvement was minimal at best. Apparently, even Porsche couldn't completely perfect the long linkage dictated by the rear-engine layout.

The Turbo was mostly a carryover for '87, but could be ordered as a Coupe, Targa, or Cabriolet. The latter cost $78,415 sans options—virtually unattainable by mere mortals. Both

Carrera and Turbo gained electric front-seat height and cushion-angle adjusters. So-called "full" power seats, with electric fore/aft and backrest-angle movement added, were standard on Turbos, optional for Carreras. Height-adjustable power lumbar support was another new separate option, borrowed from the 928S 4.

By this point, the Turbo's styling had been widely copied in aftermarket body kits for ordinary 911s. So had the hidden-headlamp "slant nose" developed for the racing 935 (see Chapter

13). Porsche's decision to end *those* rip-offs had prompted the Turbo Look option. Now came a new package, the "Turbo slant-nose modification option," stupefyingly priced at $23,244. Available for any Turbo or the Carrera coupe, it comprised the *Flachbau* ("flat profile") schnoz with flip-up headlamps surmounted by washboard louvers, plus wide 935-style back wheelarches with grilled, forward-facing rectangular air scoops and extended rocker panels reminiscent of running boards. It all came from Zuffenhausen's new *Sonderwunsch* (special wish) department, a sort of in-house customizing operation.

Outspoken Brock Yates drove a Slant Nose Turbo Cabriolet for the September 1987 *Car and Driver*. Its sticker read a breathtaking $106,254, though at least that included the optional power top (also available for Carrera cabrios) and $500 in gas-guzzler tax (another Washington invention). It had to be some kind of record price, even for a recent Porsche. Yet, the more the 911 changed, the more it seemed to stay the same. Yates carped about the awkward pedal position just like Dave Davis a decade before, and oversteer was still present, though easier to check on this particular car.

But the 911 was as compelling as ever. "We don't mean to imply that, in Turbo Cabriolet Slant Nose form, the 911 is any more reasonable than it ever was. Nor do we deny that it is a very old warhorse—and yet it never seems to age like a normal car. Annual refinements, visual tricks, and new permutations keep the 911 in a class of one. A hundred-grand window sticker by no means guarantees perfection, but it does assure you of the most potent dose ever of the Porsche essence: fearsome speed and thoroughbred sounds in a back-road dance partner that you will never forget."

The 911's 24th year was a quiet one. All '88s gained standard three-point rear seatbelts (replacing lap belts) and a new "Soft Look" leather option, while a few more extras became standard for Carreras: headlight washers, heavy-duty windshield cleaning, central locking, and cruise control, which was now electronic instead of pneumatic. The Slant Nose Modification was made a separate model called 930S, available in all body styles.

New for Carrera coupes was a special Club Sport option. Recalling the grand dual-purpose 356 Carreras, it came virtually ready to race in weekend production-class events. Specifically, it deleted the standard air conditioning, foglights, sound insulation, undercoating, power seats, and even the back seats. In exchange, it received fortified shock absorbers, front and rear spoilers, manual sports seats, and a modified engine with hollow-stem valves, reprogrammed electronics, and a correspondingly higher rev limit (6840 rpm). Apparently expecting Club Sports to be used and abused, Porsche backed them with only two-year limited-mileage warranty and did not offer its normal 10-year anti-rust guarantee.

And so the 911 just keeps going on and on. Where it goes from here is anyone's guess, although all signs at this writing point to a major redesign that will give us a virtually all-new 911 by 1989 or '90, with many new features—but the same beloved looks and layout. Four-wheel drive is rumored, probably as an option, as is a more potent Turbo with twin blowers. We can also expect a carefully reshaped nose and tail to bring aerodynamics up to modern snuff, plus a more up-to-date instrument panel.

Forecasting much of this is the car built to explore the 911's future: the 959. Finalized as a prototype in September 1983 and paraded on the 1984 international auto-show circuit, it was prompted by the advent of Group B, a production-based rally class with rules written to permit four-wheel drive, turbocharged engines, and specialized

bodywork. Typical of Porsche, exactly 200 roadgoing 959s would be built, along with the needed number of competition cars and specialized racing versions called 961.

Then the worldwide motorsports governing group suddenly cancelled Group B as too dangerous, thus ending the careers of the Ford RS 200, Peugeot Turbo-16, and other homologation specials after the 1986-87 season. But not the 959, which won the grueling Paris-Dakar rally in 1986. It may also take Zuffenhausen into a very foreign competitive arena: off-road racing.

Porsche Engineering's latest *tour de force* almost deserves a separate chapter. It's obviously 911-based, with a similar galvanized-steel center structure and the same 89.4-inch wheelbase. The cockpit is also familiar fare. Otherwise, most everything else is different.

Start with the purposeful lower body. It's not only been shaped for good surface aerodynamics but slotted (via a profusion of ducts and vents) for controlled airflow through it. The results: a 0.31 drag coefficient and—the real achievement—zero lift front and rear. To save weight, doors and the front lid are made of aluminum, the nose cap of flexible polyurethane plastic, and the rest of the front and rear structures of high-strength Kevlar composite, reinforced with fiberglass. The imposing, muscular styling speaks for itself, highlighted by a distinctive front with fixed, laid-back headlamps; ledge-type rocker skirts; and broad-beamed 935-style tail section with large, beautifully sculpted-in wing spoiler and full-width tail lamp assembly.

Hulking beneath enormously flared wheelarches are massive, state-of-the-art wheels and tires. The former are five-spoke 17-inch-diameter alloys, eight inches wide front, nine inches rear. They're shod with a special super-performance version of the Bridgestone RE71, developed by the Japanese company at Porsche's request (a big honor), sized at 235/45VR-17 fore and 255/40VR-17 aft. As first used on Porsche's 1980 Le Mans racers, hollow wheel spokes provide more air for the tires and, happily, a smoother ride than would otherwise be possible. The tires are designed to run flat for at least 50 miles after a blowout (so no spare is provided), and

As long as Porsche continues to lavish development on it, the 911 will just keep going on and on. *Car and Driver*, speaking of the '87 Turbo, said it gives "the most potent dose ever of the Porsche essence: fearsome speed and thoroughbred sounds in a back-road dance partner that you will never forget."

electronic sensors within the wheels warn of any pressure loss.

Porsche's vast experience with 911-based racers is evident in the 959 engine. Power is supplied by a special short-stroke (67-mm) flat six displacing 2849 cc (174 cid) and chockful of exotica: twin overhead cams per bank, four valves per cylinder, water-cooled heads, Motronic injection/ignition, titanium con rods and—the real kick—*twin* KKK turbochargers. A system of crossover pipes and bypass valves provides "staged" turbo operation. Only the port-side blower is used below about 4000 rpm; the starboard unit is progressively phased in as revs approach that. Despite modest 8.3:1 compression, output is a heady 450 bhp (DIN) at 6500 rpm and 369 lbs-ft peak torque at 5500 rpm.

Putting it to the ground are a six-speed transmission and a unique full-time four-wheel-drive system. The gearbox (called G 50) is basically the five-speed unit from the production Carrera with an extra-low first gear added, ostensibly for off-road use and thus labelled "G" (for *Gelände*), but needed often in town driving. Power is taken aft in the usual 911 way, to the front wheels via a tube-encased driveshaft running forward from the gearbox to a differential with an integrated multi-plate clutch running in an oil-filled chamber. Varying the clutch's oil pressure determines the amount of torque delivered to the front wheels, so there's no need for a torque-splitting center differential as used on many 4WD cars. A locking rear differential is also provided.

Front/rear torque apportioning occurs manually or by selecting one of four computer-controlled programs. The "Traction" program locks the front clutch and rear diff for maximum pulling power off-road or in mud and snow. "Ice" splits torque 50/50. "Wet" divides it 40/60, but increases rear-wheel power with increasing acceleration. "Dry" also offers a 40/60 split, but can provide up to 20/80 in all-out acceleration.

It's all done in response to wheel-mounted speed sensors that also serve the 959's anti-lock braking system (developed jointly with Westinghouse). The brakes themselves are basically production 911 Turbo with larger-diameter front discs (12.7 inches). The suspension employs double-wishbone geometry in classic racing style, plus twin shock absorbers and concentric coil springs at each wheel. The shocks in each pair have separate variable damping functions, again computer-controlled; one set stiffens as speed rises; the other set lowers the car slightly from 95 mph to improve aerodynamics. A manual override is also provided.

The 911 Carrera Targa (*bottom row*) listed for $45,830 for 1988. An additional $4485 bought the Carrera Cabrio (*top*), both shown here in European guise, which in the late Eighties differed little from American-spec models.

The ultimate Porsche, the 929, was finalized as a prototype in 1983 and paraded at the 1984 auto shows. Although 911-based, almost everything differed except the center structure. Only 200 were to be built.

What's the 959 like to drive? Mel Nichols almost ran out of superlatives in his report for the November 1987 issue of *Automobile* magazine. His was a "sport" model, lacking the rear seats, automatic air conditioning, additional sound insulation, and right door mirror of the so-called "comfort" version, but weighing 110 pounds less: 2977 pounds. That made for just 6.1 lbs/bhp (versus 7.1) and truly phenomenal acceleration: 0-60 mph in 3.7 seconds, 0-100 mph in 8.5, and a top speed beyond 190!

But what most impressed Nichols was how the 959 used its formidable power. In town it was as docile as any 911 and much quieter. On the highway it was so stable that 100 mph or more felt like 60, even in driving rain.

In corners, it was simply a revelation: "At different times, I lifted off when near maximum power, and all the car did was tighten its line neatly at the front. There was no way that tail—so deadly in these circumstances in a 911—was going to come around. So here was the 959's supreme message...supreme safety. What I liked was the clarity and accessibility of the handling that went with it." The brakes naturally played a big safety role, routinely hauling down from 150-plus with an utter lack of drama.

"No car has ever affected me as deeply as this one," Nichols concluded. "Its performance alone makes it more thrilling than any other car I have driven, but I love it most because it gave so much and asked for so little...."

That is Porsche's achievement. It has built a racing car for road drivers, with it mattering little whether the road is wet or dry. As magnificent as that achievement is, the good news is that it is the tip of an iceberg: Other Porsches will gain the 959's technology and degrees of its prowess. And other manufacturers have been shown the challenge and given the notion of what is possible."

Nichols is right. Tomorrow's 911s may not have everything that's in today's 959, but they will have some. And that's the happiest way we know to end this chapter. For the most classic of Porsches, the future not only seems assured, but rosier than ever, and enthusiasts just can't wait. Live long and prosper, 911—as we know you will.

The Production Racers: 40 Years of Improving the Breed

Ferdinand Porsche passionately believed that "racing improves the breed." So did his son Ferry and most all their associates. Add in a love of driving and no little design skill and you understand why Porsches are "engineered like no other cars in the world," to borrow a Mercedes slogan. This also explains why Porsche has won more races—and more *kinds* of races—than any of its rivals.

Of course, racing improves the breed only if you follow that old saw in most everything you do, day after day, year after year. Porsche has, and does. Nowhere is this more evident than in the stream of production-based competition cars that have been part of Porsche history from the start.

The very first one, in fact, appeared barely a month after the first prototype 356/2 was completed in Gmünd: a silver roadster driven by Herbert Kaes in an open road race at Innsbruck, Austria on July 11, 1948. It wasn't in the least modified, running with even a normal windshield and road wheels. It could do only 84 miles per hour flat out, but the little 356 won its class. With that modest success began the unprecedented story that has seen production-based Porsches win most every type of contest they've ever entered to this very day.

Porsche's earliest competition successes occurred mainly in rallying—not American-style events, where precise timing is as important as speed, but the European kind, where speed is almost everything and performance on "special stages" crucial. In 1950-51, Porsches with 1.1- to 1.5-liter engines racked up class wins in the Swedish Rally (twice), the Alpine and Tavemunde rallies, and the demanding Tour de France. These were most often specially prepared Gmünd coupes called 356SL. A 1.1-liter carried the colors on the difficult Liege-Rome-Liege Rally in '51, Huschke von Hanstein and Petermax Müller finishing

Porsche's long-tailed 935/78 "Moby Dick" racers appeared in 1978, cranking out 845 horsepower at 8200 rpm, thanks to developments like four valves per cylinder and water-cooled heads.

The Porsche factory converted five 1949 Gmünd 356 coupes for competition. The car pictured raced in Europe, was later sold to John von Neumann, who made it into a roadster and raced it in 1952-53.

second in class after achieving close to 100 mph on only 46 horsepower. The following year, the 1.5-liter coupe of Helmut Polensky and Walter Schlüter won the event outright, and other Porsches finished third, fourth, ninth, and 10th overall.

Porsche first contested Monte Carlo that same year, and again met with instant success. A coupe completed the road portion of this always-treacherous rally without a single penalty point.

The later Super 90s and Carreras went on to even greater heights. Though too numerous to list here, their championship wins stand as exciting testimony to their stamina and performance under the most trying conditions.

Porsche first assaulted the prestigious 24 Hours of Le Mans in 1951. The plan was to run four 356SLs, but two were damaged in practice and a third, pieced together from those and another car, crashed during the race. Auguste Veuillet, the French Porsche distributor, had better luck in the aluminum-bodied Gmünd coupe he'd persuaded Ferry Porsche to let him run. With nothing more than careful tuning and aerodynamic fender skirts all-round, it won its class at an average 73.5 mph and finished 20th overall against much more potent machinery. Veuillet returned in 1952 with a 1.5-liter car, upped his average to 76.7 mph and again finished first in class and 11th overall. The following year would be the SL's last at Le Mans—and disappointing too, as mechanical problems precluded a finish.

Predictably, Porsche's emergence in U.S. competition was spurred by Max Hoffman, the energetic Austrian who almost single-handedly introduced the country to import cars. In fact, the make's American racing debut came in October 1951 with his drive in a 356 cabriolet to a class win at the Mount Equinox hillclimb in Vermont. Hoffman later brought over three Le Mans-prepped coupes, though they didn't do that well. Their best showing was in July 1952 at Torrey Pines, California, where John von Neumann (who would set up Porsche's West Coast sales operations) won the 1500-cc modified class.

The 1.5-liter cars fared better in Europe. A highlight was the 1953 running of the Mille Miglia, the formidable 1000-mile dash up and down the

"boot" of Italy. Driven by Count "Johnny" Lurani and rally ace Konstantin "Tin" Berckheim, a modified 1.5 beat every car in its class and finished 46th overall.

These early victories prompted development of the Type 528/1500 Super competition engine, initially with 70 DIN horsepower, though it soon had more. It would ultimately power the first Type 550s (see next chapter), thus beginning the legend of the racing Spyders.

As its cars improved, Porsche widened its horizons. A squadron of Type 550RS prototype coupes and 1.5-liter production cars went to Mexico in 1953 for the third *Carrera Panamericana* (Mexican Road Race). The 550s finished 1-2 in the "Light Sports" class, while a 356 managed eighth overall and first in the production class at an

average 83 mph. The latter was really more impressive than it sounds, for the class was then wide open and the cars that placed higher than the Porsche were all larger and considerably more potent: Mercedes 300SLs, Ferraris, Lancias. The 550s repeated their performance in 1954 at the final *Carrera*.

The 356A, Speedster, and 1500GS Carrera greatly swelled Porsche's numbers in U.S. production-class racing. Dr. Richard Thompson, the "flying dentist" later to win fame with Corvettes, kicked things off in 1954, the year the Sports Car Club of America (SCCA) first ran national championships. He tied with Art Bunker for the F-Production crown that year, both of them having driven 1500 Super cabriolets. The light and competitive Speedster gave the same title to

Bengt Sonderstrom the following year, after which F/P became a Carrera parade. Porsche's stranglehold on the class didn't end until 1960, when SCCA no longer classified cars strictly by displacement.

The Speedster proved an ideal race car almost from the first. John von Neumann teamed with Erich Bucklers in a 1500 Super to finish eighth in the 1954 Torrey Pines six-hour event the Saturday after Thanksgiving, then won the 1500-cc production class on Sunday. Speedsters have been winning ever since, though they're now too valuable for anything but carefully staged vintage contests. Yet, it's still not uncommon for a Speedster to rocket up Mt. Equinox (now a venue for the Vintage Sports Car Club of America) in fine time or for a well-driven example to run newer iron

Porsche sent a squadron of 550RS prototypes and 1.5-liter production cars (*left*) to the *Carrera Panamericana* in 1953. The 550s finished 1-2 in "Light Sports" and a 356 finished eighth overall and first in class.

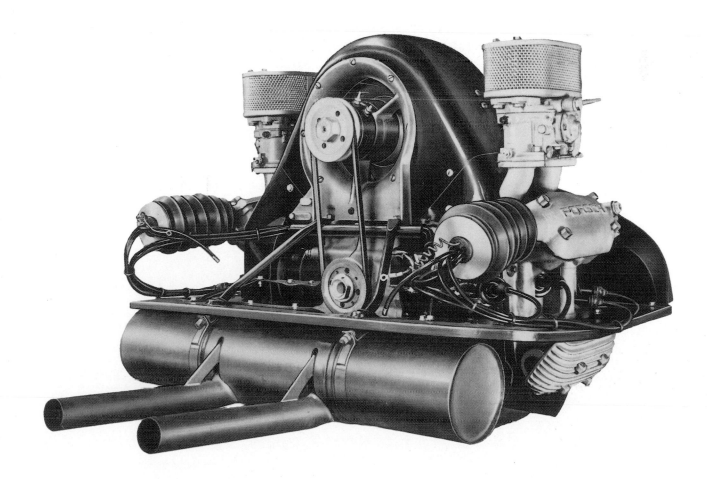

Porsche's racing Type 550 gave way to the 718, which was first made available in early 1959 and was known to the factory as RSK 718/1500.

right out of a road race. They'll probably be doing it years from now.

SCCA classification juggling directly affected the 356 Carrera. Though faster than most everything else in C-Production, it wasn't normally a match for the small-block Corvettes in B-Production. This explains a dearth of championship crowns after 1960, when Bruce Jennings won C/P going away. After that, the Carrera was bumped up to B/P. Even so, Jennings made many incredible assaults on the fiberglass Chevys and occasionally beat them, even in the rain. Race crowds, of course, were usually pro-import and cheered Jennings on, which didn't make Corvette fans very happy. SCCA returned the Carreras to C-Production in 1964 and they again dominated, Jennings winning the championship. Richard Smith was Pacific champ in 1965's divisionally divided standings, then national winner in '66. The torch then passed to the 911, but the Carreras, like the Speedsters, are still seen occasionally—and as awesome as ever.

European Carreras were mostly in charge of FIA's displacement-based 1600 GT class during 1959, but possible challenges from the Lotus Elite and Alfa Giulietta moved Zuffenhausen to commission 20 special lightweight bodies from Scaglione in Italy. That *carrozzerie* was also supplying bodies to famed engine tuner and race-car designer Carlo Abarth, who became the ostensible builder. Thus was born the Abarth-Carrera GTL.

The GTL's Abarth-designed body was executed in aluminum and bereft of all but the essentials, including bumpers. The cockpit was extremely spartan. Side windows were plastic, raised and lowered by simple leather straps. Though based on the 356B, the GTL looked more like an overgrown version of one of Carlo's Fiat-Abarths. But no one cared, for this was the fastest Carrera yet. When the first GTL arrived in Zuffenhausen, the Germans found they didn't fit, so some substantial body alterations were made to accommodate Teutonic physiques. The factory then kept four or five GTLs as team cars through 1961.

Bodywork aside, the Abarth-Carrera was all Porsche. Shocks were Koni telescopic, brakes large-diameter aluminum drums with cast-iron liners. Power was provided by the 1587-cc engine from the roadgoing 356B Carrera, with double coils and distributors to deliver the spark and a pair of twin-choke Weber downdraft carbs. This engine was a marvel of complexity, with four camshafts (one each per set of intake and exhaust valves on each cylinder bank) driven by nine shafts, 14 bevel gears and two spur gears. Crankshaft and rod bearings were roller type, but the camshafts ran in plain bearings. Output depended on exhaust system. The tamest setup was good for 115 horsepower, a "racing exhaust" liberated 128 horses, and a "Se-

bring extractor" design released 135.

The GTL's first outing came in 1960 at the grinding Targa Florio, where Paul Strahle and Herbert Linge placed sixth overall and first in class. GTLs finished 1-2-3 in the 1600-cc Sports Class at that year's Nürburgring 1000 Kilometers; the top finisher, a prototype with Porsche's ring-disc brakes, was a creditable seventh overall. There were also class wins in the Sebring 12 Hours and at Le Mans, where a GTL came in 11th.

For 1961, the new Type 692/3A engine was installed, with plain bearings

permitting higher revs (to 7800 rpm). In this form, the highest tuned GTLs (for Sebring) delivered 140 bhp. Class wins and/or high overall finishes came that year at the Targa, Le Mans, Sebring, and the Paris 1000 Km.

Records are incomplete, but 15 of the 20 GTLs built were apparently sold to private parties. These "customer cars" could lap the 14-mile 'Ring in 10 minutes, 23 seconds, and one was timed at 9:58 in 1961, the first GT car to lap that circuit in under 10 minutes. A later 1600 example was timed at 138 mph on the Mulsanne Straight at Le

The Type 718 RSK Spyder (*below*) started out with 1500 cc, but for 1959 had a 1600-cc engine that cranked out 148 bhp. The lovely and lightweight 356 Abarth-Carrera GTL (*opposite page*) was clearly built more for the track than the road; 20 aluminum bodies were commissioned, and the car scored numerous wins from 1960 to '63.

Mans, and factory driver Linge felt it might do 5 mph more.

Porsche engineers were preoccupied with their ultimately unsuccessful assault on Formula 1 (Chapter 15), so the Abarth-Carrera became the workhorse racer. Porsche had homologated it in the production 1600- and 2000-cc GT classes, and a 2.0-liter appeared at Daytona in 1963. On Saturday, Huschke von Hanstein, Zuffenhausen's well-known driver/engineer, averaged 122 mph to seventh overall and first in class in a 250-mile contest around the tri-oval. The next day, in a three-hour battle on the infield road course, Joakim Bonnier and Bob Holbert finished seventh and eighth overall and 1-2 in class, with a privately entered GTL right behind.

The Abarth-Carrera hadn't been planned for the 2.0-liter motor and none were originally built with it, the engine being retrofitted as the needs of competition dictated. All GTLs were built with drum brakes, the Porsche-made ring discs being installed later along with the bigger engine.

For a time, the Porsches most favored for GT racing were the 356B/356C Carrera 2s and a lightweight evolution, the 2000GS GT. The latter was mainly for factory teams, which nicknamed it "the wedge" because of its special droop-snoot body with squared-up roof. Many privateers continued to run GTLs (one won the Twin 400 at Bridgehampton, Long Island in 1962), though by 1964 the new 904 GTS (Chapter 16) was clearly the Porsche of choice for long-haul contests.

But the GTL had enjoyed an exceptional career. Wrote Karl Ludvigsen: "Not until the Seventies did [the name Carrera] regain the original sense of a high-performance variant of the normal production Porsche."

For the decade beginning in 1964, the 911 was Porsche's production-class warrior. SCCA initially put it in Class D, where it had little real competition. Jerry Titus won the 1966 D/P title going away in a mildly "prodified" 911 sponsored by Porsche dealer and racing enthusiast Vasek Polak. At Le Mans, meantime, a 911 that had been driven to the race over public roads finished 14th overall—after which it was driven home again, one of the more impressive finishes for a race-and-ride sports car to that time.

From the first, special equipment was available for turning the 911 into a track star at relatively low cost. Early examples include suspension package W171, with anti-sway bars, special brake pads, and a driver's footrest. There were also two engine kits, one comprising special carb jets and venturis and rudimentary carb filters, the second with blueprinted heads and manifolds. Together they raised output to 175 bhp to make the 911 formidable in C-Production. Alan Johnson owned the class in 1967-68, as did Milt Minter in '69, after which Datsun took over with its 240Zs. Johnson also won the GT class at Sebring '67 and that year's SCCA national championships at Daytona.

Back in Europe, the 911S was earning fame in the GT Hillclimb Championship and numerous rallies. Vic Elford and David Stone, two English experts with a 911T, won Porsche its first Monte Carlo Rally in 1968, a triumph Zuffenhausen had long sought. The four-cylinder 912 was also on the scene. Polish driver Sobieslaz Zasada won the 1967 European rally championship and outlasted 375 rivals for an outright win in the Argentine Grand Prix, a 2000-mile open road race that broke more cars than finished.

Just barely stock was the 911R, conceived by Ferdinand Piëch in 1967 to stretch various rules in rallying and GT racing. The first three Rs had fiberglass bumpers, front fenders, doors, engine cover, and front "hood." Elsewhere, they utilized thin-gauge steel, and had aluminum hinges, Plexiglas side and rear windows, and de-trimmed cockpits. Fenders were flared to allow wider tires, and twin oil coolers were fitted. The engine (Type 901/22) was much like that of the Type 906/Carrera 6 endurance racer (Chapter 16), with the same valve timing, oversize valves and ports, chrome-plated bores, dual ignition, and two triple-throat Type 46 Weber carbs. On 10.3:1 compression, output reached 210 bhp at 8000 rpm and 152 pounds-feet torque at 6000 rpm. One of the 911R's first triumphs was an enduro at Monza: 10,000 miles, 15,000 and 20,000 kilometers, 72 and 90 hours at an average 140+ mph, thus earning Porsche five world records in the 2.0-liter class.

In mid-1967, Porsche assigned the Stuttgart firm of Karl Baur to build 20 more 911Rs, using standard-gauge steel and adding quick-fill fuel tanks

In 1973, Porsche's emphasis shifted to a new generation of 911 warriors based on the reborn Carrera, the Carrera RSR (*above*), the all-out version of the roadgoing RS. Two other examples: a Turbo-Carrera RSR from 1974 (*below*) and a Carrera RSR 3.0 racer (*right*).

The 935/78 "Moby Dick" raced by Martini Porsche had incredible performance: 0-60 mph in 3.3 seconds; the quarter mile in 8.9 seconds and 133.5 mph.

and deep bucket seats. The plan was, eventually, to build 500 for homologation in FIA Grand Touring. But the sales department didn't think it could move that many and the project ended. A shame, as there's no telling what the car might have done in GT or SCCA B-Production. Running in the prototype class, one 911R managed an outright win in the 1969 Tour de France, thus demonstrating reliability equal to its performance.

A hoard of 911s, factory and private, would continue to do well in major rallies and enduros. A team of 911Es finished 1-2 in the 85-hour *Marathon de la Route*, held on the taxing 16-mile Nürburgring in August 1968, just as that model was making its European debut. The 911S of Björn Waldegaard and Lars Helmer gave Porsche another outright Monte Carlo win in 1969, and they repeated the feat in 1970, when 911s also took second and fourth.

Meanwhile, the intrepid Sobieslaz Zasada had followed his Argentine caper with private entries for the East African Safari in 1969-70, which encouraged Porsche to field a three-car team for 1971. Featured were 180-bhp engines, extra fuel tanks, raised suspensions, beefy torsion bars, and full rally gear. Unfortunately, the raised suspensions made shock-absorber rods vulnerable, forcing two cars to retire, but Zasada drove the remaining S

to fifth despite an erratic ignition system. Zasada tried again in 1973, Waldegaard in '74, but neither nailed a win, and Porsche wouldn't achieve an outright win in a cross-country rally until the mid-Eighties.

The 911 continued winning major races and rallies through the early Seventies thanks to a profusion of lightweight competition derivatives. Porsche produced four for the 1970 season alone: 2.2- and 2.3-liter 911STs

for production classes; S 2.4, for the Tour de France; S 2.2 Safari, the East African rally version; and the S 2.5, which saw action in both rallies and track events and was the most powerful, with up to 270 bhp. Though the deviations from stock specs among these cars are too detailed to list here, suffice it to say that all were basically 911s carefully modified for specific purposes.

Which testifies eloquently to the

amazing versatility and stamina of the showroom product, reason enough to highlight a few of the 911's more notable successes in this period. Besides the fabled Monte, 1970 brought outright victories in the Swedish Rally (Waldegaard and Helmer again, their third straight in that event), the Austrian Alpine, Danube, and Arctic rallies. Also in 1971, a 911 was first in GT and sixth overall at Le Mans. In 1972, Porsche won the GT championship and FIA Cup for GT cars in Europe, in America the GT Challenge in IMSA (International Motor Sports Association) and the Six Hours of Daytona. Zasada was runner-up in that year's East African Safari, Gerard Larousse in the Monte, while 1973 saw victories in the Baltic Rally and the tough Circuit of Ireland.

Privateers and weekend racers would add many more wins to the 911's scorecard—and still are. By 1973, the factory's emphasis shifted to a new generation of 911 warriors based on the reborn Carrera.

The first was the Carrera RSR, the all-out version of the roadgoing RS previously described (Chapter 8). Besides the usual mods, it had a flat six enlarged to 2806 cubic centimeters (171.2 cubic inches) for an astounding 308 DIN horsepower at 6200 rpm on 10.5:1 compression. The RSR had a splendid career in Group 4, beginning in 1973:

Targa Florio, 1st (Müller/Van Lennep)
Daytona 24 Hours, 1st (Peter Gregg/Hurley Haywood)
Sebring 12 Hours (Gregg/Haywood)
European GT Champion
European Hillclimb Champion
IMSA GT Champion (Gregg)
SCCA Trans-AM GT Champion (Gregg)

The engine was enlarged with some difficulty during the season for the Martini Racing Team, expanding to 2993 cc by a further bore increase (to 95 mm). With 315 bhp, it beat everything in sight at a four-hour Le Mans contest, blasting down the Mulsanne Straight at up to 179 mph.

The beat went on in 1974:
European GT champion (John Fitzpatrick)
European Hillclimb champion (Fischhaber)
IMSA GT champion (Peter Gregg)
FIA World Cup for GT Cars

There was also a wild new Group 5 RSR 3.0 with up to 330 bhp (DIN) and very purposeful body alterations (even wider rear fenders with fore and aft air ducts, wider front fenders with trailing-edge vents, and a large air dam with integrated oil cooler). This version was run mainly by the Cologne-based teams of Erwin Kremer and George Loos (Fitzpatrick alternated between them in Group 4) and would shortly lead to even greater things.

RSRs again won everywhere in '75,

The 935 was derived from the 930, although it barely resembled it, here (*right*) in "Baby" short-tail form in 1977. The 935/78 (*bottom*) is seen here in its "Moby Dick" long-tail form.

including fifth overall at Le Mans and first at the Daytona 24 Hours (Gregg and Haywood again). Porsche claimed another GT championship in IMSA and Europe (the latter courtesy of Hartwig Bertrams), as well as that year's European hillclimb crown (Swiss driver Jean-Claude Bering), and the FIA GT World Cup. The IMSA title came despite determined efforts from BMW—and even General Motors—to end their yearly embarrassment at Porsche's hands. Gregg/Haywood won eight of the 14 events. Porsche drivers also took the second and third spots. Last but not least, Porsche was 1975's German rally champ. Thus ended the era of the normally aspirated 911 and its derivatives.

Meantime, the humble little 914 had been earning its share of glory, with most of the factory's efforts predictably centered on the Porsche-powered 914/6. Competition versions were often tested on rally routes, but the emphasis was on track racing, not rallies, which were 911 territory.

Porsche + Audi made a lukewarm 1970 effort in SCCA C-Production, the always hotly contested class then dominated by the Datsun 240Z and Triumph TR6, both amply supported by their makers. The 914/6 proved competitive, winning four of seven divisional championships, but was overpowered by the Z-cars at the national runoffs, where John Morton's Datsun prevailed. Factory backing then melted, and though the mid-engine Porsche later repeated as champ in several divisions, it never captured the national crown.

For a time, the special 914/6 GT carried Porsche's colors in European Group 4 events. Ultra-wide rolling stock and bulging fenders (actually welded-on extensions) identified it. The engine remained at 2.0 liters but was highly modified, with Weber carbs instead of fuel injection, special heads, dual ignition, high-dome pistons, and aluminum cylinders. Horsepower was between 210 and 220 (DIN). Suspension and brakes were appropriately upgraded.

Four 914/6 GTs performed well at the 1970 Nürburgring 1000 Kilometers, finishing 2-5 behind the class winner, a 911L. A single car contested that year's Le Mans enduro, where it surprised everyone by taking first in class and sixth overall in a gale-lashed ordeal of severe attrition. Driven by

Guy Chasseuil and Claude Ballot-Léna of France, it averaged 99.27 mph and 13.56 miles per gallon, good for second in the Index of Efficiency. Meanwhile, 914/6 GTs breezed home 1-2-3 at the *Marathon de la Route* (two running in Group 6 because of their extra-wide tires and fender bubbles). Another pair, driven by Prince von Hohenzollern and Gunther Steckkönig, finished 1-2 at the Osterreichring, earning enough points for Porsche to clinch

the international GT trophy. But smiles turned to frowns when a GT assault on the 1971 Monte Carlo Rally was stopped cold by the Alpine-Renaults, which outran the 914s despite a 400-cc disadvantage.

Back in the States, the 914/6 fared better in IMSA's 1971 GT Challenge, swept by Gregg and Haywood in the Brumos Porsche car (sponsored by Gregg's Jacksonville, Florida dealership) that won two of the six rounds

The '78 Porsche 911SC raced in the East African Safari Rally; note the high ground clearance and screened lights.

outright, making Porsche the under-2.5-liter champ. SCCA, however, stopped the 914s cold the following season by putting them in B-Production, the category owned by Allan Barker's Corvettes between 1969 and '72.

More exciting things were brewing in Zuffenhausen with the turbocharged 911, the new Type 930, as the main ingredient. After the Martini & Rossi team's 1974 foray with a 2.1-liter development car, Porsche introduced a Group 4 Type 930 for the 1976 season. Logically tagged 934, it had a basically stock body with pop-riveted fiberglass fender flares and a huge front airdam, plus the expected "whale tail" rear spoiler. To meet the minimum weight standard (1120 kg/2740 lbs), the road car's power window lifts and many other amenities were actually left in.

Suspension was suitably fortified with coil springs atop gas-filled Bil-stein shock absorbers, and hard plastic replaced rubber in control-arm bushings. Both front and rear anti-roll bars could be adjusted to suit various tracks, while Goodyear racing specials put the rubber to the road. The brakes, borrowed from the fearsome 917 Makes Championship car (see Chapter 16), featured cross-drilled discs, finned wheel cylinders (for heat dissipation), and twin master cylinders.

Because Group 4 required a near-

253

stock engine, the 934's main mechanical changes from 930 specifications were higher turbo boost and different valve timing and overlap. In the interest of reliability and, again, to suit different track requirements, boost pressure could be varied (to a maximum 18.5 lbs/sq in.) via a dashboard knob. An interesting fillip was watercooling, not for the engine, but for the hotter turbo-compressed air, to improve volumetric efficiency. It took the form of what we now call an air-to-water intercooler, with a water/alcohol cocktail as the cooling medium. The cooler itself lived in the front airdam, much like the oil coolers on earlier Carrera RSRs. Another departure was retention of the road car's Bosch K-Jetronic fuel injection, again modified for racing.

All this literally boosted horsepower to a rated 485 (DIN) at 7000 rpm, upped by 1977 to 540. Torque measured a prodigious 420 lbs-ft at 5400 rpm. Porsche built 31 of these 3.0-liter "customer" cars (officially Type 934 Turbo RSR), and sold every one for around $40,000 apiece.

For Group 5, class requirements dictated an even wilder evolution. Called 935, it barely resembled the 930, with towering performance that compared the way a 911 does to a VW Beetle. To be sure, the 935 was derived from the 930, because FIA rules precluded purpose-designed cars. But they also resulted in what came to be called "silhouette" cars, racers that looked somewhat like street models—but only somewhat.

The first two 935s built were factory prototypes with hardly a trace of 930. Doors, fenders, deck, hood, and spoilers were fiberglass, windows Plexiglas. Porsche shaved so much weight, in fact, that it had to add 154 pounds to meet the required minimum (970 kg/2138 lbs sans fuel). Naturally, all the ballast went up front, resulting in a fine 47/53-percent front/rear weight distribution.

Things looked surprisingly stock inside except for a single racing bucket seat and the mandatory rollcage. A big 8000-rpm tach dominated the dash, surrounded by turbo boost and other gauges. A central lever allowed the driver to adjust rear anti-roll bar stiffness to suit weight distribution changes as fuel was used up. The front bar could also be adjusted. Suspension comprised adjustable front coil springs made of titanium (replacing the normal torsion bars) and rear trailing arms. Brakes, basically from the 934, sprouted extra cooling ducts. Rear tires were an eye-popping 19 inches wide, the fronts 16 inches, all mounting on 14½-inch-diameter racing rims.

Group 5 imposed a sort of "handicap" on turbo-engine displacement, which was multiplied by 1.4 for comparison with normally aspirated engines. As the latter were limited to a maximum 4.0 liters, Porsche debored the 930's flat six to 92 mm and 2857 cc, equivalent to exactly 3999.8 cc under the rules. More engine tweaks were allowed than in Group 4, so Bosch mechanical injection replaced K-Jetronic. Also, dual ignition and many lightweight internal components (such as titanium con rods) were fitted, and boost pressure set at 19-22 psi. Result: 590 DIN horsepower at 7900 rpm and 434 pounds-feet torque at 5400.

In their 1975 debut season the 935s had front bodywork much like that of the 930 and 934. But the following year brought the first of the now-familiar hidden-headlamp "droop snoot" cars, with a lower and smoother *Flachbau* (flat profile) front developed in Porsche's Weissach wind tunnel. Rear bodywork also became unbelievably wide and wild for both European and American events. Besides an assortment of radical scoops and ducts, the later 935/77 and 935/78 variations had huge spoilers, sometimes bridging tall shark-like fins molded into the lower rear quarters. Other cars wore finny "strakes" fared into the upper rear roof and extended aft to form short struts on which the wing

mounted. Configurations varied among the different teams, but all were sure to attract attention at any race.

Their performance certainly did. By the time the long-tailed "Moby Dick" of 1978 appeared, the 935 was cranking out an incredible 845 bhp at 8200 rpm, thanks to developments like four valves per cylinder and water-cooled cylinder heads.

Needless to say, the 934 and 935 had incredible performance. *Road & Track* tested both in 1977:

	934	935
0-30 mph (sec)	3.9	1.6
0-60 mph (sec)	5.8	3.3
0-80 mph (sec)	7.7	4.4
0-100 mph (sec)	10.1	6.1
0-¼ mi (sec)	14.2	8.9
¼-mi speed (mph)	121.5	133.5

Porsche was disappointed when IMSA initially banned turbocars in 1976, as it ended hopes of a GT championship; however, the ban was lifted at mid-season. There was no such problem in the Trans-Am, however, and Porsche won that championship, with George Follmer first in points (with a 934), followed by Hurley Haywood, both of Holbert Racing.

The 935s had similar troubles with the FIA when, after taking the first two events in the European GT series, they were forced to run with the 930's rear spoiler, which required adapting the 934's "waterworks" for proper cooling. Despite some mid-season stumbles after these and other modifications, Porsche pulled out the Makes Championship late in the tour by outlasting BMW's winged CSL coupes at Watkins Glen. As this was the first time a hyperaspirated car had won the title, the 935 started a revolution. From here on it took a turbo to win in Group 5: a Porsche Turbo.

And 935s continued to win—nay dominate—every series. Again a racing Porsche's record is too long to detail, but highlights include three consecutive Makes titles 1977-79 and an

The Porsche 924 Turbo Le Mans, shown in 1980 guise (*opposite*), won first-in-class and sixth overall at the famed French track in 1981. The prototype car was based on the European 924 Carrera GT, and provided a sneak preview of the new 944, which debuted shortly afterward.

outright victory at Le Mans 1979—the first production-based car to win the gruelling 24 Hours since the 1953 Jaguar C-Type. In North America, the 935 reigned as IMSA GT champion in 1978-80 and took the 1979 SCCA Trans-Am title as well. Its last victory occurred as recently as March 1984 (first overall in the Sebring 12 Hours). By then, the baton had passed to the even more specialized 936, 956, and 962 (see Chapter 16), though they, too, relied on engines firmly rooted in that of the original 911.

Remarkably, the 911 is still making history. The latest chapter concerns the 961, competition cousin to the miraculous, high-tech 959 (Chapter 12). It first appeared at the car-killing Paris-Dakar Rally of 1986, which it won going away. The 961 also did well in its first track appearance, the 1986 Daytona 24 Hours. Had not a series of tragic accidents ended the Group B rallies for which it was originally designed, production might have gone higher than the 25 units Porsche planned to build. But we've certainly not seen the last of this car's technology in rallies or production-class racing, since much of it seems destined to appear in the new-generation 911 now slated for 1989 or '90.

The 924 and the newer 944s have been successful in their own arenas. The former participated in many major rallies, though it never won one. However, a 924 managed a creditable 20th overall in the 1979 Monte against a hoard of more powerful rivals. More impressive, the 924 won national SCCA D-Production championships for "Doc" Bundy in 1980 and Tom Brennan in '81. The latter repeated in 1985, when the category was known as GT-3.

But the big event was the first-in-class and remarkable sixth overall scored by a 924 "prototype" at Le Mans 1981. Manfred Schürti and Jurgen Barth drove the car, which was actually a sneak preview of the new 944 announced two weeks later. Based on the European 924 Carrera GT, the prototype was powered by a 16-valve version of the new Porsche-designed four, thus providing a *very* early look at the new-for-'87 944S engine (though no one outside Porsche then knew that, of course).

When the 924 Turbo appeared, Group 4 versions were developed for Europe, with a basically stock body,

mounting fiberglass doors and hatch, as well as Carrera-style flared fenders to accommodate racing footwear. DIN horsepower was 310-320 with Kügelfischer injection. One of these cars proved faster than even the quickest RSR Carrera in 1980 tests at Le Mans. Two years later, Doc Bundy and Jim Busby rode to GT-class glory in the legendary French event with a 924 Carrera Turbo running on *street* tires.

Speaking of the street, the four-cylinder Porsches have found many rewards in what quickly became known as "showroom stock" racing, interest in which had exploded since the early Seventies when IMSA president Jim Bishop began reviving the kind of "run what 'ya brung" competition so popular in the early postwar years. By mid-decade, SCCA had established a professional SS class of its own, and Ken Williams captured the 1980 national crown with his 924. In 1985, a separate Escort Endurance Series (named for a brand of radar detector) was formed for SS cars in SCCA. IMSA's counterpart was the Firestone Firehawk Challenge.

Because SCCA allowed Corvettes in SS, the 944s initially fared none too well overall. But they dominated the Firehawk Challenge, winning the championship in inaugural '84. The 944 repeated in 1985, Walt Maas and John Milledge taking five of the eight events. That same year, the 944 Turbo was SCCA showroom-stock champion and non-turbo 944s grabbed the Escort series.

The "Longest Day" 24-hour enduro at the Nelson Ledges course in Ohio doesn't count toward the SS championship, but has provided several interesting Porsche anecdotes. The first running, in June 1981, saw a well-prepped 924 outlast a variety of rivals, including a squad of Ford EXP/Mercury LN7s piloted by *Car and Driver* and *Road & Track* staffers. In 1982, a then-new 944 blithely repeated the victory (this time with the *C/D* and *R&T* crews dicing it up in prototype Mustangs). The following year, a new 944 Turbo was entered but didn't win—sending the Weissach gnomes racing to devise improvements that were eventually incorporated on production models. Last but not least, the SS class in the 1984 event was won by a stock 944 with 23,000 miles on it! It was just as we always knew: racing *does* improve the breed—at least at Porsche.

And it still does. Porsche's newest four-cylinder racers are a special 300-bhp 944S and the even wilder 944 Turbo GTR, both devised for SCCA's more liberal Street Stock series. The former is a lightweight flyer with fiberglass bodywork and an aluminum-tube frame with stock 944 suspension and the big cross-drilled brakes from the 962. Top speed is 160+ mph. The Turbo GTR, the first Porsche designed and built for American road racing, is the same formula bolstered by full competition suspension and an engine coaxed to 575 bhp (by Andial of California), good for around 175 mph. At this writing, two GTRs prepared by the Bruce Jenner Racing Team of North Carolina are doing well as Porsche's unofficial entry in the 1987 Trans-Am. New Zealand native Jenner drives one. The other is piloted by 1982 T-A champion Elliott Forbes-Robinson.

Even the luxurious 928 has a credit or two. In December 1982, a European model covered over 3700 miles at an average 155 mph on the Nardo track outside Brindisi in southern Italy. Establishing themselves as "the world's fastest Sunday drivers," the international team of Gerhard Plattner (Austria), Peter Lovett (Great Britain), and Peter Abinden (Switzerland) experienced no real problems, requiring only replacement tires. With less than half the horsepower, the 928 actually went faster on the circular track than the 1982 LeMans-winning Porsche 956. And let's not forget Al Holbert's speed records at Bonneville in 1986 (see Chapter 11).

We could go on, but the point is clear: Porsche learns from competition and, perhaps more intensively than any other maker, applies that experience to the cars it sells, which in turn makes those cars—and the company that builds them—better racers. That's why a Porsche has long been the closest thing to a genuine competition machine an enthusiast can buy at a local dealer. It may also explain why so many Porsche owners get involved with racing.

Of course, in seeking competitive challenges all over the world, even in the most difficult of times, Porsche has left us not just an unparalleled racing record, but many enduring memories. That's one part of the "Porsche mystique" you don't have to be rich to enjoy.

The Early Racers: Glöckler Spyder to RS61

Although barely yet crawling as a commercial concern in the early Fifties, Porsche nonetheless wasted no time running pell mell toward racing in the great tradition of its founder. The result was the firm's first pure track car, the Type 550 Spyder, powered by Ernst Fuhrmann's four-cam version of the air-cooled opposed four that would motivate the exciting 356 Carrera (Chapter 5). In a sense, the Spyder was the spiritual descendant of the Lohner electric that Ferdinand Porsche had driven to a new record time on the Semmerling hillclimb course in September 1900. How ironic, then, that it originated not in Zuffenhausen, but some 100 miles to the north in Frankfurt.

Walter Glöckler had been a successful racer of motorcycles and 1.5-liter cars in the prewar years. After the war, he planned to build and race a car of his own design, and began constructing it at his large VW distributorship in Frankfurt. Completed in 1950, it looked so much like the eventual Spyder that Glöckler was credited as its "father."

Just 78 inches long, Glöckler's *Eigenbau* ("homemade") was a smooth, lozenge-shaped roadster with a tubular frame. An 1100-cc Porsche engine, modified to develop 53 DIN horsepower on alcohol, was mounted amidships, ahead of the rear-wheel axis, for optimum weight distribution.

Glöckler's car immediately proved itself, winning the German 1100-cc championship in 1950-52—same car, different drivers. A capable engineer in his own right, Glöckler then went on to an improved body and a 1500-cc Porsche engine with 90 bhp. This result, called Glöckler-Porsche, captured for Germany the Bugatti-class records on France's Monthlèry track in 1952. With all this and more, Porsche's reputation as a builder of durable, race-winning components was firmly established.

After a 356 had won its class at the 1951 Le Mans 24 Hours, Ferry Porsche and Karl Rabe concluded that their production pushrod engine would no longer be enough for endurance events (though it would be expanded to 1300 and then 1500 cc for road use). Accordingly, Rabe and engineer Ernst Fuhrmann explored the potential of a competition 1500 with four camshafts placed atop the cylinder barrels to serve the four widely spaced sets of valves. A prototype designated Type 547 was on the Zuffenhausen dynamometer by spring 1952, but minor development problems delayed mating with its intended body/chassis, a new design created expressly for racing and coded project 550.

To fill the gap, the Type 550 platform, a coupe style from Weidenhausen in Frankfurt, was fitted with a souped-up Type 528 pushrod engine for the 1953 season. It promptly won the *Eifelrennen* at the Nürburgring and distinguished itself on other European circuits.

The four-cam was ready by August 1953, and it propelled former Auto Union pilot Hans Stück to a class win in the Freiburg hillclimb. But its first real test was the gruelling Mille Miglia the following spring, by which time the car it powered was known as Spyder. Hans Hermann and Herbert Linge drove to victory in the 1500-cc sports class, and the 550 Spyder began making a name for itself on the international scene. The name itself was familiar, meaning a light, high-performance sports car. Porsche referred to it as 1500RS (*Rennsport*, racing sport).

Like Glöckler's racer, the Spyder had a tubular frame (with slight kickups front and rear) and a smooth, low-slung open body. Wheelbase was a compact 82.7 inches, weight a shade over 1200 pounds. A front-mounted oil radiator, four-speed Porsche gearbox, Ross-type steering, and Porsche's usual all-independent torsion-bar suspension were on hand, along with three mechanical features unique even to Porsche: a double-admission cooling blower, large separate oil tank, and dry-sump lubrication.

Spyder body production shifted several times after Karosseriebau Weinsberg built the first few hulls. It was late 1954 by the time all the engine problems were sorted out, and privateers had been waiting months for the Spyder. What they ultimately got was the Type 550S (Sport), the "customer" model with bodywork supplied by

continued on page 260

The Glöckler Spyder of 1950-51 (*above*) was a smooth, lozenge-shaped roadster with a tubular frame and a modified 1100-cc Porsche engine. The Type 550RS (for *Rennsport*, racing sport) appeared for the 1953 season. The 550RS (*right and opposite page*) also utilized a tubular frame and was fitted initially with a souped-up Type 528 pushrod engine, but by August 1953 a four-cam unit was ready for use. The cars distinguished themselves at many races, from Nürburgring to the *Carrera Panamericana* road race in Mexico.

Wendler of Reutlingen and priced at DM25,000 or about $5500 U.S. A factory car driven by Huschke von Hanstein finished eighth overall in the Sports Car Grand Prix at Caracas, Venezuela, battling a field of Maseratis and Ferraris.

Several options were offered for customer Spyders: center-lock wire wheels (modified and laced by Glöckler), the necessary axle and hub adaptors, and chrome center-lock disc wheels to match post-1954 brake drums. A later catalog listed lightweight rims for the factory RS, saving about 4.5 pounds per wheel. Swiss engineer and Spyder owner Michael May offered Porsche a specially designed aerofoil to improve rear-end adhesion, but management rejected this forecast of the later Chaparral wing because it obstructed driver vision.

By the mid-Fifties, factory-sponsored Spyders were exceeding 120 mph, yet with a degree of reliability unknown to most competitors. Wrote Ken Purdy: "So fantastically durable were these cars that it was only in the most trying races, say the 24-hour Le Mans or Sebring, that they demonstrated their uncanny ability to run flat-out hour after hour while ordinary attrition strewed the dead-car park with blown-up examples of lesser makes. As the hours passed, spectators at long-distance events came to realize that there were two dominant sounds in the cacaphony of passing exhaust howls: the high scream of the Ferraris and the lower-pitched booming of the Porsches."

But competition was rife in those days, and by mid-1956 it had prodded Porsche to produce an improved Spyder, the 550A. Retaining much of the original's appearance, it packed 135 DIN horsepower on 9.8:1 compression (previously 9.5:1), a new five-speed gearbox (though first was used only to get things rolling), and double-jointed swing axles with lower fulcrum. Fuel capacity for long-distance events, always a Porsche specialty, was 28.6 gallons (main plus auxiliary tanks). Plug reach was increased to ¾-inch and a Hirth roller-bearing crankshaft was installed along with lightweight cylinder barrels. It all made for a very free and fast-revving engine that was seemingly unbreakable. It just kept on going even when run above 7500-rpm.

Yet, the Spyder was also surprising-

continued on page 264

Porsche's 550 Spyder progressed through higher power and
more sophisticated design. Hans Hermann's number 55
(*opposite center*) saw action in the 1954 *Carrera
Panamericana*, while number 34 (*opposite bottom*) was
owned by Swiss engineer Michael May, who devised an
aerofoil for added rear wheel adhesion. Porsche
declined it because it hurt driver vision. The 550
evolved into the 550A (*above*), shown here as a '57.

Porsche's 550A RS Spyder (*both pages*) first appeared in mid-1956. It retained much of the original 550's appearance, but featured a 1500-cc four-cam engine that packed 135 DIN horsepower on a 9.8:1 compression ratio. A five-speed gearbox was new, but low gear was used only to get the car rolling. The Sypder was fondly nicknamed the "Giant Killer" because of its virtually unbreakable engine that just kept on going, even when abused, thus outlasting many bigger, more powerful rivals.

The Porsche 550A gave way to the new Type 718, officially designated RSK 718/1500. It became available in early 1958. The engine was upgraded to 1600 cc for 1959. The "K" designation vanished in 1960 in favor of RS60 (*right and bottom*).

ly tractable off the track (if less than practical as a road car). In fact, many of the 100-odd built for FIA homologation are around today, having seen little or no race action but admired as much for their functional beauty as their performance.

Predictably for a Porsche, the Spyder evolved progressively through higher power and more sophisticated design. The 550A, for example, not only had more horses but had a lighter, chest high steel-tube space frame. A works training car now known as the RSK Spyder was tested the following year, when the 550 gave way to the new Type 718. Officially designated

RSK 718/1500, it became available in early 1958.

The K referred to a new front suspension that deviated from Porsche practice in having angled upper members that looked like that letter. It wouldn't last long, but the cars usually did on the track. Variable-rate coil springs concentric with the shock absorbers replaced the Spyder's rear torsion bars, resulting in more neutral handling. Driven by the famous Jean Behra, a 1500RSK with 142 bhp (DIN) and single-seat bodywork won the 1958 Formula 2 contest at Rheims, France, besting 14 Coopers, three Lotuses, three OSCAs, and a six-cylin-

der Ferrari. It could reach 155 mph at 8000 rpm. Porsche also won that year's European Mountain Championship with the 718 Bergspyder, a special hillclimb version.

For 1959, the RSK was upgraded to a 1.6-liter four-cam with 148 bhp (DIN) at 5800 rpm. It debuted at that year's F2 race in Monte Carlo, where Wolfgang von Trips crashed it on the first lap. Rear suspension underwent a major change at season's end, with a new coil-spring/wishbone layout very much like that of the 718 F2 car (see Chapter 15), in keeping with Porsche's policy of applying competition experience to "production" vehicles.

By that point, the Spyder had apparently reached its full potential. Porsche placed third in the world sports-car championship in 1958 and '59—remarkable for 1500- and 1600-cc challengers to machines with up to 3.0 liters. And Porsche again showed its hillclimb prowess in '59, finishing 1-5 in that year's international championship.

The "K" designation vanished for 1960 in favor of RS60. Expected FIA rules changes for 1962 prompted a wait-and-see attitude in Zuffenhausen, so the Spyders were little changed in the meantime. Wheelbase was stretched 100 mm (3.94 inches) for '61, wider 16-inch-diameter wheels were adopted (previously 15s), and both 1.5- and 1.6-liter engines were run. Twelve cars went to private racers; four stayed at the factory. With the trend toward more cylinders now underway and Porsche increasingly busy with its eight-cylinder Formula 1 car (see next chapter), the Spyder program was halted in early 1962.

Inevitably, Spyders weren't built like production Porsches. Bodies were hammered out of aluminum over wooden forms, and the entire nine years of assembly work was carried out by perhaps only a dozen selected artisans who, with care and after many years of experience, put each car together piece by piece.

The Spyders were surely the ultimate expression of the three characteristics that most clearly defined early Porsches: air cooling, rear engine mounting, and giant-killing power from midget-size displacement. They also proved the worth of simple, lightweight construction, being both fast and ironclad reliable in the most gruelling of races.

Today, they testify to the formidable engineering skill Porsche could muster even in its earliest days, and are revered as part of a competition record no other make can even approach. Or probably ever will.

The RS61 appeared for 1961 as a coupe (*above*) and Spyder (*below*). Wheelbase was stretched 100 mm (3.94 inches) and 16-inch-diameter wheels replaced the 15s. Both 1.5- and 1.6-liter engines were offered.

Formula 1: Fortunes of War

The Ring of Solitude was one of those classic race courses laid out on public roads—the beautiful wooded country around *Schloss Solitude* near Stuttgart. It opened in 1922, but saw no official Grand Prix racing before the war. The great Hermann Lang drove a GP Mercedes there in a 1937 demonstration heat. He called it "a garden path."

But Dan Gurney, who did rather more in 1962, remembers it with fondness: "Solitude was a fantastic circuit. Very fast, very deceptive, very smooth, with drafting and lots of blind downhill turns," he told *Auto Motor und Sport* in 1982. "It's one of those tracks where you'd arrive at the turns together, and often it was raining, but it was a majestic circuit. It was a little more than eight miles around, and a lot of it going damn fast through the forest. It took some study to unlock the speed." Gurney had reason to remember, for it was on this narrow, tricky course that he piloted a Porsche Grand Prix car in its finest hour.

Formula 1 is the penultimate form of automotive competition, outranking the NASCAR Grand National, the Trans-Am, IMSA GT series, and everything else. To build an F1 machine and win with it is akin to scaling Mount Everest or setting foot on the moon. Thus it was that as the Fifties closed, the wizards of Zuffenhausen began thinking about the one type of racing they'd yet to try.

Porsche had already made its mark in the 1500-cc Formula 2 category with the 550A Spyders of Edgar Barth, Stirling Moss, and Wolfgang von Trips. Its venture into F1 was prompted by the FIA's decision to reduce maximum displacement for the 1961 season from 2.5 to 1.5 liters, a size with which Porsche people were

quite familiar. They also agreed with other manufacturers that this would make the competition open to more comers and thus more "interesting."

Porsche's first GP standard-bearers were four-cylinder cars based on its most recent Formula 2 machines, the 718 and 718/2. Porsche had scored its first F2 win in the 1957 German GP, and would repeat in 1-2 order at the 1960 event. From this grew a Formula 1 variant, the Type 787, built during the winter of 1960-61. Like the 718, it used wishbone suspension and a tubular frame. Power was provided by the proven Type 547/3 engine with Kügelfischer fuel injection. Wheelbase was 90.5 inches, track 51.2/50.0 inches front/rear.

Dan Gurney and Joakim Bonnier, both competitive and experienced drivers, were assigned 787s for the car's initial outings. The first two races, at Monaco and Zandvoort, were not encouraging, the drivers judging their mounts inferior to British and Italian opposition in both handling and performance. With this inauspicious beginning, Porsche switched to 718/2s and hustled the 787s back to the labs for further study. The hard-running Gurney managed to tie Moss for third in the 1961 driver's championship, but Porsche won no F1 events that season. (A privateer, Count Carel Godin de Beaufort, campaigned four-cylinder Porsches even after the eight-cylinder cars appeared, though he raced for the fun of it and never placed high.)

With interim development, the 787 was up to 185 horsepower by early 1962, but its last hurrah as a factory racer came soon and was anticlimactic. At Zandvoort, where Gurney and Bonnier had failed the year before, Ben Pon of the Dutch importer spun out of contention on lap four.

But Porsche had also been working on a definitive GP engine, begun in 1959 under the direction of a clever young engineer named Hans Metzger. Even then, Porsche had an inkling that a derivation of the four-cam Spyder/Carrera unit wouldn't be enough. Yet, the engine that ultimately emerged maintained tradition in being a flat-opposed type, necessary to give the car a low aerodynamic profile and optimum handling via a low center of gravity. The difference was that this one had eight cylinders instead of four. Designated 753, it was tried in the 787 chassis.

Designing this engine was no picnic. Neither was living with it. Porsche chronicler Karl Ludvigsen quotes Metzger as saying "it was pure hell to work on. It was as hard to adjust the valve timing on the early eight [as on the later] 917. And the assembly... required 220 skilled man-hours, an almost unbelievable 27½ 8-hour days—which of course do not exist in the world of racing." Porsche calculated the flat eight would have to produce at least 220 DIN horsepower to be competitive, and the first ones tested out at only 120.

The bore/stroke relationship was oversquare—66.0 × 54.6 mm/2.60 × 2.15 inches—the relatively short stroke chosen to minimize engine width for aero purposes. Bore could go as far as 78 mm (3.07 inches), and did for the 2.0-liter sports-racing formula. The double overhead cams were driven by a shaft and by bevel gears not unlike that of the F2 Spyder unit. Lightness was achieved with cast-aluminum heads and aluminum castings for valvegear and camshafts. Block and cam covers were of magnesium for the same reason. Two sparkplugs per cylinder were fired by twin

Porsche ran four-cylinder engines in its
earliest Formula 1 Type 787 cars of 1960-61.
They utilized wishbone suspension and a tubular
frame. For 1962, however, Porsche trotted out
the Type 804, with a lower, more slippery body,
a flat-eight engine, and a revised suspension
with double-wishbone geometry.

Bosch distributors. Carburetion was via four 38-mm two-barrel Webers.

Engineers had the 753 developing 160 bhp by early '61, still far short of the goal. Rather than run it and lose, Porsche entered four-cylinder cars while experimenting with a fuel-injection system developed by Kügelfischer in Munich. This provided a single-piston injector pump for each cylinder, the mixture metered by variations in piston stroke.

Nothing of substance occurred in the actual racing that year; Gurney came close at Rheims with a carbureted car but won no cigar. Porsche

tinkered with suspension and brakes throughout 1961, applying its experience with disc brakes (begun in 1957) and switching to double-wishbone geometry. Engineers judged the latter less worthy than their traditional trailing links, but it was needed to allow for constant small camber changes. One heartening point was that engine reliability seemed good. On test, the flat eight ran at maximum rpm for 12 hours before a con-rod bearing packed up.

The 753 was deemed ready by the start of the '62 season, by which time Porsche had devised a better car for it.

Designated Type 804 (the only time Zuffenhausen has ever used an 800 project number), it carried a lower, more slippery body, designed very much with streamlining in mind. And weight-saving: The entire car weighed only 15 pounds more than the FIA's 990-pound minimum. Wheelbase remained at 90.5 inches.

As the season opened, Hans Thomalla, who'd supervised Metzger the previous two years, replaced Klaus von Rucker as Porsche chief engineer. Determined to get into the GP fray, he entered the 804 in the lead-off contest at Zandvoort, the fast, flat track on the

Porsche contested Formula 1 in 1962 with the 804, but it was down on power and wasn't fully competitive. Nonetheless, Dan Gurney did triumph at the French Grand Prix in Rouen and also at Solitude. The rest of the season went poorly, however, and by the season closer, the South African GP, Ferry Porsche had decided to give up on Formula 1. He released his drivers in December 1962, making it official.

Dutch sands. Bonnier finished seventh, but Gurney was forced to retire when his gearshift came adrift on lap 48.

Ferry Porsche now wondered if he shouldn't give up on the whole program, but Gurney, Thomalla, and racing manager Huschke von Hanstein convinced him to stay with it for the next event—Monte Carlo. Gurney was third on the grid, but a serious pileup ended his day on the very first lap. Electing to pass up the Belgian Grand Prix at Spa, the engineers went back to their drawing boards while the racing team vowed not to shave until Porsche won.

Efforts in Zuffenhausen were directed toward further improving both aerodynamics and engine power (the 753 still wasn't above 180 bhp). The seat was raked further back, the rollbar lowered, and fuel tanks reshaped accordingly; front suspension was beefed up and a rear sway bar added; Bilstein shocks replaced Konis; horsepower was pulled up to about 185.

After Gurney ran 15 good test laps at the Nürburgring, Von Hanstein was allowed to rejoin the wars at the French Grand Prix at Rouen. This time, Gurney triumphed, giving Porsche its first—and so far only—GP championship points. To be sure, he won by attrition. Jim Clark's Lotus and Graham Hill's BRM were about a half-minute ahead when both were forced to retire in quick succession. But Gurney didn't care. "If you win a GP, why, you take it," he said later. "Some of the other guys were faster and they had difficulties, so I inherited the darn thing. I was trying my darndest, but it wasn't the same as jumping out and really legitimately blowing them all off." At least his teammates could now shave off their beards.

Solitude's 177-mile marathon was next. It wouldn't count toward the championship, but no one was conceding it to Porsche, Lotus and BRM arriving ready for battle. Some 350,000 gathered at the beautiful circuit, hoping to see the "native" cars win as they had the weekend before. They weren't disappointed. Clark grabbed the pole, but Gurney put his 804-03 out front by the end of lap one—and there he stayed, turning in a record lap of 108.37 mph for good measure. Bonnier passed Clark early on to take second, and gamely held on despite being short 300 rpm due to the

The Type 804 Formula 1 car was designed with aerodynamics in mind. And weight saving: The entire car weighed only 15 pounds more than the FIA's 990-pound minimum. Wheelbase measured 90.5 inches. The Type 753 engine developed about 180 horsepower.

loss of one of his four tailpipes. "Afterward, going around on the victory lap, all those people were throwing their hats in the air," Gurney remembered. "I was very proud of that victory."

Alas, Solitude proved the season high-point for Porsche. The team expected to do well in the German GP at the 'Ring, another "hometown" circuit famous for its twists and turns. Gurney started from the pole, but Hill had his BRM running right and John Surtess came home second in a Lola, leaving Gurney to settle for third. Despite soaking rain, all three drove a masterly race, but Gurney termed it "the most disappointing.... We had all

worked very hard—all the engineers and mechanics—and then not to win that race was very difficult to swallow. Especially because this car, even in the wet, [was] capable of winning...if we could ever have gotten back in front.... But it played hell getting around those guys because they could hold me up in the turns and then out-accelerate me."

Porsche stood to do better in the Italian GP at Monza. The 804's weight distribution was shifted forward by putting a fuel tank in the nose, and the driver could now disengage the cooling fan for 8-10 seconds when extra power was needed. But Bonnier managed only sixth, while a defective rear axle

rendered Gurney a DNF. In the U.S. Grand Prix at Watkins Glen, Gurney finished a disheartening fifth and Bonnier held on for 13th despite pranging his exhaust system. By the season closer, the South African GP at Kyalami, Porsche had decided to fold its Formula 1 tent.

Though rumors of a fresh assault circulated that winter, Ferry Porsche had decided to withdraw from Formula 1 and released his two drivers in December 1962. It made sense. Porsche was one of the few passenger-car manufacturers involved in F1— and the largest—and its competition interests were too broad to warrant

Although the Type 804 didn't bring many Formula 1
trophies home, the car Dan Gurney drove occupies a place
of honor in the Porsche Museum. Porsche's racing
interests were simply too broad to warrant the colossal
sums required to develop such a specialized car.

the colossal sums required to develop such a specialized entry. Better to concentrate on Formula 2, where Porsche had proven its mettle, and the sports-racing venues, where victories had far more benefit for showroom sales.

Today, Gurney's 804 occupies a place of honor in the Porsche Museum amidst dozens of other Zuffenhausen racers (including an F2 787). Dan drove it again for *Auto Motor und Sport*'s 1982 retrospective: "There's a certain 'time machine' aspect to it that's very, very pleasant. You identify with this old faithful horse. You've been through quite a bit together and that's a very special feeling also."

Porsche has lately returned to Formula 1, though as an engine builder, not a car constructor. It all started in the early Eighties when Zuffenhausen was commissioned by the French firm Techniques d'Avant Garde (TAG) to design a new powerplant for Team McLaren around the prevailing 1.5-liter formula. The result was an innovative V-6 with twin turbochargers and, as Porsche likes to point out, a good many features that just happen to be shared with the 5.0-liter V-8 in the current 928S 4.

As indeed they are. Both engines use aluminum alloy for block, heads, and pistons; hemispherical combustion chambers with central sparkplugs; and four valves per cylinder (two intakes and two exhausts). However, the included angle between the V-6's cylinder banks is 80 degrees instead of the V-8's 90, and bores are lined with harder nickel-silicon alloy (instead of silicon crystals) for reliability in tortuous competition conditions. Induction is via a racing version of the Bosch Digital Motor Electronics system used in the 924S and 944 Series. Here it manages the twin turbochargers as well as multiport fuel injection (with two injectors per cylinder) and integrated electronic ignition. With four intercoolers, the TAG-Porsche V-6 can spin out 1000 horsepower for race qualifying—all from 1.5 liters!

Fitted to the TAG-McLaren MP4, the Porsche-designed V-6 proved so dominant in its debut 1984 season that the only real question was which of the two team drivers would win the overall championship. Between them, Niki Lauda and Alain Prost won 12 of the 16 scheduled events and dueled for points down to the last laps of the season finale in Portugal, where Lauda eked out his third world driver's crown by just half a point. The constructor's championship was sewn up by mid-season, as only four events (Belgium, Canada, Detroit, and Dallas) eluded the TAG-McLarens.

Given the events of 22 years earlier, this overwhelming victory tasted especially sweet to Porsche, and there was more to come. The 1985 season was much more closely fought, but Prost managed wins at Brazil, Monaco, England, Austria, and Italy, and Lauda came home first in Holland. Prost collected the driver's crown he'd wanted so badly, and TAG-McLaren won its second consecutive constructor's championship.

The 1986 story had the same ending but a different plot. It was the first all-turbo season in Formula 1 history, with no fewer than 14 different makes representing 20 chassis and 10 engine types. Two teams quickly took charge: the TAG/Porsche-McLarens and the Honda-powered Williams FW11s.

Prost and teammate Keke Rosberg battled against Nigel Mansell and Nelson Piquet through 15 of the 16 scheduled events. Rosberg's best showing was a second at Monaco, while Prost notched three firsts to Team Williams' seven.

Both driver's and constructor's championships hinged on the season closer, the second Australian GP at Adelaide. Rosberg again failed to finish, as he had eight times before, but canny tire strategy brought Prost home 17 seconds ahead of Piquet, giving him a second straight driving title (by a slim two-point margin over Piquet) and TAG-McLaren its third straight constructor's crown (143½ points to Team Williams' 141).

The 1987 campaign is still being

fought at this writing, but the TAG-McLarens and their Porsche-designed engines are again in the thick of the F1 wars. Though the displacement limit will be lowered to 1.2 liters for 1988 and beyond, Porsche engineers believe they can preserve the TAG engine's incredible power through honing of induction, the twin turbos, and the quadruple intercoolers, as well as making the engine electronics "smarter."

Meantime, Porsche enthusiasts everywhere can rejoice in the marque's return to Formula 1, however indirect, for no other make is more deserving of a place on the Mount Olympus of automotive competition. It may have taken over two decades, but Porsche is back where it belongs.

Porsche likes to point out that the Type 804 Formula 1 car was mid-engined like the Auto Union racers Ferdinand Porsche designed in the '30s. Here, Dan Gurney is behind the wheel of the 804 at Rouen.

Conquering All: 904 to 962

By 1963, the days of the great 550 Spyder and its developments were over. With competition in the "big leagues" heating up, the time had come for Porsche to move to more specialized racing designs that owed less to road-car technology than their forebears.

The car that marked this historic turn was the 904 Carrera GTS. It was the last competition Porsche with anything like a "stock" engine, and thus the last that might be used on the street—if you insisted—yet it set the pattern for every "deluxe" competition Porsche built since.

Which is a bit surprising because, except for a fiberglass body, the 904 broke no new technical ground for Porsche. David Owen wrote that it "was beautiful, but it wasn't as aerodynamically efficient as it could have been. It was tough...but it wasn't as light as it should have been. And it used the old four-cam four-cylinder engine, stretched in this case to 1966 cc [120 cubic inches] and producing (ultimately) 195 bhp [some sources list 185 DIN] ahead of the rear wheels." The 904's boxed-rail chassis, said *Car and Driver* magazine, "might be straight out of Frank Kurtis' design book."

All true enough. But it must also be said that the 904 was one of the prettiest Porsches of all time: low, sleek, exquisitely shaped. And it went like almighty clappers. "Time and again," Owen continued, "in races like the 1964 Rheims 12 Hours, the Porsches would come roaring home just behind the big Ferraris." With it, Porsche returned to prominence in international sports-car competition.

Work on the 904 had begun in 1962, when a wood body buck was built to a design by Ferdinand "Butzi" Porsche, grandson of the company founder and creator of the 901/911. This was sent in February 1963 to Heinkel, the aircraft firm, which returned the first finished body the following November.

Certain 904 elements were influenced by Porsche's abortive 804 Formula 1 car, notably the all-round double-wishbone suspension. The rear employed four-link geometry, with upper and lower pairs of parallel trailing arms and reversed wishbones. Telescopic shocks and coil springs appeared at both ends in lieu of lateral torsion bars. Steering was the new ZF rack-and-pinion mechanism from the recently announced 901/911, which also supplied the 904's five-speed transaxle. Brakes were outboard Dunlop/Ate four-wheel discs; tiny drums were provided inside the rear rotors for the handbrake *a la* 356C.

To speed pit stops, bodywork behind the doors was a one-piece assembly that lifted up on rear hinges, and the engine could be easily removed for more serious servicing. Such convenience didn't extend to body repairs, however, as Porsche found it extremely difficult to fix broken panels quickly.

FIA rules at the time required 100 units to qualify a car for GT-class racing, and Porsche completed the requisite number of 904s by April 1964. The first six were retained as factory team cars and were eventually seen with four-, six-, and eight-cylinder engines. The first dozen or so customer cars went to the U.S., where the racing

season started earlier than Europe's. Unfortunately, only these 100 would be built. All were quickly snapped up, but a number of buyers were left wanting as orders far exceeded cars.

Fitted for road work, the 904 greeted its driver with a full set of gauges dominated by a 9000-rpm tachometer. Deep bucket seats were provided but didn't adjust; the pedals did instead. Different size seats were available to further accommodate various physiques. A huge single wiper swept side-to-side on a pantograph arm for maximum windshield coverage.

It all sounds quite civilized, but the Carrera four didn't like stop-and-go traffic, and the car as a whole wasn't as successful for touring as it was in racing. Most 904s now used on the road have been retrofitted with 911 engines, which does nothing for nonexistent sound insulation, nor a cockpit that was never designed for relaxed highway cruising. But then, this *was* a racing car.

"Ze machine," cracked *C/D*'s Brock Yates, "ist chust an oldt Carrera mohtorr vis only 130 horses. Ist much better vis too-litah 180-horrsepowerr rracing enchine....Oh sure, only 130 hp. It didn't seem hardly enough to do any more than pool all our blood along our jellied spine, break our glasses across the bridge of our nose and leave the impression of our belt buckle on our stomach." Huschke von Hanstein, giving Yates his first 904 ride, was doing 100 mph three blocks from the factory. "You're sure President Johnson does this?" Yates asked. "Ja shoor—look!" Huschke removed both

The Carrera GTS 904 was Porsche's first "specialized"
racing design. It owed less to the production cars, and
was the last with anything like a "stock" engine.

The original model of the 904 (*above*) is in the Porsche Museum. The racer (*top row*) did well, but was not as happy as a road car; 100 were built. The 1966-cc flat four was located *ahead* of the rear axle (*opposite, bottom*); the body and frame weighed 320 pounds.

hands from the small woodrim wheel. "The 904 tracked along as steadily at 120 mph as a Yankee Clipper."

Test results showed 0-60-mph times of 5.5-6.1 seconds and a 160-mph observed top speed—fast enough for government work. And no surprise when you realize that, pudgy though it was, the 904 was the first Carrera with a sub-10 pounds/bhp power-to-

weight ratio: about 8 lbs/bhp—smack dab in muscle-car territory. And it could run at 160 all day long if necessary, as reliable as Big Ben.

The 904 looked a sure winner after factory pilot Herbert Linge drove an early one around the Nürburgring in 9 minutes, 30 seconds. And so it would be. The quadcam Carrera engine may have been 10 years old by now, but it

was at its development peak, while the mid-engine layout made for superb handling. Though the highish weight reduced the 904's effectiveness in short-distance "sprint" contests, it proved no great handicap in longer races on less-than-perfect surfaces. A 904 might not outrun competitors, but it could almost certainly outlast them.

Successes, both factory and private,

came quickly for the 904, with longer events the predictable forte of this almost too-sturdy machine. Clutch problems prevented a finish at Sebring in 1964, the car's debut outing, but things went better a month later when 904s ran first and third in the Targa Florio, leading a fleet of Ferraris and Shelby Cobras. Next came a third overall in the Nürburgring 1000 Kilometers. Five cars contested Le Mans that year and all finished in the top 12, the highest placing seventh overall. In the Tour de France, 904s ran third through sixth (behind a brace of Ferrari GTOs) and were first and second on handicap.

For 1965, Porsche fitted a revalved Carrera engine with reprofiled cam-shaft. Horsepower went up again in 1966 via higher compression. As mentioned, a few 904s were seen with more than four cylinders: the 2.0-liter flat six from the 911, tuned for up to 210 DIN horsepower, and the potent 2.2-liter Type 771/1 eight, derived from the 804 F1 engine of 1962, with up to 270 bhp.

The 904 was nothing if not versatile, and it did well in major rallies. For example, Porsche acquired the services of ace Mercedes driver Eugen Bohringer for the 1965 Monte Carlo. One of only 22 of 237 starters to finish, he placed second overall in one of the snowiest Montes ever.

Though costly by 1964 standards, the 904 was a remarkable bargain all things considered: $7425 at the factory. A pity that more weren't made, for it was a glorious machine, special even for Porsche. Those fortunate enough to own one, wrote Yates, "won't be dissuaded by the awkward-ness of getting in and out, by the expense of maintaining the four-cam engine, by the harsh ride, nor by the insufficient steering lock. No sir, they're utter fools, and we wish we were among them."

A semblance of production power appeared in Porsche's next "deluxe" racer, only now it was the 911 flat six. It mounted amidships in an all-out competition machine, the Type 906. Also called Carrera 6, it was the first Porsche designed by Dr. Ferry

The 904 was the first Carrera with a pounds/bhp ratio
under 10 (actually about 8:1). It stormed from 0-60 in
5.5-6.1 seconds and could run at 160 mph all day long if
necessary, as reliable as Big Ben.

Porsche's young nephew, Ferdinand
Piëch, who'd helped develop the
engine.

The 906 was built around an ultra-
light tubular space-frame topped by a
very streamlined body giving an overall height of only 38.6 inches. The engine, turned 180 degrees from its 911
positioning, was quite similar to the
production unit in basic design but
much lighter, making extensive use of
magnesium and aluminum alloys.
With dual ignition, 10.3:1 compression, two triple-throat Weber 46IDA
carburetors and special manifolds and
exhaust system, this Type 901/20 put
out 210-220 bhp (DIN) at 8000 rpm
and a peak 145 pounds-feet torque at
6000 rpm. Clutch and transaxle were
911-based, and a variety of gearsets
was devised for various tracks and race
distances.

First outing for the 906 was the 1966
Daytona 24 Hours, where a dark blue
car finished sixth, beaten only by a factory team of fleet Ford GTs and a single Ferrari. The lead car at Sebring
spun out, but 906s nailed fourth, sixth,
and eighth. At the Targa Florio that
year they ended up 1-3-4-8. Ford GTs
dominated Le Mans, but Carrera 6s
were right behind, 4-5-6-7.

The Carrera 6's lineal successor was
the 1967 Type 910/6, which used the
same engine in an even lighter space-
frame topped by more handsome and
slippery fiberglass bodywork. There
was also a 270-bhp flat-eight variation,
the 910/8, powered by the 2.2-liter
Type 771/1 engine. One of these appeared at the 1967 Targa Florio, where
910/6s placed second and third. Six-
cylinder cars also finished high at Daytona, Sebring, Monza, and Spa, while a

trio cleaned up at the Nürburgring
1000 Kilometers. (A 910/8 might have
led them home but suffered an electrical failure on the last lap.) Porsche
outscored Ferrari in 1967 Manufacturers Championship points (helped
by a class win at Le Mans by one of the
new 907s), but Ferrari prevailed because only the best five races counted.

Racing developments came thick
and fast in the late Sixties—one new
car after another. Predictably,
Porsche's were logical evolutions.
Thus, the 904's suspension and brakes
went into the 906, whose frame was
lightened and modified for the 910.
Next came the 907, which started out
as a more aerodynamic 910, with the
same six- and eight-cylinder engines
and somewhat smoother bodywork,
again in K (*Kurzheck*, short-tail) and L
(*Langheck*, long-tail) configurations.

Criticism was made that the Carrera GTS 904 (*both pages*) was too pudgy. But the quadcam Carrera engine, already a decade old, was at its development peak and the mid-engine layout allowed for superb handling. Handicapped by its weight in short-distance events, the 904 usually outlasted the competition in long-distance races. The '64 model seen here was originally the personal car of a factory team driver, Count de Beaufort, and has never been raced.

The next step was the 908, basically a 907 with a new and simpler 3.0-liter flat eight.

It was prompted by the FIA's 3.0-liter displacement ceiling on prototype-class racing for 1968, echoing an earlier move by the Le Mans organizers after Ford's GTs swept the 24 Hours for the second time in 1967. Porsche probably didn't influence these decisions, but racing manager Huschke von Hanstein was certainly close enough to keep track of them.

Work on the new engine got underway in July 1967. With 2977 cc (181.6 cid) and a formidable 350 DIN horsepower, it was exactly right for the new formula. More important, it enabled Porsche to compete at last with any rival for overall wins, not just class victories. As time would prove, the 908 and its new powerplant spelled the end of the vaunted Ford GTs.

Piëch and his engineers faced but one obstacle in developing the Type 908 engine: money. But an expensive ground-up design wasn't necessary. Instead, they merely added two cylinders to the 911 engine, changed to magnesium-alloy construction, bolted on twincam cylinder heads, and stretched bore 5 mm (to 85 mm). Completing the transformation were titanium-alloy flywheel and con rods. Putting power to the ground was a hefty transaxle with six forward speeds for coupes, five on the later (1969) 908 spyders. Porsche insiders jokingly termed this the "injection gearbox" because lubrication was via an oil jet directed at each pair of gears.

Outside, the first 908s were difficult to distinguish from 907s—mainly because they *were* 907s with aerodynamic refinements; only minimal chassis modifications were needed to accommodate the new engine. But after a "907/8" won the Daytona 24 Hours, Porsche shifted from 13- to 15-inch wheels and tires, which made for higher front fenders that reduced aerodynamic efficiency.

High-speed stability was one of several problems that plagued the 908s in '68. By mid-season, the K-body had acquired a strut-mounted rear wing with suspension-controlled flaps, Porsche's first use of a such a device. An earlier K won the Nürburgring 1000 Kilometers, which would prove the 908's only victory that year. Continued teething troubles, particularly with the new transaxle, prevented

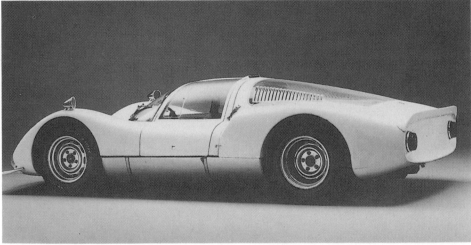

This page: The Porsche 906—also known as the Carrera 6—was designed by Ferdinand Piëch around a modified 911 flat six and an ultra-light tubular space frame, topped by a 38.6-inch-high streamlined body. Its frame was further lightened for the '67 910 (*opposite*).

further wins. Meanwhile, the Fords took Le Mans a third time.

This underwhelming performance led to some personnel changes at Weissach. The charming Huschke von Hanstein, Porsche's long-time racing manager, stepped down but continued as a consultant. His successor, Rico Steinemann, picked up new drivers: Britain's Richard Attwood and Brian Redman, Formula 2 maestro Kurt Ahrens, and rally aces Pauli Toivonen, Björn Waldegaard, and Gérard Larousse—one of the most daunting factory teams in the business. Steinemann decided to use the open spyders for shorter courses, long-tail coupes for fast tracks like Monza, and 908Ks for in-between situations. He also decided to ignore events not counting toward the championship. It was win or nothing and let the privateers worry about non-point matches.

Not everything went Porsche's way in '69. The initial contests at Daytona and Sebring were plagued by breakdowns, and Ford won again at Le Mans in September. In between, though, the plan worked: 908s finished 1-2 at Monza, 1-2-3-4 in the Targa, and 1-2-3-4-5 at the 'Ring. In short, Porsche won the Makes Championship going away, trouncing Ford 76 points to 26. And 908s would continue doing well. In 1981—12 years after the first examples appeared—a 908/80 won the Nürburgring 1000. Few machines can claim as much.

Arriving with the 908 was the 909 *Bergspyder* (*Berg* = mountain). It lasted only a year, after which Porsche withdrew from hillclimbs to concentrate on Makes Championship events in 1970. But while it was around, the 909 was unbeatable.

Not that Porsche had anything more to prove. Edgar Barth had won the European Hillclimb Championship in 1959, 1963, and '64 in stubby, purpose-built versions of the Type 718 and RS 60/61. Gerhard Mitter followed by winning it in 1966-67 using similar open derivatives of the 906 and 910.

The 909 evolved from the 910 Bergspyder of 1967, with the same aging but still capable 2.0-liter flat eight (Type 770/0) coaxed up to 275 bhp (DIN), as high as this engine would go. Weighing a hair under 950 pounds, the 909 could see 155 mph on the straight, and with extra-wide tracks (57.9/57.6 inches front/rear) and a compact 89.1-inch wheelbase (versus the 908s' 90.6

inches), it was simply amazing on the curves. As on the 910 Berg, bodywork was low and squat, but even more streamlined, with a pair of small downward-pointing "spoilerettes" on the nose and two up-tilting flaps on the tail. Beneath was a tubular spaceframe that placed engine and driver relatively far forward. In fact, the driver's legs actually extended over the centerline of the front anti-sway bar. Titanium was used extensively in the all-coil suspension and for the fuel tank.

Mitter made it three in a row by winning the '68 Hillclimb Championship. But the triumph was overshadowed because teammate Ludovico Scarfiotti, the greatest of the con-temporary Italians, was killed at Rossfeld when his 909 leaped off the road and plastered itself against a tree. It was the first death at a Porsche racing wheel and a black day for Zuffenhausen. In the wake of "Lulu's" loss, Mitter decided he'd had enough of the hills.

The stage was now set for Porsche's biggest, fastest, and most successful sports-racer yet—a car that would recall as no other the screaming silver *Deutschlanders* of prewar fame: the supercharged Auto Unions, also designed by Porsche hands. It would so completely dominate the sport that nothing else could be properly compared to it. Today it's been enshrined with the Grand Prix Mercedes and In-dianapolis Offys as one of racing's giants. We can only be speaking of the 917.

The FIA's 3.0-liter displacement limit for prototypes back in '67 had been accompanied by a 5.0-liter ceiling on Group 4 sports cars. Though aimed at curbing Ford, it prompted Porsche to move on two levels: the 908 for the prototype class, the 917 for Group 4. Of course, no one outside Zuffenhausen knew about the latter until the 917 showed up at the 1969 Geneva Salon. And since Porsche had never ventured into 4.0/5.0-liter territory, it sent shock waves throughout the racing world. Enzo Ferrari at first doubted that anyone could build an air-cooled flat-12, let alone win with it. He soon

learned otherwise—the hard way.

The 917 chassis was basically that of the 908, enlarged and strengthened for the new engine. It wasn't feasible to make the eight into a twelve simply by adding cylinders; that would have meant a long, undesirably "whippy" crankshaft. Still, Porsche managed to retain the 908 engine's reciprocating parts and its 85-mm bore and 66-mm stroke for the new 917 unit, ending with 4494 cc (274.2 cubic inches)—exactly 50 percent more capacity. (Porsche also built a flat 16 but never raced it.) Thanks to their experience in lightweight engines and chassis, designers kept curb weight very close to the 800-kg (1764-pound) Group 4 minimum. In fact, the 917 ended up so light—and its engine so powerful—that they found it unnecessary to use the full 5.0 liters allowed.

To minimize critical vibration, a two-piece crankshaft was used with a power take-off from a central gear cut into it. A second shaft above the crank drove twin electronic distributors; a

The 910 was a winner for Porsche, whose policy was to build a new car for every major event and then to sell the cars to privateers for racing. This late-chassis short-tail 910 competed with both six- and eight-cylinder engines.

Bosch fuel injection unit was belt-driven from the left intake camshaft. For optimum crank balance, each pin had two con rods, which also allowed wider flange and bearing widths. With 10.5:1 compression, the twelve as raced at Le Mans and Spa developed 580 bhp at 8400 rpm and 375 lbs-ft torque at 6600. This, plus extreme lightness, promised to make the 917 the fastest car in the class—and the FIA knew it.

Porsche duly presented the 917's homologation papers. What followed is one of those stories race fans love to tell about bureaucratic regulators. Porsche had more than the minimum 25 cars under construction when the

FIA's International Sporting Commission (CSI) first visited, but the inspection team demanded that they be *ready to roll* before they'd certify the 917. After a marathon effort by all hands, 25 fully finished cars were lined up in a Le Mans-start sort of formation for CSI's second look on April 21, 1969. The Porsche folk invited their guests to drive any one at random. The inspectors meekly declined.

Porsche again raced *Kurz* and *Lang* versions of its latest fiberglass-bodied streamliner. As before, the aft sections could be exchanged to suit distance and track conditions. The long-tail, designed for high-speed circuits, had a drag coefficient of 0.33, good for 236

mph at Le Mans. Both *Hecks* incorporated suspension-controlled aero flaps, though they caused intense debate and were banned at some '69 events. Without them, the 917 was a real handful at racing speeds.

Like the 908, the 917 needed a full season to be completely sorted out. One car led at Le Mans for 20 hours before retiring with a cracked bell housing, leaving Jacky Ickx in a Gulf-Weyer GT40 to make it four straight for Ford—but only by a scant two seconds over a screaming 908.

Suitably impressed, Gulf-Weyer agreed to sponsor a team of 917s for 1970. There was a second sponsor, one old hands highly approved: Porsche-

Porsche's 907 started out as a more aerodynamic 910, with the same six- and eight-cylinder engines and smoother bodywork in K (short-tail) and L (long-tail) versions. This '68 long-tail 907 (*both pages*) is the last known copy of five built for Le Mans. It boasts a Cd of 0.27, weighs 1240 pounds, and tops 180 mph.

Salsburg, operated by Ferry Porsche's sister, Louise Piëch. The Martini Racing Team would also field its first 917 in 1970, at Le Mans, a purple-and-green monster for Larrouse/Kauhsen.

Inevitably, these teams and the works entries simply dominated Le Mans 1970, sweeping home 1-2-3 at

speeds that have not been equalled to this day. Confounding the wind-tunnel crew, which had labored long and hard on a special 917 LH (*langheck*) just for this race, the winner was a *short*-tail Porsche-Salzburg entry piloted by Dickie Attwood and veteran Hans Hermann. Though marred by crashes

and the death of a corner marshal, it was the crowning moment of Hermann's career. He retired from racing soon afterwards, depressed by the tragic events, but his work was complete, his greatest ambition realized. The victory was just as sweet for the Austrian team. The land that 22 years before had given birth to the strange teardrop-shape 356 had produced a winner in the world's most prestigious road race.

Having won every 1970 contest except the Sebring 12 Hours, the Targa, and the Nürburgring 1000, the 917s were now "the cars to beat," as Don Vorderman put it. But in 1971, nobody tried. The only apparent challenger was Ferrari's 512M, faster and lighter than its 512S—but not as light as the 917.

To thwart any potential threat from the Italian quarter, Porsche engineers decided to take advantage of their remaining half-liter, bringing the twelve first to 4907 cc (299.4 cid), then to 4998 cc (305 cid) for 600 and 630 bhp, respectively. The 5.0, found to be the more reliable, was selected for Le Mans '71. But Ferrari elected not to contest the Manufacturers Championship that year, so Porsche again won all the big races—Daytona, Sebring, Monza, Spa, the Osterreichring, and Le Mans—on the efforts of Gulf-Weyer and Martini Racing. The latter took over from Porsche-Salzburg and repeated its triumph at the Sarthe circuit, Helmut Marko and Gijs van Linnep doing the honors.

A memorable factory car at Le Mans '71 was the 917/20, a low-drag special built to see whether the L-body's superior aerodynamics could be achieved without its long tail. This rather bloated-looking coupe with vast lateral overhang was developed by the SERA design office in France and chosen over a rival proposal by Porsche's own stylists. The company consoled them by letting them paint and decorate the thing, which they nicknamed "Big Bertha" and "The Pig" and finished in bright piggy-pink with dotted lines to mark off various sections like a butcher's diagram. Their disdain made little difference: "Bertha" crashed and few tears were likely shed among the stylists.

The end of the '71 season ended the 917's Group 4 career. As Porsche knew from the outset, 5.0-liter sports cars wouldn't be eligible for the Makes Championship from 1972. All due credit, then, to Weissach's determination to build a winner—and the speed with which they did it.

Porsche built 37 Group 4 917s, and many survive today. Count Gregorio Rossi of Martini & Rossi had Porsche put one in concours condition (painted silver like its German forebears from decades past) for display at his Paris offices. Porsche also salvaged the 917/20 "Pig" and treated it to a complete res-

toration in 1985. Today it rests in the Porsche Museum alongside long- and short-tail 917s and 908s, assorted Bergspyders, the 908, 910, Carrera 6, 904, and all the rest.

But the 917 was far from finished after 1971—it was ready, in fact, to write more history in the Canadian-

This 907 (*opposite and below*) is powered by the Type 771 two-liter eight-cylinder engine, good for about 260 horsepower. Compare its tail with that of the short-tail 907 (*bottom*), seen here as a '67 set up for racing at Germany's Nürburgring.

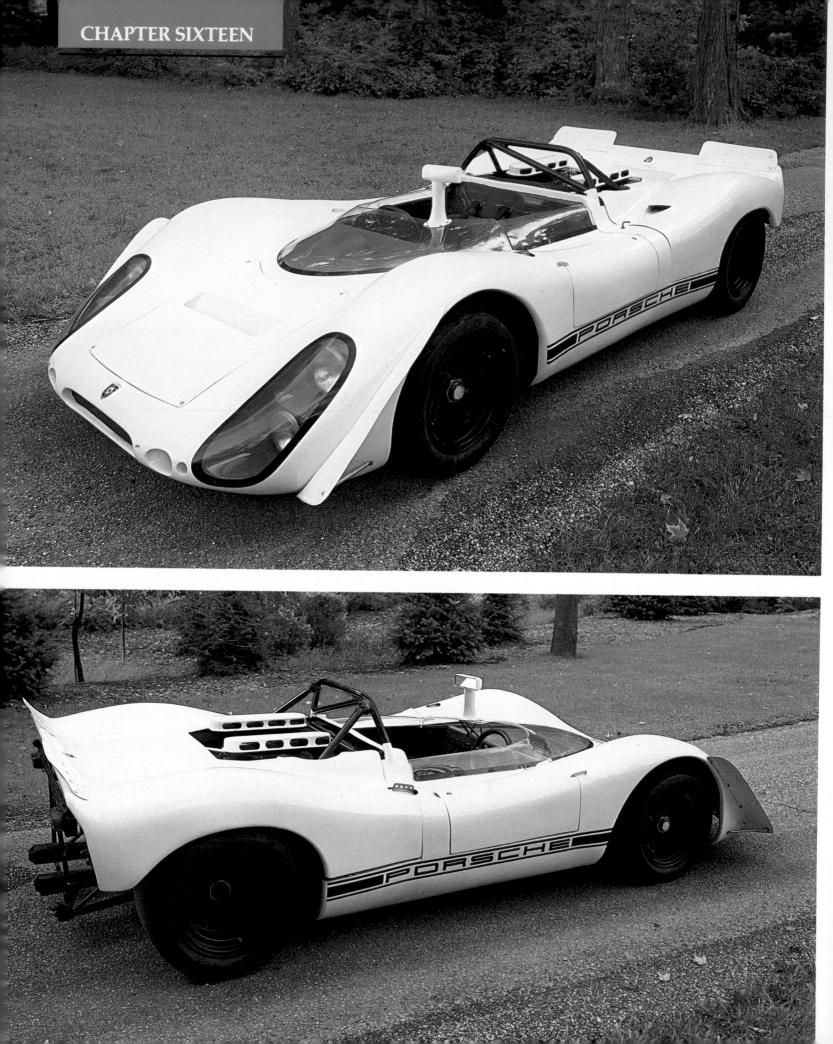

Porsche developed the 908, shown here as a '69 model (*both pages*), with an eye toward the FIA's new three-liter displacement ceiling on prototype-class racing for the 1968 season. The 908 was basically a 907 with a new, simpler 2977-cc (181.6-cid) flat eight that cranked out a formidable 350 DIN horsepower.

American Challenge Cup. Established by the Sports Car Club of America (SCCA) in 1966 as North America's premiere road-racing series, the Can-Am was initially run under what amounted to Formula Libre rules that permitted almost anything at all. This resulted in a diverse assortment of cars and not much action, so regulations were rewritten to make things more interesting.

Still, Can-Am rules in the early Seventies were surprisingly liberal. Competitors had to qualify as FIA Group 7, which basically required little more than fenders and some semblance of a cockpit. There were certain restrictions on aerodynamic aids, weight, and engines (nothing below 2.5 liters, no gas turbines), but the series was pretty wide open otherwise.

On paper, the 917 was not good Can-Am material. Up to now, the dominant cars had run cheap, uncomplicated American V-8s, mainly Chevys. Practicality dictated an off-the-shelf engine for Porsche, and the biggest one available was the 917's. (Weissach again contemplated its flat 16, which stood to deliver about *2000* horsepower with turbocharger, but progress with the twelve rendered it superfluous.)

Porsche had tasted Can-Am action as early as 1969. Two open cars designated 917PA (for Volkswagen of America's Porsche + Audi division) were built, and one was sent to North America late in the season. As expected, it was no match for the American V-8s, its best finish being a third at Bridgehampton. The chief problem was the competition's tremendous low-end torque.

Once ousted from the Makes Championship, Porsche turned in earnest to developing a Can-Am 917, approaching the project from two directions. One was an enlarged 5.4-liter twelve which, despite a creditable gain in torque, produced only 30 more horsepower than the 5.0-liter version. The second was turbocharging, via an Eberspacher system boosting at 18-20 pounds per square inch. Though considerable work was required to insure reliability, the turbo released astonishing power: 850 bhp (DIN) from the original 4.5-liter, 950-1000 on the 5.0. Having helped with development, Penske Racing agreed to campaign the 5.0-liter version of the Type 917/10, with Mark Donohue driving.

The 917 (*both pages*), one of Porsche's all-time great racers, came about when Porsche decided to contest Group 4, which restricted displacement to five liters. The chassis of the 908 was enlarged and strengthened to accommodate the new 4494-cc air-cooled flat-12, which in Le Mans form yielded 580 bhp on 10.5:1 compression.

Donohue went to Germany to work with chief program engineer Helmut Flegel. "I've got a unique relationship in this project," Donohue said, "a kind...I've never had before. Helmut Flegel...is capable in every respect. I can talk to him. I can say things to him and he to me and we understand each other perfectly....I've never really had a relationship like that before." Donohue added, "When Porsche ships you a car, it's not like with McLaren or Lola. With a Porsche, you unload it off the airplane, put the key in the ignition, turn it on and you race it....We've never seen a car so complete."

The affable Donohue thus summarized a close, friendly partnership with Porsche over months of trial and error in bringing the 917/10 to that race-ready state. For example, the extra power required a completely new gearbox, strengthened chassis, improved cooling system, and deeply finned, vented aluminum disc brakes. They also watched weight. A secret here was using magnesium alloy instead of aluminum for the tubular space-frame. Questioned hard by *Road & Track*'s Pete Lyons, Donohue said the material involved was "Unobtainium."

Lyons pointed out that the 917/10's great strength wasn't power (McLaren M20s had that too) but handling. Porsche had revived an anti-dive suspension from earlier 917 prototypes, with the upper-wishbone pivot axes angled down toward the rear and converging toward the front. Donohue "was a lot faster than anybody else in the corners," Lyons wrote, "by a factor of 5 percent—which is a bunch."

With such a well-prepared car, the Penske team proved virtually unbeatable by McLaren or anyone else. One of the turbo relief valves denied Mark the opening race at Mosport, and during practice for the next, Road Atlanta, he was injured in a shunt. Teammate George Follmer then took over, winning in Georgia, then at Mid-Ohio,

Road America, Laguna Seca, Riverside—and naturally the Can-Am Championship. In Europe, Leo Kinnunen matched this performance in the similar Interserie competition, giving Porsche its third championship in a row (after non-turbo 917s won it in 1970-71.)

Over the winter, Donohue and Flegel improved the body and built reliability into the 5.4-liter turbo, which by springtime was pumping out 1100 bhp at 7800 rpm and 810 lbs-ft torque at 6500. (These were merely the nominal outputs. At 32-psi boost, the dyno showed an amazing 1560 bhp!) With this new and better car, the 917/30, the 1973 Can-Am was a Donohue cakewalk.

It began to seem that every time Porsche started dominating competition, authorities would rewrite the rules to even things up (though so far, they've been only temporarily successful in that). That's just what they did for the '74 Can-Am season, effectively

Opposite page: The 917 was available in either long- or short-tail form (*bottom*). As introduced, it was priced at $35,000 for the few entitled to buy one. The 917 evolved with time, of course, with Mark Donohue driving a 917/10 (*top*) in the Can-Am. Above is a 917/30.

barring the 917s from yet another series. But Petermax Müller took the Interserie—and for good measure won it once more in 1975 with a turbocharged 908/03. With that, Porsche had achieved supremacy in almost all forms of road racing.

One final triumph awaited. At Daytona in August 1975, driving a specially prepared 917/30, Donohue set a new closed-course speed record of 221.120 mph, breaking A.J. Foyt's 217.854. Alas, it would be Mark's last hurrah. Little more than a week later, he was killed when his Formula 1 Penske crashed at the Osterreichring. He had accomplished great things, for Porsche and motorsports in general, and he's still missed.

Though the 917 really *was* finished this time, Porsche felt ready by now to tackle anything the fickle FIA could throw at it. When Porsche needed a sports-racer in the new 3.0-liter Group 6 unsupercharged class for 1976, its engineers promptly reeled off a fabulous contender in the image of "the big one," the Type 936.

Here, Porsche returned to its mainstay powerplant, the 911 flat six, albeit in 2142-cc (130.7 cid) Carrera RSR form (precisely 2998.8 cc under the 1.4

handicap factor for turbocharged cars). Designed mainly for short hauls, the engine could tolerate 20-psi boost that provided a maximum 520 bhp (DIN) at 8000 rpm—242 bhp per liter! It naturally rode ahead of the rear wheels, tied to a 917-type transaxle. Suspension and steering were also in the 917 mold, as was the aluminum space-frame. Fiberglass was again used for the bodywork, a new spyder style that looked for all the world like a cleaned-up, slicked-down Can-Am 917, dominated by a huge air intake above and behind the cockpit and equally large tailfins cradling an adjustable aerofoil.

The 936 had a splendid first season. The climax was Porsche's triumphant return to Le Mans, where Jacky Ickx and Jochen Mass drove the winning car. The 936 also collected the World Sports Car title that year. It then repeated as Le Mans winner in 1977, giving Porsche its fourth outright victory at Sarthe, with Ickx, Hurley Haywood, and Jurgen Barth sharing the driving honors.

Alas, the 936s would later run into mechanical faults at times (and one was disqualified on a technicality). But Porsche never put all its competition

eggs in one basket, and the 935 produced the marque's highest-ever Le Mans finishes in 1978-79 (see Chapter 13). A 750-bhp 935/78 placed eighth overall in 1978; a twin-turbo 935K3 (K for Kremer) turned back the Mirage M10s to win for Ludvig/Wittington in '79. In 1980, a 908 (still hanging in there) took second, with 935K3s in fifth, eighth, and ninth. Thanks to privateers, Porsche again won the Makes Championship that year, and in 1981.

One significant race had yet to see a Porsche, though it nearly did in 1980. It was the Indianapolis 500, brightest star on the United States Auto Club's (USAC) champ-car circuit. Porsche announced in late '79 that it would field an Indy challenger: the P6B, derived from the Parnelli VPJ6C, to be run by the Interscope Racing Team. Though the "Parnelli" part seemed odd, it really wasn't. As *Road & Track*'s Joe Rusz reminded us: "Anyone who recalls the Abarth-Carrera coupes...knows that Porsche has often had to rely on other coachbuilders for its racing cars."

Once again, the amazing 911 flat six was at the heart of a racing Porsche. Actually, it was the 2649-cc (179.8 cid) unit from the 935 "silhouette" racer. Designated 935/76, this was the ulti-

mate "high tech" engine of its day. Its crankcase was air-cooled, its cylinder heads water-cooled—and welded to the block to eliminate leakage at the gaskets. There were four valves per cylinder operated by two gear-drive camshafts, allowing cup followers to replace rocker arms. Two water pumps for the hybrid cooling system were run from the exhaust cams, while the intakes drove another pair of water pumps for twin intercoolers, through which intake air passed after turbo pressurization. Dry-sump lubrication was employed per USAC rules.

Interscope had planned to assign the Indy Porsche to 37-year-old Danny Ongais, USAC Indy Division Rookie of the Year in 1977 and co-driver of the winning 935 at Daytona '79. But the project was nipped in the bud when USAC limited boost to a maximum 48 psi—this a mere half-hour before the green flag! Porsche claimed it had been allowed 54 psi (pushrod turbo engines could use 58, Offys 60) and said that couldn't be reduced because of the welded heads. Raising compression to accommodate the lower pressure would have required a major rebuild.

After angry words between USAC and Porsche racing director Manfred Jantke, Porsche withdrew, taking a serious financial loss. Rusz spoke for many when he expressed disappointment "for Porsche, a small dedicated company which has contributed much to...motor racing.... I can't help but wonder if they'll ever be back."

For 1982, the FIA established a new Group C category, which spawned a

North American counterpart in the GTP division (P for prototype) under the International Motor Sports Association (IMSA). This was very much a return to the kind of way-out factory sports-racers that had thrilled so many in the late Sixties, so perhaps it was no surprise that Porsche's contenders—the 956 for Group C, the 962 for IMSA—evoked memories of the fabled 917 coupes, much like the 936 resembled a modernized Can-Am car.

These new Porsches looked somewhat alike: imposing and very smooth. The difference was the 962 had an extra 100 mm (3.94 inches) in wheelbase toward the front to satisfy IMSA's rule that a driver's feet rest behind the front-wheel centerline. Both 956 and 962 employed unit construction, something Porsche hadn't used on a sports-racer since the 904, prompted by Group C rules for driver-protecting "crushable" structures and the greater rigidity a monocoque would provide.

Because Porsche already had the essentials, the 956 came together with astonishing speed, racing a little more than a year after budget approval (on June 22, 1981). Peter Falk, who'd replaced Jantke, was in charge, aided by racing-development engineer Norbert Singer, engine designer Valentine Schafer, and body/chassis expert Horst Reitter.

Salvaging work from the aborted Indy effort, Schafer endowed the 935/76 engine with a special racing version of the Bosch Motronic integrated electronic ignition/fuel injec-

tion system. Result: 620-630 bhp (DIN) at 8200 rpm. Borrowing 936 chassis concepts, Reitter produced a riveted-and-bonded aluminum affair that was 50-percent stiffer. This was overlaid as before with plastic panels, only now they were made of reinforced Kevlar carbon-fiber. Curb weight thus came in only 20-50 kg (44-110 pounds) over the 800-kg (1764-pound) minimum, though some suggested the frame could have been lighter still. The only other change from 936 chassis specs was double-stiff springs to avoid unwanted "porpoising" at racing speeds.

Like the 917s, the 956 was raced in long- and short-tail forms. The former, for Le Mans, had a 0.35 drag coefficient; the latter, measuring 0.42, was for other Makes races. The latest "ground effects" design thinking was very evident: ultra-deep side skirts; short, downsloped nose; "bubble" top; and 936-style fins-mit-aerofoil. Fuel economy in enduros was a concern, so compression ratios were varied during the season (between 7.1 and 7.5:1), as were boost pressures (ultimately settling at 1.2 bar/17.6 psi).

Unlike its famous forebear, the 956 was a winner from its very first race. Ickx and Derek Bell (who drove a 956 "mule" faster than any previous Porsche in tests at France's Paul Ricard circuit) led a 1-2-3 Le Mans sweep in a season that brought Porsche another Makes championship and made Ickx the world's top endurance driver. Porsche added three more Le Mans vic-
continued on page 304

The 936 (*opposite page*) featured a huge air intake above and behind the cockpit and an adjustable aerofoil. It was victorious at Le Mans in both 1976 and 1977, and also won the World Sports Car title in '76. The 956 (*above*) competed in Group C. It utilized unit construction to meet required safety regulations.

Like the 917s, the 956 (*both pages*) was raced in long-
and short-tail forms. The former (pictured) had a 0.35
drag coefficient, ground effects design, and 620-630 DIN
bhp. A winner from the start, it swept Le Mans 1-2-3
in 1982, and was victorious again in 1983-84-85.

tories and three consecutive championships in 1983-85, after which it switched to the 962C.

That car was a development of the 962 that had been evolving in North America since 1983 when IMSA impresario John Bishop, fearing a Porsche steamroller in GTP would reduce attendance, reluctantly let in a suitably modified version of the 956 for the '84 season. Al Holbert Racing had been Porsche's main standard-bearer in the IMSA GT wars (his Porsche-powered March had won the '83 championship), and Holbert himself participated in much of the 962's development. Also on board were Alwin Springer from Andial of California, and Jurgen Barth and Valentine Schafer from Weissach.

Aside from bodywork differences—mainly tail configurations and a more radically sloped nose (to accommodate the longer wheelbase)—the 962's chief distinction was its powerplant. Initially, this was the 2.8-liter all-air-cooled 934 unit, with single turbo and ignition. In this form, the 962 scored its first win, at Mid-Ohio, but the team was already working on a 3.2-liter extension for some needed extra power.

Problems with the Motronic engine system precluded a winning season in '84, but the 962 came into its own the following year, walking away with the GT championship. It repeated in '86, giving Holbert (by now director of Porsche Motorsport, the firm's North American racing arm) his fifth IMSA driving title. That same year, Derek

Bell captured his second endurance-driver's title with a 962C.

These days it's almost bigger news if a Porsche doesn't win, be it a single race or an entire series. At this writing, 962s are still conquering all on both sides of the Atlantic, some fitted with the experimental PDK—Porsche *Doppel-Kupplung* (double-clutch)—semi-automatic transmission that allows shifting under power to reduce the speed-sapping effects of turbocharger lag. Rulemakers are once again rejiggering requirements in an attempt to stem Porsche's dominance (IMSA by cutting maximum displacement to 3.0 liters), but they'll have to burn at least as much midnight oil as the visionaries of Weissach—if not more.

And Porsche is having another go at

After 1985, the 956 (*opposite*) gave way to the 962C
(*above*), a development of the 962 that had been evolving
in North America. The 962 didn't win in '84, but did
take the IMSA GT championship in 1985 and '86.

"Indycar" competition, with a new turbocharged V-8 car first appearing late in the 1987 Championship Auto Racing Teams (CART) season. It's an all-Porsche effort, unusual in a series where chassis and engine have traditionally come from different constructors. The engine is a water-cooled 90-degree V-8 of 2.6 liters (the maximum allowed with "limited" turbocharging), with gear-driven twin overhead camshafts operating four valves per cylinder in magnesium cylinder heads. Output is in the vicinity of 700 bhp with 8.7-psi boost. It all sounds a lot like the production 928 S 4 engine—as it should, for at Porsche the distinction between racing and production technology has always been delightfully blurred.

Though this second Indy-Porsche won't get its first real test until the '88 season, Weissach is going slow with the project, which bodes well for at least a few wins if not overall victory. Then again, what else from the winningest make in motorsports?

And whether it's Indy, IMSA, SCCA, or FIA, Porsche racers will still be in there swinging—and winning. Every one of them, from 904 to 962, has been brilliant, and the 917 stands alone: the "King," the fastest sports car ever seen. The owner of every road-going Porsche can take justifiable pride in these all-conquering competition relatives. They stand as irrefutable proof of Porsche's ability to make history on and off the track.

CHAPTER SEVENTEEN

At the Crossroads: Porsche Today and Tomorrow

Porsche's first cars were born in adversity, and the company has weathered its fair share of storms in the four decades since. Yet for most of its existence, Porsche has been the very model of success, increasing production almost every year while compiling an unprecedented competition record and unparalleled worldwide engineering fame.

Now, suddenly, Porsche seems to be falling apart. With the dollar's precipitous drop against the Deutschmark in 1987 came the first sales decline most anyone could remember, unmasking an over-reliance on the American market and long-standing internal dissention among company managers. Things seemed so serious, in fact, that Porsche became rumored as a takeover target. Lending credence to such speculation was a statement by Daimler-Benz vice-chairman Werner Neifer that D-B would buy Porsche to keep it from falling into non-German hands.

Only a few days later, in an unusual move for a German company, the Porsche board released chairman Peter Schutz from his contract a year ahead of schedule. Why? According to some company insiders, his policies had led to Porsche's late-Eighties troubles. Others said that, like Lee Iacocca versus the late Henry Ford II, Schutz had grown too big for his britches, becoming an annoyance to the Porsche and Piëch families who still control a majority of the firm's voting stock. Yet, this was the same German-born, American-educated *wunderkind* who had rejuvenated the 911 (to the delight of enthusiasts everywhere) and boosted total sales to record levels. At

the same time, he had taken Porsche into the aero-engine business and modernized production facilities to lower costs and increase profitability.

What was going on? Had Porsche lost its touch? Could it survive as an independent? Did Schutz clash once too often with the board and "ruling families" over strategy, or were he and his plans merely a victim of economic forces he could not have foreseen or controlled? Such were the questions being asked by many observers pondering Porsche's future as this book went to press.

Let's try to assess that future by beginning with a few facts. First and foremost, it shouldn't be forgotten that for all its success, Porsche remains a small automaker by world standards. Its annual volume at this writing is only about 50,000 cars, sales of which represent some 65 percent of total profits (down from around 80 percent in the early Eighties). Remaining revenues continue to come from engineering consultancy contracts with clients ranging from SEAT in Spain to Lada in Russia, plus parts sales. More recently, some income is generated from royalties on the light-aircraft version of the 911 flat six, conceived in 1982 and now offered as a production part by Mooney Aircraft in Texas.

It should be noted that income does *not* accrue from Porsche Design, the industrial-design and marketing firm famous for pricey leather goods, Carrera sunglasses, and other personal-use items. That company has always been a separate entity, established by Butzi Porsche after his father took the family out of running the car business

in 1972, when Porsche KG (limited-partnership company) became today's Porsche AG (*Aktiengesellschaft*, public stock corporation).

That Porsche depends more heavily on the U.S. market than most any other automaker is indisputable. At this writing, American car sales account for some 61 percent of total production, up from 54 percent in 1986. That's ironic, as U.S. laws and driving conditions make it virtually impossible to use any Porsche's full performance, which was true even *before* the 55-mph speed limit took effect.

So why has America's appetite for Porsches been so strong for so long? Most observers cite two factors: exclusivity (the aforementioned limited volume, enhanced in recent years by rapidly escalating prices), and the well-known "Porsche Mystique." The latter derives from the make's German heritage and engineering reputation (designed for the unlimited-speed *Autobahnen*), plus the aura that always surrounds a marque active in competition. In the 911's case, exclusivity also means uniqueness. As the "traditional" Porsche (air-cooled rear engine), it remains for many the only "real" Porsche.

But heavy reliance on U.S. sales means that Porsche's financial health depends to a greater extent on the value of the dollar than it does for most car companies. And since late 1985, the dollar has been plunging like a rock: by late 1987, down some 50 percent against the Deutschmark to new lows. While this partly results from recent Reagan Administration fiscal policies, it also reflects waning confidence among foreign investors in the face of continuing huge deficits in America's national budget and balance of trade.

Predictably, Porsche has had to raise prices to make up for the widening currency gap. It's not alone in this, of course. To some extent, all automakers—even Detroit—have suffered from the weakening dollar since 1985. Japanese producers in the same two-year period had to contend with a similar 50-percent dollar decline against the yen. Yet, while they compensated with price hikes on the order of 10 to 20 percent, Porsche's increases have been around 30 percent—some 20 percent on its '87s alone.

This isn't the first time German automakers have been hurt by a weak dollar. The inflation touched off by the 1973-74 Energy Crisis also necessitated stiff price increases. But unlike today, Porsche's U.S. sales were little affected then; in fact, they went up. Since the market seemed happy to bear higher prices through the Seventies and into the Eighties, Porsche saw no reason not to continue moving up-market. And in fairness, it offset "sticker shock" somewhat with mechanical improvements and additional standard equipment.

But 15 years ago, there were virtually no alternatives to Porsche performance and quality. Today there are—and they're far cheaper. Most strongly challenged are the "budget" Porsches, the 924S and the standard 944. Sporty Japanese cars like Mazda's second-generation RX-7 may not have Porsche's illustrious competition heritage or that extra degree of handling at the limit. But is a great name and performance that's seldom usable in America really worth up to $10,000 extra? That's the current price gap between a well-equipped RX-7 and the base 944—a gap that's grown by some $4700 in just two years (1985-87).

For many who have looked at all this, the answer to that question is a resounding "no." Said *AutoWeek* in late 1987: "As far as the RX-7 (and similar Japanese sports cars) are concerned, the 944 has simply priced itself out of contention. Were we to recreate our 1986 RX-7/944 test today, the RX-7's...price advantage would all but ensure victory for the Mazda." Two years before, they thought the Porsche worth its extra cost. It should also be born in mind that Detroit's reborn performance cars—Chevy's Cor-

vette and Camaro IROC-Z, the Pontiac Trans-Am, and Ford Mustang GT—also offer a lot more performance per dollar. "The bottom line," concluded *AutoWeek*, "is that Porsche is abandoning the lower end of the sports-car market, the $15-25,000 bracket where the Japanese have established such a stranglehold."

It's thus no real surprise that 924/944 sales have been sinking: in 1987, down some 30 percent from '86 levels in both the U.S. and Germany. More disturbing, for the first time in anyone's memory, the 911 hasn't been selling as well as it used to: off 27 percent in Germany for the first eight months of 1987. Only the 928 seemed to hold its own, with a 52-percent home-market gain in the same period. But that only represented an increase from 487 to 740 units, still small potatoes.

The Wall Street crash of October 19, 1987, not only evoked memories of 1929 but threw Porsche's vulnerabilities into dramatic relief (along with those of many other companies). It also added insult to the injury of an 18-percent decline in total U.S. sales. A month later, Schutz, reflecting the attitude that may have prompted his dismissal, confessed to CONSUMER GUIDE®: "I don't know that anyone really *needs* a Porsche. It is a purchase you *can* postpone."

A good many have evidently done just that—or bought elsewhere—and not solely because of price, we think. Consider that Porsche hasn't introduced a truly new car in over a decade. Its newest, the 928, is 11 years old now, the 924/944 a year older, the 911 an elderly quarter-century along in years. That's not to overlook Porsche's penchant for slow, steady development, of course, nor its ability to keep its cars fresh and exciting come what may. But that these same basic cars continue year after year must surely be a factor in the recent sales slump. Newness still sells cars. That's why the Japanese keep changing theirs every four years or so.

A major reason there hasn't been a really new Porsche for so long is the heavy expenditures being made in new manufacturing and engineering facilities at Zuffenhausen, investments instituted under Schutz. This is hardly bad. Commencing spring 1988, these new plants will allow Porsche to produce more model variations more eco-

nomically than before, and to control its entire output for the first time (which means taking over four-cylinder production from Audi). But because Porsche's resources are far more limited than those of a GM or Ford, this investment has necessarily diverted funds that might have speeded introduction of new products. And it's this lack of same that some critics say has weakened Porsche in the marketplace despite heretofore strong demand for the familiar offerings.

So that leaves Porsche in the situation of being a small independent with a line of aging—though still very capable—cars, selling in diminishing numbers at least partly because of stickers that are fast approaching those of an airplane or yacht. Indeed, a U.S. dealer publication admitted that for some folks the latter are often alternatives to a Porsche. The high price tags stem largely from economic forces Porsche can't control, of course, but likely also reflect the fact that Porsche has gotten away with stiff yearly price hikes for so long. And even if the public hasn't really tired of the current models, it must surely wonder how high prices will go and what it's getting for those sums. Again, the four-cylinder Porsches invite the most criticism, but the 911 and 928 aren't exactly immune. Even Schutz allowed that Porsche may not have done enough to justify spiraling prices, telling *AutoWeek* shortly before his ouster, "What we should have done was to ask buyers to pay more for better cars."

Which leads to the subject of what Porsche is doing and *will* do to combat these problems. Right now it seems that though Schutz is out, most of his plans will go forward under new chairman Heinz Branitski, a 22-year company veteran. Because Branitski is a financial type, his appointment is a clear indication that Porsche will be watching its *pfennigs* a lot more closely in the near future, scaling back some projects, and postponing or even eliminating others.

Two key decisions were made even before Schutz's dismissal: a cutback in four-cylinder production (from 134 to 100 units a day) to match reduced demand, and a halt in development on the 984 and 995, Porsche's latest attempts at a "budget" model. The 984 envisioned a compact, low-nose coupe with VW Golf transaxle and 1.8-liter

four-cylinder engine placed transversely amidships. The same power package in front-engine/rear-drive configuration was planned for the 995, though other inline fours were contemplated, along with flat fours, a V-4 (the 928 V-8 sliced crosswise), and even a 2.0-liter V-6 derived from Porsche's Indy V-8. Alleged 995 spy photos actually showed the experimental PEP (Porsche Experimental Prototype) "modular" car built for testing different suspensions, engines, powertrain locations, and other variables in the same platform. But it's all shelved now. Apparently, a new, more affordable Porsche just isn't in the cards.

As for what is, a few near-term developments can be confirmed. January 1988 sees release of the 944 Turbo S, essentially a blown version of the 16-valve 944S with 247 horsepower in U.S. trim, stiffer suspension and wider tires than the normally aspirated S, plus 928 brakes. (The Turbo S has already seen racing action in the European Porsche Cup series.)

Shown at Frankfurt 1987, but not due for production until 1989, is the much-awaited revival of the Speedster. It's not a replica of the highly coveted 356 model, but rather a 911 Carrera Cabriolet with a lower, reshaped windshield raked five degrees further back, no door ventwings or power windows, and a simpler, unlined top. These changes reportedly reduce curb weight by 154 pounds, though claimed top speed is unchanged at 150 mph. An as-yet-unseen hardtop will be offered. There's also a Club Sport option that converts the car into a single-seater for weekend racing via a large passenger's-side tonneau incorporating an even smaller windshield (thus requiring that the normal screen be removed).

Unfortunately, the styling of the new Speedster has generated mixed reactions among the press and Porsche dealers, some judging it unhappily bulbous next to the 911-based one-off built for Schutz and shown earlier in 1987. Worse, perhaps, *AutoWeek* correspondent Giancarlo Perini reported after a short test drive that much greater wind turbulence was the new model's only real difference.

It's enough to make you wonder whether Zuffenhausen hasn't finally run out of ideas for the 911. Britain's *Motor* magazine said the Speedster "could have easily come from one of Germany's second-rate tuning shops. How installing a different windscreen and a lump of plastic over the rear justifies a price tag likely to be well over £45,000 no one knows. Yes, the car will

Porsche continues to evolve. A limited-volume model for
1988 is the 911 Anniversary Edition (*opposite page*).
Coming in 1989 is the revival of the Speedster (*above*),
basically a 911 Carrera Cabriolet with cut down
windshield and a plastic boot over the rear.

undoubtedly be a major sales success [a view echoed by some U.S. Porsche dealers] but it must be seen as a rather wasted opportunity."

Due for simultaneous European and American release in January 1989 is the 944 Cabriolet, unveiled at the 1985 Frankfurt Show but delayed by problems in achieving acceptable structural strength in a roofless 944 with turbo power. In late 1987, Porsche revealed that it tapped ASC in Michigan, designer and builder of many latterday U.S. convertibles, for engineering assistance. Now ASC will supply some

components and tooling for Cabrio production at a new plant near the Neckarsulm coupe facility. Final specifications weren't available at this writing, but the 944 Cabrio is likely to arrive with both turbo and non-turbo versions of the 16-valve 944 engine. Interestingly, Schutz had declared that the 944's early-Nineties replacement will be designed as a convertible and then developed into a coupe, mainly because doing things that way is easier and less expensive in the long run.

For the same reason, don't expect a Porsche with active rear-wheel steer-

ing. While the firm is watching Japanese developments in this area, it's not keen on RWS because of its cost and weight penalties. Then too, Porsche can ill afford to squander its limited resources on such peripheral engineering, especially now.

Little is known about the 924/944 replacement, except that it probably won't appear before 1991 and may have a new V-6. Just what that engine might be and where it might be located are open to question, however, at least judging by "scoop" stories that popped up as we went to press. These speak of a much-modified 944 with shortened wheelbase, 928-style nose, 959-type tail and—the intriguing part—a rear-engine configuration. Is this a prototype for the successor model a possible interim offering to perk up lagging four-cylinder sales, or just another interesting Weissach experiment? Your guess is as good as ours.

Meantime, the 924S seems almost certain to disappear before the new junior generation arrives, a predictable belt-tightening move given the present circumstances. Schutz told CONSUMER GUIDE® that the 924 has never outsold the base 944 and that Porsche has never made money on it. Depending on what Herr Branitzki concludes on studying the balance sheet, the low-end 944 might vanish, too.

But we will definitely see a new-generation 911, if for no other reason than the fact that it's too far along to stop. Most likely to debut in late 1989 (at the next Frankfurt Show), it retains the familiar basic shape, but wears a moderately revised tail and a 959-style nose as seen in published spy photos. An all-new dash is rumored, and some simplified engineering features from the 959—notably a version of its four-wheel-drive system—seem certain. Engine developments are said to involve more displacement (reportedly to 3.4 liters) and four valves per cylinder, good for 180 mph in turbocharged form, according to *The Autocar*.

More remote is a long-wheelbase four-door version of the 928. First broached by Britain's *CAR* magazine in 1986, it was hinted as an outside possibility in late '87 when chairman Schutz took British journalists on a tour of the partly completed new Zuffenhausen body plant. Schutz described this 928 "sedan" as "a tremendous styling challenge, but we won't do it unless we can make it look and feel like a true Porsche." Again, it remains to be seen whether the Branitzki regime deems it worth doing at all.

As for competition, it appears that all current programs, including those begun by Schutz, will continue. In conversations with CONSUMER GUIDE® shortly before his dismissal, Schutz said that a new eight-cylinder engine of about 3.5 liters is in the works for the 1989 Formula 1 season, when turbos will be banned in favor of engines with any number of cylinders. He also hinted that the Indy-car V-8

Unveiled at the 1985 Frankfurt Auto Show, the
944 Cabriolet has had a long gestation period
in order to solve structural strength problems.
Look for it at your dealership in early '89.

may be enlarged from its present 2.65 to 3.2 liters for 1988, and could form the basis for a new passenger-car engine (perhaps the V-6 rumored for the 944 replacement). Porsche also plans to contest the entire CART series in 1989, as well as '88, despite a notable lack of success in 1987.

Only time will tell whether these and other measures are sufficient to ensure Porsche's future. The late Eighties have been difficult for specialty producers, as reflected in the recent takeovers of Maserati and Lamborghini (by Chrysler), Lotus (GM), and AC and Aston Martin (Ford). A major question is how long Porsche can remain independent in light of its current problems, which will take at least two to four years to resolve (assuming a stable or slightly improved market). Though takeover talk has died down as this is written, a few Porsche insiders have been quoted as saying that a buyout, most likely by Daimler-Benz, is inevitable—perhaps even before 1990. According to an *AutoWeek* story, the reason—in their view—is that Schutz's departure leaves Porsche without a young, dynamic leader precisely at the time it needs one most.

Further, there's apparently no one in Zuffenhausen's corridors of power with similar vision or the ability to inspire renewed confidence in the company. As one long-time American Porsche "insider" told *AutoWeek*: "The brains, the enthusiasm, the genius that created these cars until the last few years is no longer there ... because these people have retired or they're dead. Ferry Porsche, my God, he's pushing 80. [Veteran chief engineer Prof. Helmut] Bott is the last of that breed, and although he's wonderful, he's near the end of his rope."

Rumors also abound concerning another Schutz legacy: Porsche Cars of North America. One is that PCNA will take on another maker's luxury sedan (again, your guess) to placate dealers pleading for new, less costly, and more saleable products. Another scenario has PCNA being disbanded and Volkswagen of America resuming sales, service, and warranty administration to rid the parent company of this expense. (*Automotive News* reported a London stockbroker as estimating that Porsche added some $6.5 million to its annual costs—about 10 percent of 1984-85 profits—simply by extending its new-car warranty from one to

Porsche will likely offer the 944 Cabriolet with both
turbo and non-turbo versions of the 16-valve 944 engine.
ASC, a Michigan firm and builder of many latterday
American ragtops, was hired for engineering assistance.

two years.)

For all the uncertainties, one thing seems clear: Porsche will survive, but not before enduring some tough times, especially in the U.S. "We know it won't be good," Schutz admitted to *AutoWeek* in late '87. "The question is: How bad will it be? We're not worried about the competition. If the Japanese copy us, we must be doing something right. It's when nobody copies us that I worry.... Porsche will continue to build cars the way it knows best. Around 50,000 units a year is ideal for us. To go for a bigger mass market would be to degrade the name. Look what happened to Packard."

We have, and we hope that Herr Branitzki, Prof. Bott, and their colleagues have, too. As Porsche begins its second 40 years, we sincerely wish them all the wisdom and inspiration necessary to meet the formidable challenges ahead. They'll need it.

MAJOR SPECIFICATIONS: U.S. PRODUCTION MODELS FROM 1948

1948 Type 356 Prototype
Engine: Four-cylinder horizontally opposed with Porsche-modified cylinder heads. Bore and Stroke: 75×64mm (2.853×2.52 in.), 1131cc (169.0 cid). Bhp: 40 (DIN), 46 (SAE) at 4000 rpm. Compression ratio: 6.5:1. Overhead valves, four plain bearings, single Solex Type 26VFJ carburetor.
Chassis: Trailing-arm front suspension, swing-axle rear suspension, VW brakes and worm-gear steering, VW 9-inch drum brakes (cable actuated), single dry-disc clutch, VW non-synchromesh gearbox. Final drive ratio: 4.43:1.
Measurements: Weight (lbs): 1324 (unladen). Tire size: 5.00×16. Track: 53.4" front, 53.5" rear. Wheelbase: 84.6". Overall length: 152.4". Overall width: 65.7". Overall height: 49.8". Maximum speed: 90 mph. Fuel consumption: 35 mpg.

1949 Early Production Type 356 1100
Engine: As per 1948 prototype except twin carburetors.
Chassis: As per 1948 prototype.
Measurements: Weight (lbs): 1332 (unladen). Tire size: 5.00×16. Track: 50.8" front, 49.2" rear. Wheelbase: 82.7". Overall length: 152.3". Overall width: 65.5". Overall height: 51.2". Maximum speed: 90 mph. Fuel consumption: 33.6 mpg.

1950-54 Type 356 1100
Engine: Porshe Type 369, four-cylinder flat-opposed. Bore and Stroke: 73.5×64mm (2.89×2.52 in.), 1086cc (66.3 cid). Bhp: 40 (DIN), 46 (SAE) at 4000 rpm. Compression ratio: 6.5:1. Overhead valves, four plain bearings, twin Solex Type 32PBJ carburetors.
Chassis: Trailing-arm front suspension, swing-axle rear suspension, torsion bars front and rear, VW worm-gear steering, Ate hydraulic brakes, single dry-disc clutch, VW non-synchromesh transmission (through Autumn 1952) or Porsche Type 519 all-synchro transmission. Final drive ratio: 4.43:1.
Measurements: Permissible total weight (lbs): 2425. Tire size: 5.00×16. Track: 50.8" front, 49.2" rear. Wheelbase: 82.7". Overall length: 151.6". Overall width: 65.4". Overall

height: 51.2". Maximum speed: 90 mph. Fuel consumption: 35 mpg.

1951-54 Type 356 1300
Engine: Porsche Type 506, four-cylinder flat-opposed. Bore and Stroke: 80×64mm (3.14×2.52 in.), 1286cc (78.5 cid). Bhp: 44 (DIN), 50 (SAE) at 4200 rpm. Compression ratio: 6.5:1. Overhead valves, four plain bearings, twin Solex Type 32PBI carburetors.
Chassis: As per 1950-54 1100.
Measurements: As per 1950-54 1100 except Overall length: 152.4". Overall width: 65.5". Maximum speed: 92 mph. Fuel consumption: 32 mpg.

1953-55 Type 356 1300S
Engine: Porsche Type 589, four-cylinder flat-opposed. Bore and Stroke: 74.5×74.0mm (2.93×2.91 in.), 1290 cc (78.8 cid). Bhp: 60 (DIN), 71 (SAE) at 5500 rpm. Compression ratio: 8.2:1. Overhead valves, four roller-type bearings, twin Solex Type 32PBI carburetors.
Chassis: As per 1950-54 1100 except Porsche Type 519 all-synchromesh gearbox all years. Final drive ratio: 4.375:1.
Measurements: As per 1950-54 1100, except Overall length: 155.5". Maximum speed: 100 mph. Fuel consumption: 32 mpg.

1951-52 Type 356 1500
Engine: Porsche Type 527, four-cylinder flat-opposed. Bore and Stroke: 80×74mm (3.14×2.91 in.), 1488cc (80.8 cid). Bhp: 60 (DIN), 71 (SAE) at 4800 rpm. Compression ratio: 7:1. Overhead valves, four roller-type bearings, twin Solex Type 40PBI carburetors.
Chassis: As per 1950-54 1100.
Measurements: As per 1953-55 1300S except Maximum speed: 96 mph. Fuel consumption: 29 mpg.

1952-55 Type 356 1500
Engine: Porsche Type 546, four-cylinder flat-opposed. Bore and Stroke: 80×74mm (3.14×2.91 in.), 1488cc (90.8 cid). Bhp: 55 (DIN), 64 (SAE) at 4400 rpm. Compression ratio: 6.5:1. Overhead valves, four plain bearings, twin Solex Type 32PBI carburetors.

Chassis: As per 1953-55 1300S.
Measurements: As per 1951-52 1500.

1952-55 Type 356 1500S
Engine: Porsche Type 528 (528/2 from November 1954), four-cylinder flat-opposed. Bore and Stroke: 80×74mm (3.14×2.91 in.), 1488cc (90.8 cid). Bhp: 70 (DIN), 82 (SAE) at 5000 rpm. Compression ratio: 8.2:1. Overhead valves, four roller-type bearings, twin Solex Type 40PBI carburetors (Type 40PBIC from May 1954).
Chassis: As per 1953-55 1300S.
Measurements: As per 1953-55 1300S except Maximum speed: 105 mph. Fuel consumption: 21 mpg.

1954-55 Type 356 1300A
Engine: Porsche Type 506/2, four-cylinder flat-opposed. Bore and Stroke: 74.5×74mm (2.93×2.91 in.), 1290cc (78.7 cid). Bhp: 44 (DIN), 50 (SAE) at 4200 rpm. Compression ratio: 6.5:1. Overhead valves, four plain bearings, twin Solex Type 32PBI carburetors.
Chassis: Trailing-arm front suspension, swing-axle rear suspension, torsion bars front and rear, VW type worm-gear steering, Ate Hydraulic brakes, single dry-disc clutch, Porsche Type 519 transmission. Final drive ratio: 4.375:1.
Measurements: Permissible total weight (lbs): 2425. Tire size: 5.00×16. Track: 50.8" front, 49.2" rear. Wheelbase: 82.7". Overall length: 151.6". Overall width: 65.4". Overall height: 51.2". Maximum speed: 87 mph. Fuel consumption: 35 mpg.

1954-55 Type 356 1300S/A
Engine: Porsche Type 589/2, four-cylinder flat-opposed. Bore and Stroke: 74.5×74mm (2.93×2.91 in.), 1290cc (78.7 cid). Bhp: 60 (DIN), 71 (SAE) at 5500 rpm. Compression ratio: 8.2:1. Overhead valves, four roller-type bearings, twin Solex Type 32PBI carburetors.
Chassis: As per 1954-55 1300A.
Measurements: As per 1954-55 1300A except Maximum speed: 100 mph. Fuel consumption: 31.5 mpg.

1954-55 Type 356 1500A
Engine: Porsche Type 546/2, four-cylinder

Porsche Spyder Specifications

year	model	bore × stroke	cc	CR (:1)	bhp @ rpm	gears	WB (in.)	length (in.)	width (in.)	height (in.)	weight (lbs.)
1953	550/528	74.0 × 80.0	1488	9.0	79 @ 5200	4	82.8	141.8	61.0	40.0	1512
1953	550/547	66.0 × 85.0	1498	9.0	110 @ 7000	4	82.8	141.8	61.0	40.0	1500
1954	550/547	66.0 × 85.0	1498	9.0	110 @ 7000	4	82.8	141.8	61.0	40.0	1500
1955	550S	66.0 × 85.0	1498	8.8	110 @ 6200	4	82.8	140.0	60.0	40.0	1440
1956	550/1500RS	66.0 × 85.0	1498	9.8	135 @ 7200	5	82.8	149.5	63.8	36.0	1301
1957	718/1500RSK	66.0 × 85.0	1498	9.8	142 @ 7500	5	82.8	149.8	58.3	34.6	1146
1958-59	718/1600RSK	66.0 × 87.5	1598	9.8	165 @ 8000	5	82.8	149.8	58.3	34.6	1148
1960	718/RS60	66.0 × 87.5	1598	9.8	165 @ 8000	5	82.8	149.8	57.8	34.9	1058
1961	718/RS61	66.0 × 85.0	1498	9.8	150 @ 7800	5	82.8	149.8	57.8	34.9	1058
1961	718/RS61	66.0 × 87.5	1598	9.8	165 @ 8000	5	82.8	149.8	57.8	34.9	1058

BHP is DIN measurement.

flat-opposed. Bore and Stroke: 80 × 74mm (3.14 × 2.91 in.), 1488cc (90.8 cid). Bhp: 55 (DIN), 64 (SAE) at 4400 rpm Compression ratio: 6.5:1. Overhead valves, four plain bearings, twin Solex Type 32PBI carburetors.
Chassis: As per 1954-55 1300A.
Measurements: As per 1954-55 1300A except Maximum speed: 96 mph. Fuel consumption: 29 mpg.

1954-55 Type 356 1500S/A
Engine: Porsche Type 528/2, four-cylinder flat-opposed. Bore and Stroke: 80 × 74mm (3.14 × 2.91 in.), 1488cc (90.8 cid). Bhp: 70 (DIN), 82 (SAE) at 4400 rpm. Compression ratio: 6.5:1. Overhead valves, four roller-type bearings, twin Solex Type 40PBIC carburetors.
Chassis: As per 1954-55 1300A.
Measurements: As per 1954-55 1300A except Maximum speed: 105 mph. Fuel consumption: 21 mpg.

1955-57 Type 356A 1300
Engine: Porsche Type 506/2, four-cylinder flat-opposed. Bore and Stroke: 74.5 × 74mm (2.93 × 2.91 in.), 1290cc (78.7 cid). Bhp: 44 (DIN), 50 (SAE) at 4200 rpm. Compression ratio: 6.5:1. Overhead valves, four plain bearings, twin Solex Type 32PBIC carburetors.
Chassis: Trailing-arm front suspension, swing-axle rear suspension, torsion bars front and rear, VW type worm-gear steering, Ate hydraulic brakes, single dry-disc clutch, Porsche Type 519 transmission (Type 644 from 1956). Final drive ratio: 4.375:1.
Measurements: Permissible total weight (lbs): 2425. Tire size: 5.60 × 15. Track: 51.4″ front, 50.1″ rear. Wheelbase: 82.7″. Overall length: 155.5″. Overall width: 65.7″. Overall height: 51.6″. Maximum speed: 90 mph. Fuel consumption: 35 mpg.

1955-57 Type 356A 1300S
Engine: Porsche Type 589/2, four-cylinder flat-opposed. Bore and Stroke: 74.5 × 74mm (2.93 × 2.91 in.), 1290cc (78.7 cid). Bhp: 60 (DIN), 71 (SAE) at 5500 rpm. Compression ratio: 8.2:1. Overhead valves, four roller-type bearings, twin Solex Type 32PBI carburetors (Type 40PBIC from 1956).
Chassis: As per 1955-57 1300.
Measurements: As per 1955-57 1300 except Maximum speed: 100 mph. Fuel consumption: 31.5 mpg.

1955-59 Type 356A 1600
Engine: Porsche Type 616/1, four-cylinder flat-opposed. Bore and Stroke: 82.5 × 74mm (3.24 × 2.91 in.), 1582cc (96.5 cid). Bhp: 50 (DIN), 70 (SAE) at 4500 rpm. Compression

ratio: 7.5:1. Overhead valves, four plain bearings, twin Solex 32PBIC carburetors (Zenith Type 32NDIX from engine number 67001).
Chassis: As per 1955-57 1300 except ZF Type 7155 steering (from September 1957). Final drive ratio: 4.43:1.
Measurements: As per 1955-57 1300 except Permissible total weight (lbs): 2425, 2750 from 1958. Maximum speed: 100 mph. Fuel consumption: 31.5 mpg.

1955-59 Type 356A 1600S
Engine: Porsche Type 616/2, four-cylinder flat-opposed. Bore and Stroke: 82.5 × 74mm (3.24 × 2.91 in.), 1582cc (96.5 cid). Bhp: 75 (DIN), 88 (SAE) at 5000 rpm. Compression ratio: 8.5:1. Overhead valves, four roller-bearings (Alfing crankshaft from September 1957), twin Solex Type 40PBIC carburetors (Zenith Type 32NDIX from engine number 81201).
Chassis: As per 1955-59 1600.
Measurements: As per 1955-59 1600 except Maximum speed: 110 mph. Fuel consumption: 29.5 mpg.

1959-63 Type 356B
Engines: Porsche four-cylinder flat-opposed. Bore and Stroke: 82.5 × 74mm (3.24 × 2.91 in.), 1582cc (96.5 cid). 1600: 60 bhp (DIN) at 4500 rpm, compression ratio 7.5:1. 1600S: 75 bhp (DIN) at 5000 rpm, compression ratio: 8.7:1. 1600 Super 90: 90 bhp (DIN) at 5500 rpm, compression ratio 8.7:1, later 9.1:1.
Chassis: As per 1955-59 Type 356A 1600 except Al-Fin aluminum brakes.
Measurements: As per 1955-59 356A/1600, except Curb weight (lbs): 1980. Permissible total weight (lbs): 2750. Tire size: 5.60 × 15. Factory official maximum speeds (mph): 100 (1600), 110 (1600S), 116 (Super 90).

1963-65 Type 356C
Engines: Porsche four-cylinder flat-opposed. Bore and Stroke: 82.5 × 74mm (3.24 × 2.91 in.), 1582cc (96.5 cid). 1600C: 75 bhp (DIN) at 5200 rpm, compression ratio: 8.5:1. 1600SC: 95 bhp (DIN) at 5800 rpm, compression ratio: 9.5:1.
Chassis: As per 1959-63 Type 356B except four-wheel disc brakes.
Measurements: As per 1959-63 Type 356B, except factory official maximum speeds (mph): 110 (1600C), 116 (1600SC).

1966-69 Type 912
Engine: Four-cylinder flat-opposed. Bore and Stroke: 82.5 × 74.0mm. Displacement: 1582cc (96.5 cid). Bhp (SAE): 102 at 5800 rpm. Torque (lbs/ft SAE): 90 at 3500 rpm. Compression ratio: 9.3:1. Overhead valves, two twin-choke Solex carburetors.

Chassis: MacPherson-strut front suspension with lower A-arms, coil springs, transverse torsion bars, anti-roll bar; semi-trailing arm rear suspension with transverse torsion bars; rack-and-pinion steering; four-wheel disc brakes with vacuum assist; Porsche four-speed or (optional) five-speed overdrive manual transmissions; single dry-disc diaphragm clutch. Final drive ratio (five-speed): 4.43:1.
Measurements: Curb weight (lbs): 2100. Tire size: 6.95 × 15. Track: 52.6″ front, 51.8″ rear. Wheelbase: 87.0″. Overall length: 163.9″. Overall width: 63.4″. Overall height: 52.0″.

1964-68 Type 911/911L
Engine: Six-cylinder, flat-opposed. Bore and Stroke: 80.0 × 66.0mm. Displacement: 1991cc (121.4 cid). Bhp (DIN): 130 at 6100 rpm. Torque (lbs/ft SAE): 143 at 4300 rpm. Compression ratio: 9.0:1. Single overhead camshaft per cylinder bank, eight main (forged-steel) bearings, light-alloy crankcase and cylinder block, aluminum-alloy cylinder head, six Type 40PJ Solex carburetors (Weber 40IDA 3C from February 1966).
Chassis: As per 1966-69 Type 912 except Porsche five-speed manual transmission standard. Sportomatic four-speed semi-automatic transmission optional Type 911.
Measurements: As per 1966-69 Type 912 except Curb weight (lbs): approx 2270. Tire size: 165HR-15.

1966-67 Type 911S
Engine: As per 1964-68 Type 911/911L except bhp (DIN): 160 at 6600 rpm (180 SAE). Torque (lbs/ft SAE): 144 at 5200 rpm. Compression ratio: 9.8:1.
Chassis: As per 1964-68 Type 911/911L except rear anti-roll bar standard. Final drive ratio (five-speed): 4.43:1.
Measurements: As per 1964-68 Type 911/911L except Curb weight (lbs): approx 2280. Rear track: 52.2″.

1969 Type 911 T/E/S
Engine: As per 1964-68 Type 911/911L except bhp (DIN): 110 at 5800 rpm (T), 140 at 6600 rpm (E), 170 at 6800 rpm (S). Compression ratio: 8.6:1 (T), 9.1:1 (E), 9.8:1 (S). Carburetors on T, Bosch mechanical fuel injection on E and S.
Chassis: As per 1964-68 Type 911/911L except Boge self-adjusting hydropneumatic front struts standard on E, optional on T and S.
Measurements: As per 1964-68 Type 911/911L except Tire size: 184-14 standard on T and E, 185/70HR-14 optional E, 185/70HR-15 optional S. Wheelbase: 89.3″.

1970-71 Type 911 T/E/S
Engine: As per 1964-68 Type 911/911L except Bore and Stroke: 84 × 66mm. Displacement: 2195cc (133.9 cid). Bhp (DIN): 125 at 5800 rpm (T), 155 at 6200 rpm (E), 180 at 6500 rpm (S). Zenith Type 40TIN carburetors on T.
Chassis: As per 1969 Type 911 models except Porsche four-speed manual transmission standard T, five-speed standard E and S.
Measurements: As per 1969 Type 911 models.

1972-73 Type 911 T/E/S
Engine: As per 1964-68 Type 911/911L except Bore and Stroke: 84 × 70.4mm. Displacement: 2341cc (142.9 cid). Bhp (DIN): 140 at 5600 rpm (T), 165 at 6200 rpm (E), 190 at 6500 rpm (S). Compression ratio: 7.5:1 (T), 8.0:1 (E), 8.5:1 (S). Bosch mechanical fuel injection all models; Bosch K-Jetronic fuel injection on T from mid-1973.
Chassis: As per 1964-68 Type 911/911L except softer shock absorber valving and adoption of Type 915 five-speed manual transmission with conventional shift pattern.
Measurements: As per 1969 Type 911 models except Curb weight (lbs): approx 2480-2550. Tire size: 165HR-15 (T), 185/70VR-15 (E and S). Overall length: 168.4". (1973 models).

1974-77 Type 911/911S/Carrera
Engine: As per 1964-68 Type 911/911L except Bore and Stroke: 90.0 × 70.4mm. Displacement: 2687cc (164 cid). Bhp (DIN): 150 at 5700 rpm (911), 175 at 5800 rpm (1974 S and Carrera), 165 at 5800 rpm (1975-77 S and Carrera). CIS electronic fuel injection. Air pump or twin thermal reactors and exhaust-gas recirculation from 1975.
Chassis: As per 1972-73 Type 911 T/E/S except rear anti-roll bar optional 911 and 911S, standard Carrera.
Measurements: As per 1972-73 Type 911 T/E/S except Overall length: 168.9".

1976 Type 912E
Engine: Volkswagen four-cylinder flat-opposed. Bore and Stroke: 94.0 × 71.0mm. Displacement: 1971cc (120.3 cid). Bhp (SAE net): 86 at 4900 rpm. Torque (lbs/ft SAE): 93 at 4000 rpm. Compression ratio: 7.6:1. Overhead valves, light-alloy cylinder head, cast-iron block, forged crankshaft with four plain bearings, Bosch L-Jetronic fuel injection, air pump, thermal reactors, exhaust-gas recirculation.
Chassis: As per 1974-77 Type 911 except non-ventilated disc brakes, different five-speed manual transmission.
Measurements: As per 1974-77 Type 911 except Curb weight (lbs): 2560. Tire size: 165HR-15.

1978-83 Type 911SC
Engine: As per 1964-68 Type 911/911L except Bore and Stroke: 95.0 × 70.4mm. Displacement: 2994cc (183.0 cid). Bhp (SAE net): 172 at 5500 rpm. Torque (lbs/ft SAE): 175 at 4200 rpm. Compression ratio: 9.3:1. CIS fuel injection with oxygen sensor.
Chassis: As per 1974-77 Type 911 models except front and rear anti-roll bars standard, Sportomatic transmission no longer available. Final drive ratio: 3.875:1.
Measurements: Curb weight (lbs): 2756. Tire size: 185/70VR-15 front, 215/60VR-15 rear (205/55VR-16 front and 225/50VR-16 rear optional). Track: 53.9" front, 54.3" rear. Wheelbase: 89.5". Overall length: 168.9". Overall width: 65.0". Overall height (unladen): 51.6".

1983-88 Type 911 Carrera
Engine: As per 1964-68 Type 911 except Bore and Stroke: 95 × 74.4mm. Displacement: 3164cc (193 cid). Bhp (SAE net): 200 at 5900 rpm (1983-86), 214 at 5900 rpm (1987-88). Torque (lbs/ft SAE): 185 at 4900 rpm (1982-86), 195 at 4900 rpm (1987-88). Compression ratio: 9.5:1. Bosch Digital Motor Electronics (DME) injection/ignition control.
Chassis: As per 1964-68 Type 911 except Final drive ratio: 3.87:1 (1984-86), 3.44:1 (1987-88).
Measurements: As per 1978-83 Type 911SC except Curb weight (lbs): 2740-2750. Tire size: 195/65VR-15 front, 215/60VR-15 rear (205/55VR-16 front, 245/55VR-16 rear optional).

1970-73 Type 914/4
Engine: Volkswagen four-cylinder, flat-opposed, mid-mounted. Bore and Stroke: 90.0 × 66.0mm. Displacement: 1679cc (102.5 cid). Bhp (DIN): 80 at 4900 rpm. Torque (lbs/ft SAE): 103 at 2800 rpm. Compression ratio: 8.2:1. Overhead valves, light-alloy cylinder head, cast-iron block, forged crankshaft with four plain bearings, electronic fuel injection.
Chassis: MacPherson-strut front suspension with coil springs, transverse torsion bars, lower A-arms; semi-trailing-arm rear suspension with coil springs; front-disc/rear-drum brake system with vacuum assist; rack-and-pinion steering; five-speed overdrive manual transmission. Final drive ratio: 4.43:1.
Measurements: Curb weight (lbs): approx 2100. Tire size: 155-15 (165-15 optional). Track: 52.6", front, 54.1" rear. Wheelbase: 96.4". Overall length: 156.9 " (159.4" 1973 models). Overall width: 65.0". Overall height: 48.0".

1970-71 Type 914/6
Engine: As per 1964-68 Type 911 except mid-mounted. Two Weber Type 40JDT3C carburetors.
Chassis: As per 1970-73 Type 914/4 except ventilated front disc brakes and solid-rotor rear disc brakes.
Measurements: As per 1970-73 Type 914/4 except Curb weight (lbs): 2195. Tire size: 185HR-14 (on light-alloy wheels). Track: 53.6" front, 54.4" rear.

1974-75 Type 914/4
Engine: As per 1970-73 914/4 except Bore and Stroke: 93.0 × 66.0mm. Displacement: 1795cc (110 cid). Bhp (SAE net): 73 at 4800 rpm. Torque (lbs/ft SAE): 89 at 4000 rpm. Compression ratio: 7.3:1.
Chassis: As per 1970-73 Type 914/4.
Measurements: As per 1970-73 Type 914/4 except Curb weight (lbs): approx 2160. Tire size: 165SR-15. Overall length: 161.2".

1973-76 Type 914 2.0 Liter
Engine: As per 1970-73 Type 914/4 except Bore and Stroke: 94.0 × 71.0mm. Displacement: 1971cc (120 cid). Bhp (SAE net): 91 at 4900 rpm (84 bhp after 1973). Torque (lbs/ft SAE): 109 at 3000 rpm (108 at 3500 rpm after 1973). Compression ratio: 7.6:1.
Chassis: As per 1970-73 Type 914/4 except solid-rotor four-wheel disc brakes with vacuum assist.
Measurements: As per 1970-73 Type 914/4 except Curb weight (lbs): approx 2150. Tire size: 165HR-15. Overall length: 161.2" (159.4" on 1973 models).

1976-77 Type 930 Turbo Carrera
Engine: Six-cylinder, flat-opposed, turbocharged. Bore and Stroke: 95.0 ×

70.4mm. Displacement: 2993cc (183 cid). Bhp (DIN): 245 at 5500 rpm (234 SAE net). Torque (lbs/ft SAE): 246 at 4500 rpm. Compression ratio: 6.5:1. Single overhead camshaft per cylinder bank, eight main (forged-steel) bearings, light-alloy crankcase and cylinder block, aluminum-alloy cylinder head, Bosch CIS electronic fuel injection.
Chassis: As per 1964-68 Type 911 except front and rear anti-roll bars standard, Porsche four-speed manual transmission. Final drive ratio: 4.22:1.
Measurements: As per 1974-77 Type 911 models except Curb weight (lbs): approx 2800. Tire size: 185/70VR-15 front, 215/60VR-15 rear. Track: 56.4" front, 59.1" rear. Overall width: 69.9".

1978-79 Type 930 Turbo
Engine: As per 1976-77 Type 930 except Bore and Stroke: 97 × 74.4mm. Displacement: 3299cc (201.3 cid). Bhp (DIN): 265 at 5500 rpm (253 SAE net). Torque (lbs/ft SAE): 282 at 4000 rpm. Compression ratio: 7.0:1.
Chassis: As per 1976-77 Type 930.
Measurements: As per 1976-77 Type 930 except Curb weight (lbs): approx 2860. Tire size: 205/55VR-16 front, 255/50VR-16 rear.

1986-88 Type 911 Turbo/Type 930S
Engine: As per 1978-79 Type 930 Turbo except bhp (SAE): 282 bhp at 5500 rpm. Torque (lbs/ft SAE): 288 at 4000 rpm.
Chassis: As per 1976-77 Type 930 except brakes vented and cross-drilled.
Measurements: As per 1978-79 Type 930 except Curb weight (lbs): 2960-3312. Tire size: 205/55VR-16 front, 245/55VR-16 rear.

1977-82 Type 924
Engine: Four-cylinder inline, water-cooled. Bore and Stroke: 86.5 × 84.4mm. Displacement: 1984cc (121 cid). Bhp (SAE net): 95-115 at 5500-5750 rpm. Torque (lbs/ft SAE net): 109-111.3 at 3500 rpm. Compression ratio: 8.0:1-9.0:1. Single overhead camshaft, five main (forged-steel) bearings, cast-iron cylinder block, cast-aluminum alloy cylinder head, CIS electronic fuel injection (with oxygen sensor from 1980).
Chassis: MacPherson strut front suspension with coil springs and negative roll radius geometry (anti-roll bar optional), independent rear suspension with integral transaxle, diagonal control arms, transverse torsion bars, anti-roll bar (optional); rack-and-pinion steering; front-disc/rear-drum brakes with vacuum assist; Porsche five-speed overdrive manual or Audi three-speed automatic transmission; single dry-disc clutch. Final drive ratio: 3.44 to 5.00:1 (manual transmission), 3.73:1 (automatic transmission).
Measurements: Curb weight: 2625-2675 lbs. Tire size: 165HR-14, 185/70HR-14 from 1979 (205/60HR-15 optional from 1980). Track: 55.9" front, 54.0" rear. Wheelbase: 94.5". Overall length: 170.0". Overall width: 66.3". Overall height (unladen): 50.0".

1980-82 Type 924 Turbo
Engine: As per 924 except bhp (SAE net): 143 at 5500 rpm. Torque (lbs/ft SAE net): 147 at 3000 rpm. Compression ratio: 7.5:1.
Chassis: As per 924 except standard 23mm-diameter front anti-roll bar; 14mm-diameter rear anti-roll bar optional with Sport (S) Group. No automatic transmission option. Final drive ratio: 4.71:1.
Measurements: As per 924 except Curb weight (lbs): approx 2825. Tire size: 185/70VR-15 (205/55VR-16 optional with Sport Group). Overall length: 168.9".

1987-88 Type 924S
Engine: As per 1983-88 Type 944 (below).
Chassis: As per 1983-88 Type 944 (below).
Measurements: As per 1977-82 Type 924 except Curb weight (lbs): 2734. Tire size: 195/65VR-15. Track: 55.8" front, 54.8" rear. Overall length: 168.9". Overall height (unladen): 50.2".

1983-88 Type 944
Engine: Porsche four-cylinder inline, water-cooled. Bore and Stroke: 100 × 78.9mm. Displacement: 2479cc (151 cid). Bhp (SAE net): 143 at 5500 rpm (1983-85), 147 at 5800 rpm (1986-87), 158 at 5900 rpm (1988). Torque (lbs/ft SAE net): 137 at 3000 rpm (1983-85), 140 at 3000 rpm (1987), 155 at 4500 rpm (1988). Compression ratio: 9.5 to 10.2:1. Single overhead camshaft, five main (forged-steel) bearings, silicon/aluminum-alloy cylinder block, aluminum-alloy crossflow cylinder head, electronic fuel injection with oxygen sensor, Bosch Digital Motor Electronics injection/ignition control. **Chassis:** As per 924 except standard 20mm-diameter front anti-roll bar (21.5mm diameter optional) and 14mm-diameter rear anti-roll bar, four-wheel ventilated disc brakes. Final drive ratio: 3.89:1 (manual transmission), 3.45:1 (automatic transmission). **Measurements:** As per 924 except Curb weight (lbs): 2778-2844. Tire size: 215/60VR-15. Track: 58.2" front, 57.1" rear. Overall width: 68.3". Overall height (unladen): 50.2".

1986-88 Type 944S
Engine: As per 1983-88 Type 944 except Dual overhead camshafts, 4 valves per cylinder. Bhp (SAE net): 188 at 6000 rpm. Torque (lbs/ft SAE): 170 at 4300 rpm. **Chassis:** As per 1983-88 Type 944 except automatic transmission not available. **Measurements:** As per 1983-88 Type 944 except Curb weight (lbs): 2866.

1978-79 Type 928
Engine: Eight-cylinder in 90-degree "V," water-cooled. Bore and Stroke: 95.0 × 78.9mm. Displacement: 4474cc (273 cid). Bhp (SAE net): 218 at 5250 rpm. Torque (lbs/ft SAE): 254 at 3600 rpm. Compression ratio: 8.5:1. Single overhead camshaft per cylinder bank, five main (forged-steel) bearings, silicon/aluminum-alloy cylinder head and block, iron-coated aluminum pistons, CIS electronic fuel injection. **Chassis:** Coil spring/strut front suspension with twin control arms, anti-roll bar, negative offset steering geometry; coil spring/strut rear suspension with integral transaxle, "Weissach axle" lower control arms, anti-roll bar; rack-and-pinion steering with speed-variable power assist; ventilated four-wheel disc brakes with hydraulic assist; Porsche five-speed overdrive manual or Daimler-Benz three-speed automatic transmission; double dry-plate clutch with hydraulic actuation. Final drive ratio: 2.75:1 (manual), 2.00:1 (automatic). **Measurements:** Curb weight (lbs): 3300. Tire size: 225/50VR-16. Track: 61.1" front, 60.2" rear. Wheelbase: 98.4". Overall length: 175.7". Overall width: 72.3". Overall height: 50.5".

1980-82 Type 928
Engine: As per 1978-79 Type 928 except bhp (SAE net): 220 at 5500 rpm. Torque (lbs/ft SAE): 265 at 4000 rpm. Compression ratio: 9.0:1. Bosch L-Jetronic electronic fuel injection with oxygen sensor and three-way catalyst. **Chassis:** As per 1978-79 Type 928 except 2.12:1 final drive ratio with automatic transmission on 1981-82 models. **Measurements:** As per 1978-79 Type 928 except Tire size: 215/60VR-15 (225/50VR-16 with optional Competition Group). Curb weight (lbs.): 3351 (manual), 3385 (automatic).

1983-84 Type 928S
Engine: As per 1978-79 Type 928 except Bore and Stroke: 97.0 × 78.9mm. Displacement: 4644cc (285 cid). Bhp (SAE net): 234 at 5500 rpm. Torque (lbs/ft SAE): 263 at 4000 rpm. Compression ratio: 9.3:1. **Chassis:** As per 1978-79 Type 928 except optional four-speed automatic transmission from late-1983. Final drive ratio: 2.27:1 (manual), 2.20:1 (automatic). **Measurements:** As per 1978-79 Type 928 except Tire size: 225/50VR-16.

1985-86 Type 928S
Engine: As per 1983-84 Type 928S except Dual overhead camshafts, 4 valves per cylinder. Bore and Stroke: 100.0 × 78.9mm. Displacement: 4957cc (302 cid). Bhp (SAE net): 288 at 5750 rpm. Torque (lbs/ft SAE): 316 at 6000 rpm. Compression ratio: 10.0:1. Bosch LH-Jetronic fuel injection. **Chassis:** As per 1983-85 Type 928S. **Measurements:** As per 1983-85 Type 928S.

1987-88 Type 928S 4
Engine: As per 1985-86 Type 928S except bhp (SAE net): 316 at 6000 rpm. Torque (lbs/ft SAE): 317 at 3000 rpm. **Chassis:** As per 1985-86 Type 928S except Single-disc dry-plate clutch. Final drive ratio (automatic transmission): 2.20:1 (1987), 2.64:1 (1988). **Measurements:** As per 1985-86 Type 928S except Curb weight (lbs): 3505 (manual transmission), 3549 (automatic transmission). Tire size: 225/50VR-16 front, 245/45VR-16 rear. Overall length: 178.1". Overall height (unladen) 50.2".

1987-88 Type 959
Engine: Six-cylinder, flat-opposed, air-cooled. Bore and Stroke: 95.0 × 67.0mm. Displacement: 2849cc (173.8 cid). Bhp (DIN): 450 at 6500 rpm. Torque (lb/ft DIN): 369 at 5500 rpm. Compression ratio: 8.3:1. Dual overhead camshafts, 4 valves per cylinder, aluminum block and water-cooled heads, Bosch Digital Motor Electronics injection/ignition control, dual sequential turbochargers. **Chassis:** Independent front and rear suspension with upper and lower A-arms, coil springs, anti-roll bar, and twin shock absorbers; power-assisted rack-and-pinion steering; ventilated cross-drilled four-wheel disc brakes; computer-controlled variable-torque-split four-wheel drive via six-speed manual rear transaxle and integrated differential/multi-plate clutch. Final drive ratio: 4.12:1. **Measurements:** Curb weight (lbs): 2977/3197 (Sport/Touring versions). Tire size: 235/45VR-17 front, 255/40VR-17 rear. Track: 59.2" front/61.0" rear. Wheelbase: 89.4". Overall length: 167.7". Overall width: 72.4". Overall height: 50.4".

Condensed Specifications: Porsche Sports/Racing Cars 1964-date

years built	type	body type	no. cyls.	cc	bore × stroke	CR (:1)	bhp @ rpm	top speed (mph)
1964-66	904	coupe	4	1966	92.0 × 74.0	9.8	180-195 @ 7000	160
1966-67	906	coupe	6	1991	80.0 × 66.0	10.3	210-220 @ 8000	165
1966-68	907	coupe	6	1991	80.0 × 66.0	10.3	220 @ 8000	165 (907L: 186)
1968	908	coupe	8	2997	85.0 × 66.0	10.4	310-350 @ 8400	180 (K/L: 190)
1968	909	spyder	8	1981	76.0 × 54.6	10.4	275 @ 9000	155
1967	910/6	coupe	6	1991	80.0 × 66.0	10.3	220 @ 8000	165
1967	910/8	coupe	8	2195	80.0 × 54.6	10.2	270 @ 8600	175
1969-70	917	coupe	12	4494	85.0 × 66.0	10.5	560-580 @ 8400	210 +
1970-71	917	coupe	12	4907	86.0 × 70.4	10.5	600-615 @ 8400	240
1970	917	coupe	12	4999	86.8 × 70.4	10.5	630 @ 8300	200
1970	917	coupe	12	5374	90.0 × 70.4	10.5	660 @ 8300	240
1972	917/10	spyder	12*	4494	85.0 × 66.0	8.5	850 @ 8000	220 +
1972	917/10	spyder	12*	4999	86.8 × 70.4	8.5	950-1000 @ 7800	230 +
1973	917/30	spyder	12*	5374	90.0 × 70.4	8.5	1100 @ 7800	245
1976-date	936	coupe	6*	2142	83.0 × 66.0	6.5	520-540 @ 8000	200 +
1981-85	956	coupe	6*	2649	92.3 × 66.0	7.0-7.6	600-700 @ 8200	205 +
1985-88	962	coupe	6*	3200	NA	NA	600 @ 8200	205 +

*turbocharged.

INDEX